Those '80s Cars

Published by

James H. Kaster

Concord, NC

Printed in the United States of America

ISBN 978-0-615-34620-5

The information contained within this book is true and complete to the best of my knowledge. Material was gathered from manufacturers' brochures, advertisements and media kits. Information is provided without any guarantee on the part of the publisher. Publisher also disclaims any liability incurred from use of this information.

© 2010 by James H. Kaster

All rights reserved. No part of this publication may be reproduced or transmitted in any form or by any means, electronic or mechanical, including photocopy, scanning, recording or any information retrieval system without permission in writing from the publisher. Permission is never granted for commercial purposes.

Manufacturer, vehicle, model, trim names and/or designations are the trademarks of the respective companies. They are used for identification purposes only. This is not an official publication of any of these companies or manufacturers.

Table of Contents

Table of Contents	2
Foreword	3
The 80's Measured	4
1980	5
1981	38
1982	74
1983	106
1984	138
1985	167
1986	195
1987	226
1988	255
1989	282
Index	309

Chapters are organized by year and then alphabetically by manufacturer within year. See the Index for a list of manufacturers within each year.

1980 Pontiac Phoenix LJ 5-door

Foreword

The 80's. Like many of the decades before it, it was a decade of change. As the disco era was coming to a close, the glamour cars representing that time were becoming obsolete. Over the 80's decade, the industry began phasing out vinyl roofs, opera windows, opera lights, velour upholstery and other remnants of glitz. (Although pillow-type seats remained very popular in upper level trim cars.) Consumers demanded more function and feedback from their cars. As a result, cars became more driver-oriented, without sacrificing comfort.

The 80's. Unlike, the times before, however, it was a time when lines blurred even more. Re-badged, foreign assembled vehicles were sold on domestic car lots. Were cars considered "domestic" based on their assembly point or their content of U.S. made components? Did it matter as long as the profits went to a U.S. globally headquartered corporation? This debate still continues today.

Much like the blurring line of domestic/foreign definitions was the blurring of vehicle lines. In this decade we saw the introduction of the minivan with the Dodge Caravan/Plymouth Voyager and the introduction of the SUV by Jeep Cherokee. Though the manufacturers classified these vehicles as light trucks, they were used mostly by families with needs to haul people and their "stuff", replacing the role of the station wagon.

Trends in society found their ways into automobiles. Video game consoles became more popular and personal computers began appearing on household desks. A great use of electronics permeated in cars from controlling various mechanical systems to displaying instrumentation in digital readouts and even warning systems that talked.

The economy and a second gas crisis also had a significant impact, shaping manufacturers' responses throughout the 80's. Cars shrank in size and engine displacements. Many platforms migrated to front-wheel drive. And with a few years of experience building smaller cars, auto companies learned how to make smaller engines more powerful through an increased use of turbo-charging.

Yet, in the 80's, there were some contrasts. While cars continued to downsize and follow function, hairstyles grew. Women wore large, frizzy, crimped and messy styles while men wore mullets (business in the front, party in the back).

I began the 80's in college, studying computer science. Secretly, I pondered whether I should have considered more seriously a career in the automotive industry. There was just something about automobiles that kept my focus. Yet, my interest in computer technology proved equally strong. While software applications became a career, automobiles would become my passion.

The 80's, like 2008-2010 (the time of this composition) was a time of economic strife that threatens the survival of the U.S. auto industry. We find that Chrysler's survival, yet again, depends on government intervention. Yet, the struggle for the industry goes beyond Chrysler. GM is on life support, also using taxpayer money to rebuild. Chrysler survived the 80's and came out a stronger, more profitable corporation. It is yet to be seen if the same scenario holds true for Chrysler and GM as the economy of the Great Recession recovers.

As a young boy, my father inspired my passion for automobiles. We spent Sundays (there were blue laws then) on car lots, free from salespeople. We looked at cars, considered their styles, materials, features and options. We compared and noted other manufacturer's comparable vehicles to each car we studied. There was something we could find to appreciate in a base Pinto as well as the top of the line Lincoln. It wasn't about horsepower. For us, it was about the artistry of design, the folds and creases in the metal, styling cues that paid loyal homage to previous generations, extra comforts and conveniences, appointments and new technologies.

Today, my modest collection of cars include four cars from the 80's: the last year of the Lincoln Versailles, a Mercury Cougar XR-7, a Chrysler LeBaron Mark Cross convertible and a Chrysler LeBaron Mark Cross turbo coupe. I delight in driving them as they are now unique on the roads and reliable for everyday driving.

I hope you enjoy this trip through the 80's memory lane as much as I enjoy compiling the material.

James H. Kaster

The 80's Measured

The chart below shows the pattern of costs for various items throughout the decade. While the cost of bread was increasing, the cost of gasoline was decreasing and by the middle of the decade, a loaf of bread cost more than a gallon of gasoline. Housing prices made a big jump in 1989. Together, these two metrics ushered in the 90's SUV craze. Homeowners, using their newfound equity, took out second mortgages to purchase larger cars and SUVs than had been available in the 80's. With gas prices so low, the MPG concerns that started the early 80's recession was no longer a concern by the end of the decade. Interestingly, as we enter the 2010 & 2011 model years, we find ourselves in a similar, if not worse, predicament. The U.S. is in its most severe recession since World War II and the volatile cost of gasoline has consumers demanding fuel efficient vehicles. History is repeating.

Cost Comparison Chart

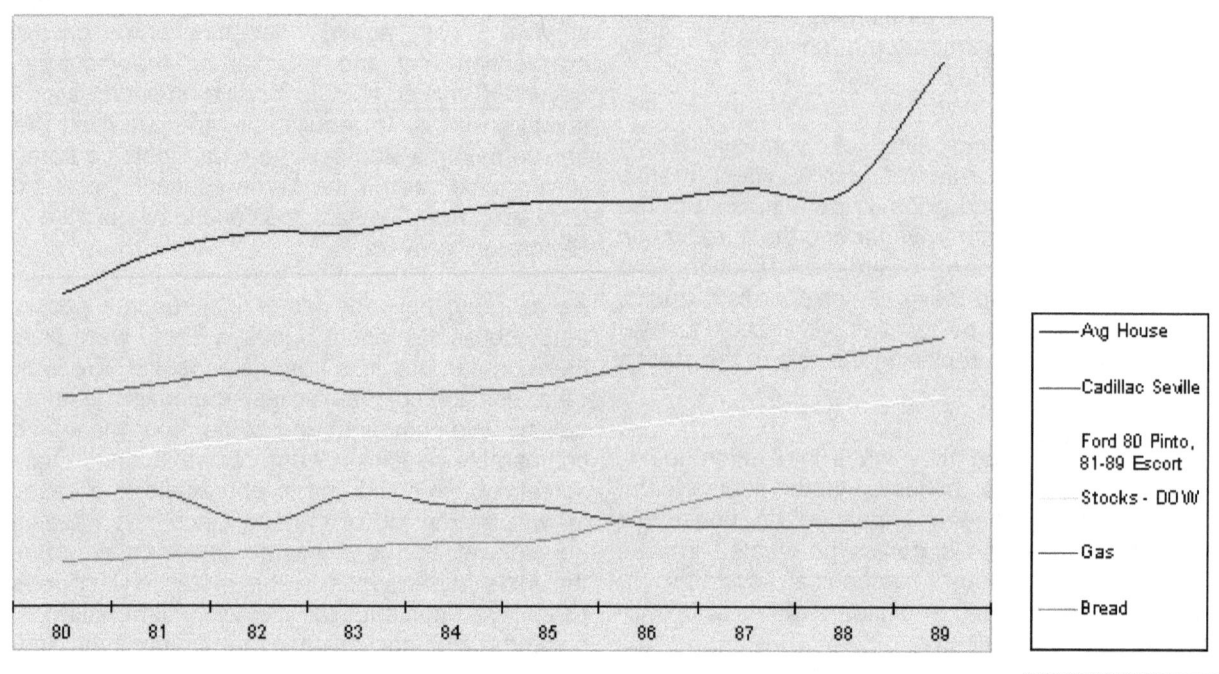

Percentage of change, comparing 1989 to 1980

Average House Price	74.7%
Cadillac Seville	29.1%
Ford '89 Escort / '80 Pinto	51.2%
Stocks – DOW	185.0%
Gallon of Gas	-18.5%
Loaf of Bread	168.6%

1980

1980 - Facts at Glance

News Headlines

- US operation failed to free hostages in Iran
- Ronald Reagan elected President
- Mount St. Helen Erupts
- John Lennon is killed
- Fire destroys MGM Grand Hotel in Las Vegas
- Winter Olympics held in Lake Placid
- Pac-Man introduced

Tops in Pop Culture

Music
- Call Me, Blondie

Movies
- Star Wars Episode V: The Empire Strikes Back

TV Show
- Dallas

Sports Champions

Basketball
- LA Lakers

Football
- Pittsburg Steelers

Baseball
- Philadelphia Phillies

MT – Car of the Year

Chevrolet Citation

Those '80s Cars

1980 - AMC / EAGLE

1980 AMC Concord Limited Wagon

1980 AMC 4-WD EAGLE • CONCORD SPIRIT • PACER • AMX

1980 AMC Concord Limited Sedan

1980 AMC Concord DL Coupe

1980 AMC Concord available leather interior

1980 AMC Concord instrument panel

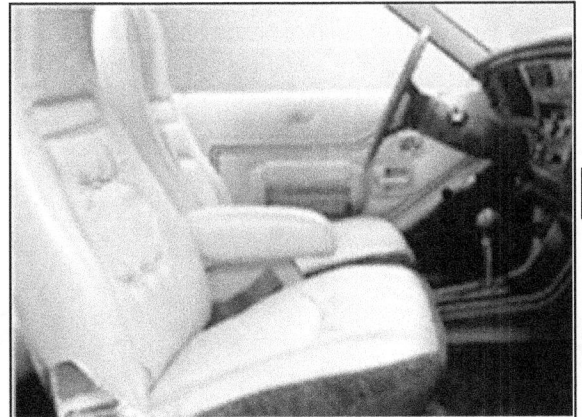
1980 AMC Spirit Limited leather interior

Standard G.T. Rally-tuned suspension system

Last Model Run: 1980 AMC AMX

1980 AMC Spirit Sedan

2.5 liter 4-cylinder power

1980 AMC Eagle Sedan

1980 AMC Spirit Liftback

1980 AMC Eagle Sport Wagon, 2-door & 4-door

Last Model Run: 1980 AMC Pacer Sedan

Last Model Run: 1980 AMC Pacer Wagon

Those '80s Cars

1980 - BUICK

3.8 liter (231) 4-bbl, turbocharged V6

1980 Buick Riviera S Type

From the Brochure: "Perhaps you're the sort of person who remembers, with fondness, the early Corvette Stingray, the fabled Skylark GS 400, or the original Riviera. To you we dedicate the 1980 Buick Riviera S Type... For many, it truly represents an American luxury car with impressive road manners."

1980 Buick Riviera available leather interior

1980 Buick Electra Park Avenue interior

Refreshed: 1980 Buick Electra Limited Coupe

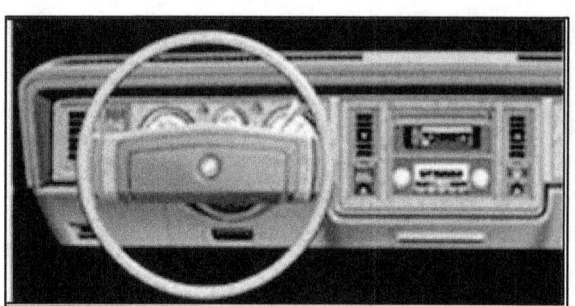

1980 Buick Electra instrument panel

Refreshed: 1980 Buick LeSabre Sedan

1980 Buick Regal Coupe

1980 Buick Century Sedan

1980 Buick Regal Limited interior

Last Model Run: 1980 Buick Century Coupe (aero)

1980 Buick Regal Sport Coupe

1980 Buick Regal instrument panel

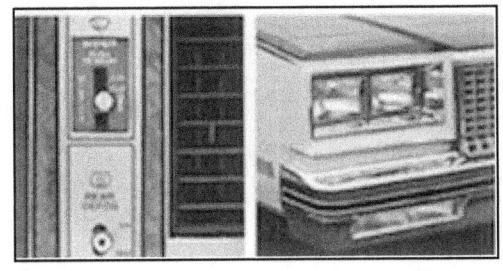

Those '80s Cars

Last Model Run: 1980 Buick Skyhawk

New Model: 1980 Buick Skylark Limited Sedan

1980 Buick Skyhawk bucket seat interior

1980 Buick Skylark instrument panel

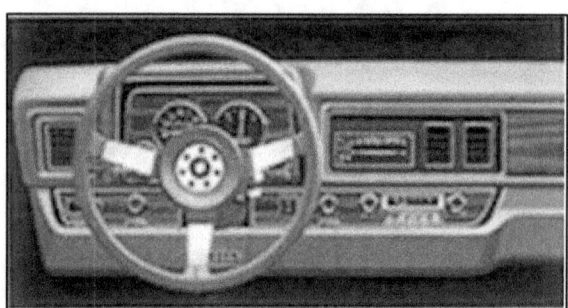
1980 Buick Skyhawk instrument panel

1980 Buick Skylark Limited interior

1980 Buick Skyhawk shifter and optional wheel

1980 Buick Skylark Coupe

From the Brochure: "A great suspension. Nimble size. Sleek, aerodynamic shape. A just right 2+2 seating configuration. And a three-door design with an eminently practical hatchback." – 1980 Buick Skyhawk

Those '80s Cars

1980 - CADILLAC

New, standard 6.0 liter gas V8

Refreshed: 1980 Cadillac Coupe deVille

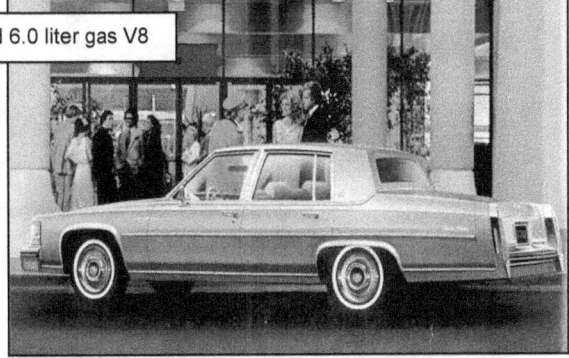

Refreshed: 1980 Cadillac Fleetwood Brougham

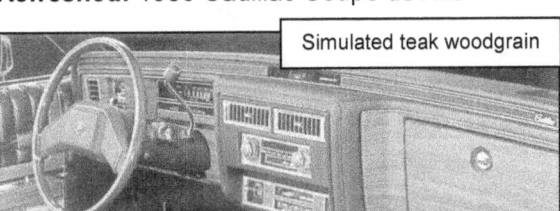

Simulated teak woodgrain

1980 Cadillac deVille instrument panel

1980 Cadillac Fleetwood Brougham interior

Durand knit cloth with Renaissance velour inserts

1980 Cadillac deVille interior

From the Brochure: "…quite possibly the most distinctive car in the world today… and the most advanced. This is Seville for the 80's. A masterwork of classical and contemporary elements united in an undeniably beautiful automobile." – 1980 Cadillac Seville

Standard 5.7 liter, fuel-injected diesel V8

New Model: 1980 Cadillac Seville Elegante

1980 Cadillac Seville Elegante interior

1980 Cadillac Eldorado interior

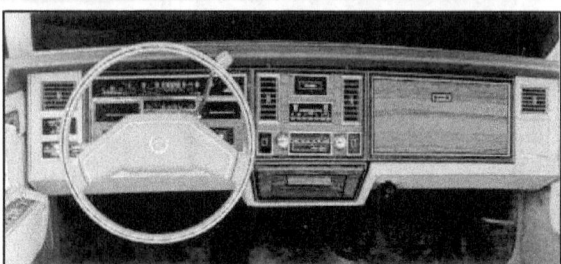
1980 Cadillac Seville instrument panel

New electronic climate control

From the Brochure: "World class in engineering. Cadillac in luxury. A legend on the road. Eldorado, one of the cars that pioneered front-wheel drive in the U.S. is still one of its finest expressions."
– 1980 Cadillac Eldorado

6.0 EFI V8 gas engine standard, 5.7 liter diesel V8 optional

1980 Cadillac Eldorado

1980 - CHEVROLET

350 CID, 4-speed manual standard

1980 Chevrolet Camaro Z28

1980 Chevrolet Camaro interior

From the Brochure: "Chevy Camaro. The Hugger. Take a look. Here's the shape that turns heads and quickens heartbeats. Camaro is a car that helps recapture the fun and excitement and challenge of driving."
– 1980 Chevrolet Camaro

1980 Chevrolet Camaro instrument panel

5.7 liter, 4bbl, V8 gas, 4-speed manual transmission are standard (5.0 in CA). 5.7 L82 with high lift cam is optional.

1980 Chevrolet Corvette

1980 Chevrolet Corvette interior

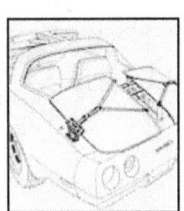

Those '80s Cars

1980 Chevrolet Caprice Classic dash

Refreshed: 1980 Caprice Classic Sedan

Caprice / Impala engine options: 3.8 liter V6 gas, 4.4 liter V8 gas, 5.0 liter V8 gas, 5.7 liter diesel

1980 Chevrolet Caprice Classic interior

Refreshed: 1980 Caprice Classic Coupe

Refreshed: 1980 Chevrolet Impala Sedan

New Model: 1980 Chevrolet Citation 4-door

Citation standard power team: 2.5 liter, 151 CID, 90hp, 4-speed manual

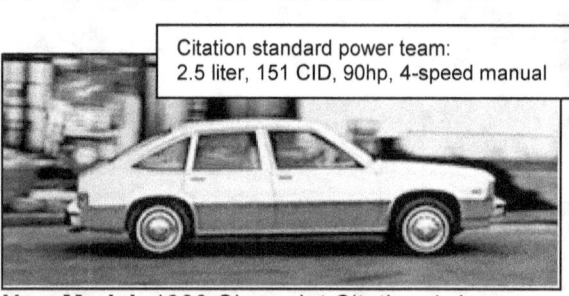
New Model: 1980 Chevrolet Citation 4-door

1980 Chevrolet Impala interior

1980 Chevrolet Citation standard interior

1980 Chevrolet Citation instrument panel

Those '80s Cars

Malibu engine options: 3.8 liter V6 gas, 4.4 liter V8 gas, 5.0 liter V8 gas

1980 Chevrolet Malibu Sedan

1980 Chevrolet Malibu Classic Landau Coupe

1980 Chevrolet Malibu Classic Wagon

1980 Chevrolet Malibu Classic interior

1980 Chevrolet Monte Carlo Coupe

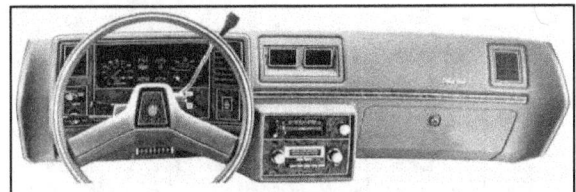

1980 Chevrolet Monte Carlo instrument panel

Monte Carlo engine options: 3.8 liter V6 gas, 3.8 liter turbo V6 gas, 4.4 liter V8 gas, 5.0 liter V8 gas

1980 Chevrolet Monte Carlo bucket seat interior

1980 Chevrolet Monte Carlo Special Custom

Monza engine options: 2.5 L4, 3.8 liter V6 gas

1980 Chevrolet Monza 2+2 Sport interior

Last Model Run: 1980 Chevrolet Monza 2+2

Those '80s Cars

1980 - CHRYSLER

1980 Chrysler New Yorker Fifth Avenue

5.2 liter V8 (318) standard & 5.9 liter (360) optional

1980 Chrysler New Yorker instrument panel

1980 Chrysler New Yorker Standard Richton cloth interior

From the Brochure: "Every facet of its brilliant design speaks eloquently for itself. The long, graceful sweep of its classic profile. The understated beauty of its chrome grille topped by the striking pentastar hood ornament. Concealed headlamps."
– 1980 Chrysler New Yorker

1980 Chrysler Newport interior

1980 Chrysler Newport

3.7 liter (225) slant six standard on Newport; 5.2 liter V8 (318) & 5.9 liter (360) optional

From the Brochure: "Friend. Seldom has the term been more appropriate in describing a car. The right car at the right time. A Chrysler in the true sense. Capably equipped, superbly appointed and yet so wonderfully affordable in light of its standard attributes."
– 1980 Chrysler Newport

3.7 liter (225) slant six standard & 5.2 liter V8 (318) optional

112.7" wheelbase
209.8" length
3,362 lbs

New Model: 1980 Chrysler Cordoba

1980 Chrysler Cordoba crest

New trim: Crown Corinthian Edition with exclusive Black Walnut Metallic or Designer's Cream-on-Beige paint treatments.

1980 Chrysler Cordoba instrument panel with tilt steering wheel

1980 Chrysler Cordoba available leather interior

From the Brochure: "Cordoba 1980. A car whose striking new resized form strides into the new decade with poise and assurance befitting its proud tradition. From its Franklin Minted hood ornament to its tri-lens taillamps, Cordoba 1980 is an exceptional automobile. But extraordinary styling marks the beginning.

Cordoba. The car that redefined the term "contemporary classic" during the 1970's returns to set new standards of personal luxury for the 1980's."

– 1980 Chrysler Cordoba

3.7 liter (225) slant six standard & 5.2 liter V8 (318) optional

2-doors shortened to a 108.7" wheelbase

Refreshed: 1980 Chrysler LeBaron LS

1980 Chrysler LeBaron LS instrument panel

1980 Chrysler LeBaron 4-door

From the Brochure: "The whole idea of elegance in a personal-sized car is rapidly changing Chrysler LeBaron has a great deal to do with this changing attitude."
– 1980 Chrysler LeBaron

1980 Chrysler LeBaron bucket seat interior option

1980 Chrysler LeBaron Town & Country

1980 - DODGE

1980 Dodge Diplomat S-Type bucket seat interior, 4-door sedan, illuminated entry, electronic stereo

Diplomat & Mirada: 3.7 liter (225) slant six standard & 5.2 liter V8 (318) optional

Refreshed: 1980 Dodge Diplomat S-Type 2-door Coupe

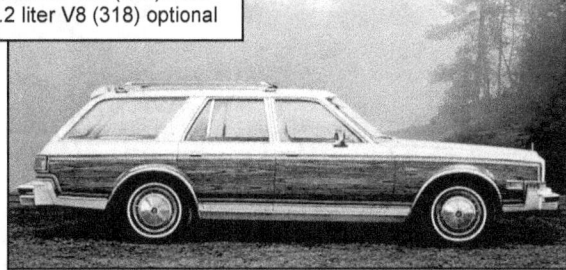

1980 Dodge Diplomat Salon Wagon

6 different Aspen coupe series

Last Model Run: 1980 Dodge Aspen Value Sedan & Sunrise Coupe

New Model: 1980 Dodge Mirada

Aspen pricing starts under $5,000

Last Model Run: 1980 Dodge Aspen Special Edition Wagon

1980 Dodge St. Regis

New for 1980: Touring Edition series
Touring Edition instrument cluster shown

1980 Dodge St. Regis interior, instrument panel & optional glass sunroof

1980 Dodge Omni 024

1.7 liter 4-cylinder w/4-speed manual are standard

1.6 liter & 2.6 liter 4-cylinder engines

1980 Dodge Challenger

1980 Dodge Omni 4-door with Premium Exterior Package

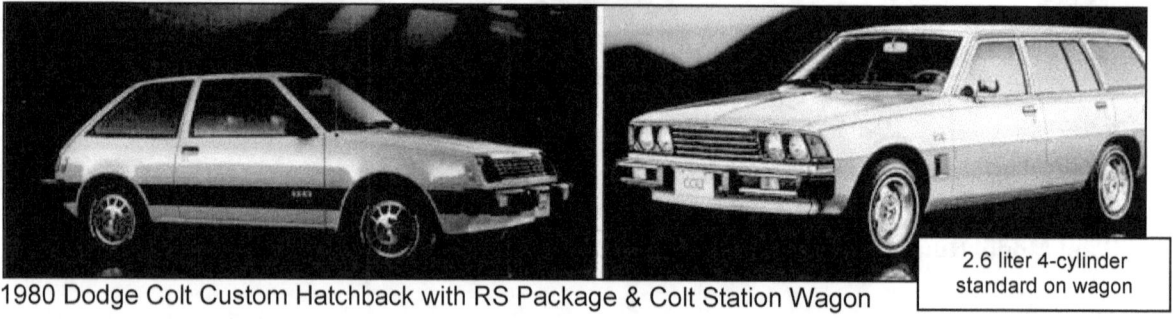
1980 Dodge Colt Custom Hatchback with RS Package & Colt Station Wagon

2.6 liter 4-cylinder standard on wagon

Those '80s Cars

1980 - FORD

New Model: 1980 Ford Thunderbird Silvery Anniversary

1980 Ford Thunderbird optional electronic instrument panel

1980 Ford Thunderbird Interior Luxury Group with leather

New Model: 1980 Ford Thunderbird with Exterior Luxury Group

1980 trim series:
Thunderbird
Silver Anniversary
Town Landau
Exterior & Interior Luxury
Exterior & Interior Decor
Standard Exterior & Interior

Granada engine choices: 4.1 liter inline 6-cylinder, 4.2 & 5.0 liter V8s

Last Model Run: 1980 Ford Granada Ghia 4-door Sedan

3 trim series: Granada, Granada Ghia, Granada ESS

New 4.2 V8 engine & new 4-speed automatic overdrive for 5.0 engine only option

1980 Ford Granada optional leather bucket seats

Granada ESS

Those '80s Cars 21

Standard power team 2.3 liter OHC 4-cylinder w/4-speed manual

1980 Ford Fairmont Ghia 4-door

2.3 liter turbo 4-cylinder

1980 Ford Fairmont Futura Ghia Turbocharger

1980 Ford Fairmont Wagon

Ghia luxury steering wheel with fingertip speed control

1980 Ford Fairmont dash panel

Ghia flight bench seat in new luxury velour cloth

1980 Ford Fairmont Futura interior

1980 Ford LTD 4-door

5.8 liter V8 is optional

1980 Ford LTD 2-door

5.0 liter (302) V8 w/3-speed automatic are standard

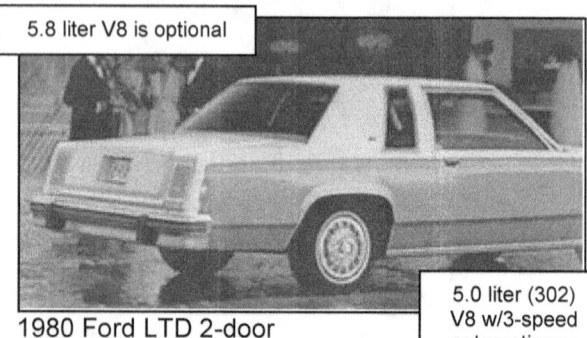

Optional 4-speed AOD

22

Those '80s Cars

Mustang engines: 2.3 liter 4-cylinder, 2.3 turbo, 3.3 liter inline 6 & 4.2 liter V8

1980 Ford Mustang 3-Door Turbocharger (2.3 liter) with Michelin TRX tires

1.6 liter OHV 4-cylinder w/4-speed manual are standard

Last Model Run: 1980 Ford Fiesta with Décor Group option

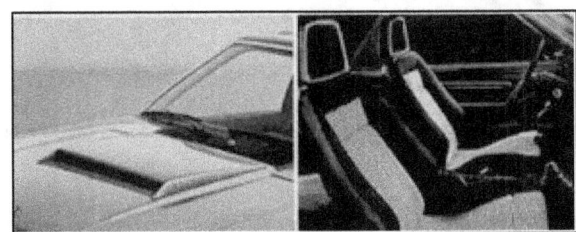

1980 Ford Mustang hood scoop & new for 1980: Recaro Seats

1980 Ford Fiesta & Ghia interior

2.3 liter OHC 4-cylinder w/4-speed manual are standard

Last Model Run: 1980 Ford Pinto interior, Wagon & 2.3 liter OHC 4-cylinder engine

Pinto Models:
2-door sedan
3-door Runabouts
2-door wagons

Last Model Run: 1980 Ford Pinto 3-Door Runabout with Exterior Décor Group Option

Those '80s Cars

1980 - LINCOLN

5.0 liter V8 w/3-speed auto

Last Model Run: 1980 Lincoln Versailles

Last Model Run: 1980 Lincoln Versailles

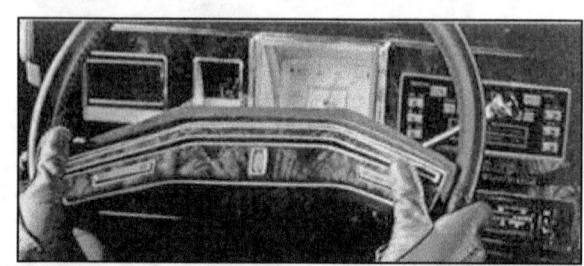

1980 Lincoln Versailles instrument panel

New Twin Comfort Lounge Seats replace last year's flight bench seat

1980 Lincoln Versailles standard Twin Comfort Lounge Seat cloth interior

1980 Lincoln Versailles optional leather bucket seat interior

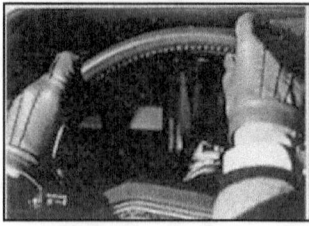  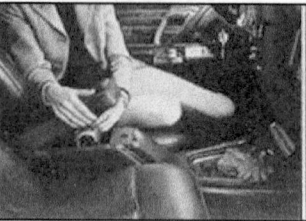 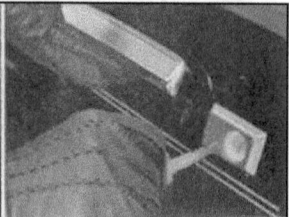

Those '80s Cars

New Model: 1980 Lincoln Continental Coupe

5.0 & 5.8 liter V8s with new 4-speed AOD

New Model: 1980 Lincoln Continental Mark VI Signature Series

1980 Lincoln Town Car interior

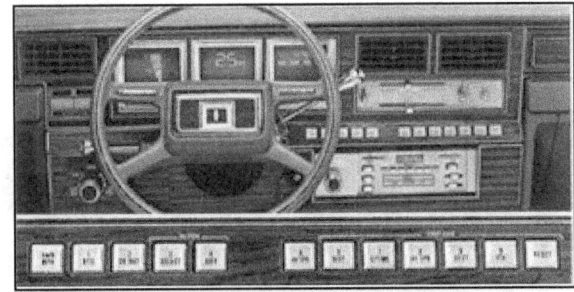
1980 Lincoln Continental Mark VI instrument panel

New Model: 1980 Lincoln Continental Town Car

New Model: 1980 Lincoln Continental Town Car

1980 Lincoln Continental Mark VI Signature Series 2-door interior

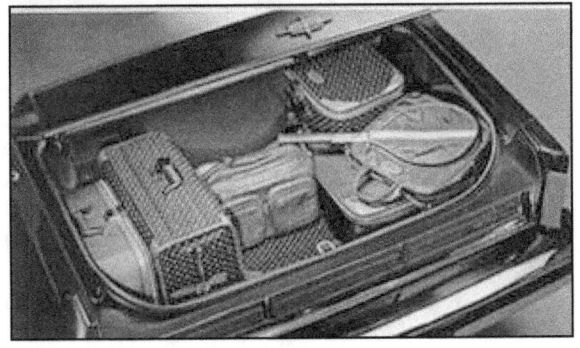

New Model: 1980 Lincoln Continental Mark VI Bill Blass Designer Series

Those '80s Cars

1980 - MERCURY

Last Model Run: 1980 Mercury Monarch Ghia 4-door

Monarch power team choices:
4.1 liter inline 6-cylinder, 4.2 & 5.0 liter V8
4-speed manual overdrive & 3-speed automatic

1980 Mercury Monarch flight bench with optional luxury cloth

Capri engines:
2.3 liter 4-cylinder, 2.3 turbo
3.3 liter inline 6, 4.2 liter V8

1980 Mercury Capri RS Turbo

Last Model Run: 1980 Mercury Monarch 2-door with ESS option

1980 Mercury Monarch options

2.3 liter 4-cylinder

Last Model Run: 1980 Mercury Bobcat with Sport Option

Press Kit: "With its blend of European styling and American performance, U.S.-built Capri was an instant hit in 1979. For 1980 Capri will generate more excitement with a new optional 4.2 liter (255 CID) V-8 engine and new powertrain combination matching the 2.3-liter turbocharged engine with an automatic transmission." – 1980 Mercury Capri

Press Kit: "The Sport Option --- another exciting new styling innovation --- will feature a front air dam, a rear spoiler, a special black two-tone paint/tape treatment, and distinctive lower bodyside tape-striping."
– 1980 Mercury Bobcat

1980 Mercury Zephyr Sports Instrumentation Group option

1980 Mercury Zephyr Interior Accent Group option

Zephyr engines:
2.3 liter 4-cylinder, 2.3 turbo
3.3 liter inline 6, 4.2 liter V8

1980 Mercury Zephyr Z-7

1980 Mercury Zephyr 2-door with 2.3 Turbo

1980 Mercury Zephyr 2-door Sedan

Dual beam halogen headlamps are now standard

1980 Mercury Zephyr Station Wagon and Villager option

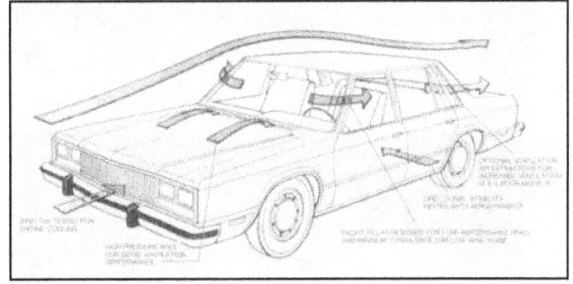

Those '80s Cars

4.2 & 5.0 liter V8s
3-speed auto & 4-speed AOD

New Model: 1980 Mercury Cougar XR-7

New Model: 1980 Mercury Cougar XR-7 with Luxury Group

1980 Mercury Cougar XR-7 Twin Comfort Lounge Seats

1980 Mercury Cougar XR-7 electronic dash

1980 Mercury Grand Marquis interior

1980 Mercury Cougar XR-7 Features & Options

5.0 & 5.8 liter V8s
3-speed auto & 4-speed AOD

New coach roof

1980 Mercury Grand Marquis 4-door Sedan

1980 - OLDSMOBILE

Refreshed: 1980 Oldsmobile Custom Cruiser

Delta 88 engine options: 3.8 liter V6 gas, 4.3, 5.0 & 5.7 liter V8 gas, 5.7 liter diesel

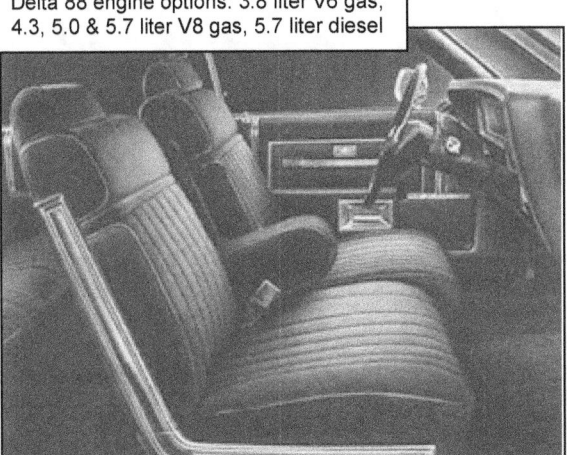
1980 Oldsmobile Delta 88 Royale interior

Toronado engine options: 5.0 & 5.7 liter 4-bbl V8 gas engines & 5.7 liter diesel engine

1980 Oldsmobile Toronado Brougham

1980 Oldsmobile Toronado instrument panel

Refreshed: 1980 Oldsmobile Delta 88 Royale Brougham Coupe & Ninety-Eight Regency Sedan

Ninety-Eight/Custom Cruiser engine options: 5.0 & 5.7 liter 4-bbl V8 gas engines & 5.7 liter diesel

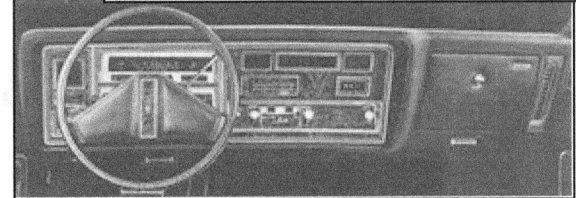
1980 Oldsmobile Ninety-Eight instrument

1980 Oldsmobile Ninety-Eight Regency interior

1980 Oldsmobile Toronado Brougham interior

1980 Oldsmobile Cutlass Supreme Brougham Coupe & Omega Brougham Sedan

1980 Oldsmobile Cutlass Supreme Brougham Coupe interior

1980 Oldsmobile Cutlass Cruiser Brougham

Cutlass engine options: 3.8 liter V6 gas, 4.3 & 5.0 liter V8 gas, 5.7 liter diesel

1980 Oldsmobile Cutlass Supreme Brougham Sedan

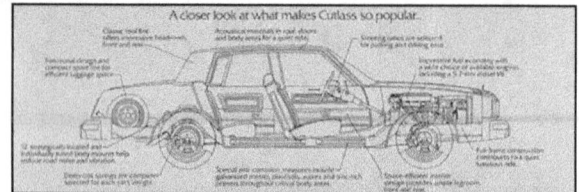

1980 Oldsmobile Cutlass instrument panel

1980 Oldsmobile Cutlass Calais interior

1980 Oldsmobile Cutlass Salon Brougham

Last Model Run: 1980 Oldsmobile Cutlass Salon Brougham (aero)

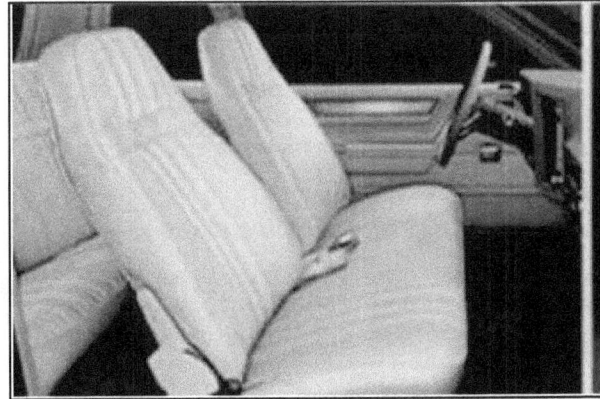

New Model: 1980 Oldsmobile Omega Sedan

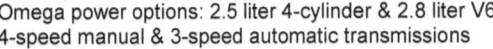

Omega power options: 2.5 liter 4-cylinder & 2.8 liter V6
4-speed manual & 3-speed automatic transmissions

New Model: 1980 Oldsmobile Omega Brougham Coupe with available bucket seats

1980 Oldsmobile Omega instrument panel

8-track tape player & power window options

New Model: 1980 Oldsmobile Omega Brougham Sedan

Starfire engine options:
2.5 liter L4, 3.8 liter V6

New Model: 1980 Oldsmobile Omega SX

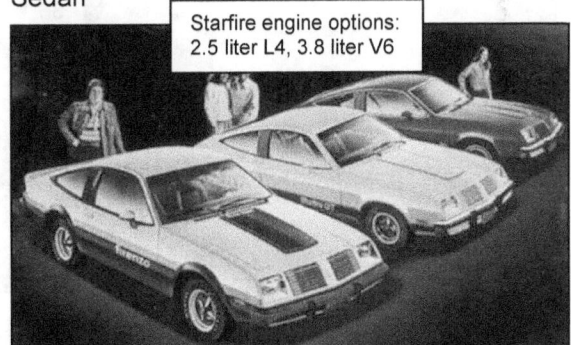

Last Model Run: 1980 Oldsmobile Starfire
Starfire standard features shown below

Those '80s Cars

1980 - PLYMOUTH

Optional 5.9 liter 4bbl V8

New Model: 1980 Plymouth Gran Fury Pursuit Package

Last Model Run: 1980 Plymouth Volare 4-door with Premier Package

2-doors: Volare, Custom, Special, Premier, & Duster
4-doors: Volare, Custom, Special, Premier
Wagons: Volare, Custom & Premier

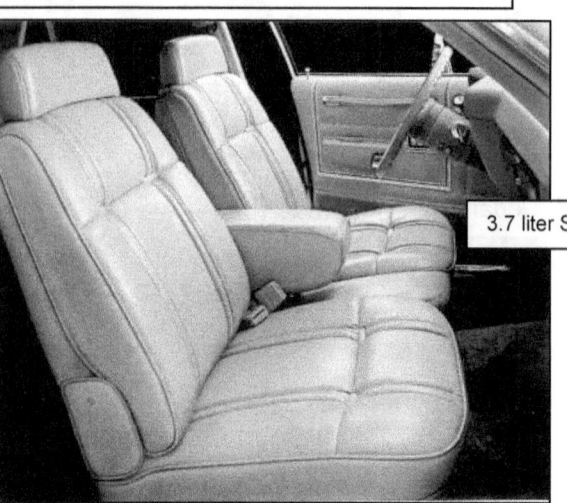

1980 Plymouth Volare with all-vinyl 60/40 seats

1980 Plymouth Volare instrument panel

3.7 liter Slant Six, 5.2 liter V8 & 5.9 liter V8 engine options

New Model: 1980 Plymouth Gran Fury

1980 Plymouth Gran Fury interior and optional features

3.7 liter Slant Six & 5.2 liter V8

Last Model Run: 1980 Plymouth Duster

Last Model Run: 1980 Plymouth Volare Wagon with Custom Package

Last Model Run: Plymouth Arrow (1979 above) **Last Model Run:** 1980 Plymouth Arrow

1980 Plymouth Horizon TC3 with Sports Appearance Package & Horizon 4-door

1.7 liter 4-cylinder w/4-speed manual are standard

1980 Plymouth Horizon Custom Interior Package (woodgrain dash appliqués, locking glove box, cigarette lighter, knit-cloth covered headliner, custom door trim, rear armrests, custom vinyl bucket seats)

1980 Plymouth Horizon instrument panel with optional deep-dish 4-spoke sport steering wheel

2.6 liter 4-cylinder

1980 Plymouth Sapporo

1980 Plymouth Horizon with Premium Woodgrain Package

Those '80s Cars

1980 - PONTIAC

From the Brochure: "It's a whole new decade. Calling for dramatically new kinds of American cars. Cars that are trim. Cars that are roomy. Cars that are efficient. Cars that are designed to last. Pontiac is committed to answering your call for these cars, not by relying on past successes, but by creating new ones."

– 1980 Pontiac

1980 Pontiac Firebird Esprit with Yellow Bird appearance package

1980 Pontiac Firebird Formula

1980 Pontiac Firebird Special Edition Trans Am interior

1980 Pontiac Firebird Trans Am

Firebird/Esprit engines: 3.8 V6, 4.3 V8, 4.9 V8, 5.0 V8 (CA)
Formula/Trans Am engines: 4.9 V8, 5.0 V8 (CA), new 4.9 turbo V8

New Model: 1980 Pontiac Phoenix LJ Coupe

Phoenix engine choices: 2.5 liter L4 & 2.8 liter V6

New Model: 1980 Pontiac Phoenix LJ 5-Door Hatchback

Grand Prix engines: 3.8 V6, 4.3 V8, 4.9 V8, 5.0 V8 (CA)

1980 Pontiac Grand Prix SJ

1980 Pontiac Phoenix interior with available cloth bucket seats

1980 Pontiac Grand Prix instrument panel & interior with available leather bucket seats

1980 Pontiac Phoenix 5-Door hatchback interior

Those '80s Cars

Bonneville Catalina engines: 3.8 V6, 4.3 V8, 4.9 V8, 5.7 V8

Refreshed: 1980 Pontiac Bonneville Safari Wagon

Refreshed: 1980 Pontiac Bonneville Brougham Coupe

1980 Pontiac Bonneville Brougham Coupe interior with available cloth bucket seats

1980 Pontiac Bonneville Brougham available leather interior

1980 Pontiac Catalina interior

Refreshed: 1980 Pontiac Catalina

Refreshed: 1980 Pontiac Bonneville Brougham Sedan

36 Those '80s Cars

1980 Pontiac Grand LeMans Safari

LeMans engines: 3.8 V6, 4.3 V8, 4.9 V8, 5.0 V8 (CA)

1980 Pontiac Grand LeMans Sedan

1980 Pontiac LeMans instrument panel

1980 Pontiac Grand Am instrument panel with custom bucket seats

Last Model Run: 1980 Pontiac Sunbird Sport Coupe

Last Model Run: 1980 Pontiac Grand Am Coupe

Last Model Run: 1980 Pontiac Sunbird Sport Hatch with available Formula Package

1980 Pontiac Sunbird with available luxury cloth bucket seats

Those '80s Cars

1981

1981 - Facts at Glance

News Headlines

- Reagan fires striking air traffic controllers
- Researchers find the wreck of the Titanic
- Muhammad Ali retires
- Lady Diana marries Prince Charles
- Egyptian President Anwar Sadat is assassinated
- Sandra Day O'Connor appointed to Supreme Court
- 1st test tube baby is born
- Microsoft introduces MS-DOS
- MTV launched

Tops in Pop Culture

Music
- Bette Davis Eyes, Kim Carnes

Movies
- Raiders of the Lost Ark

TV Show
- Dallas

Sports Champions

Basketball
- Boston Celtics

Football
- Oakland Raiders

Baseball
- L.A. Dodgers

Motor Trend – Car of the Year

Chrysler K Cars:
Dodge Aries & Plymouth Reliant

1981 - AMC / EAGLE

1981 AMC Spirit Hatchback & 2-door Sedan

1981 AMC Spirit interior

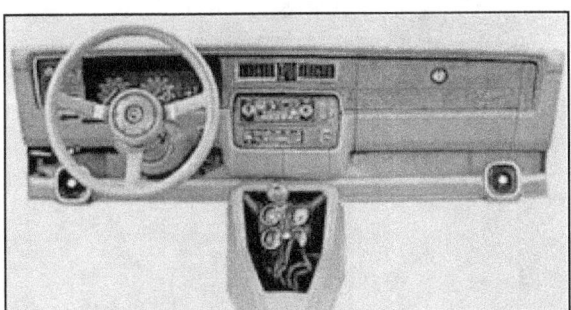
1981 AMC Spirit instrument panel

1981 AMC Spirit interior

1981 AMC Concord Station Wagon

1981 AMC Concord 4-door Sedan

1981 AMC Concord DL interior

1981 AMC wheels and wheel covers

From the Brochure: "Choose a Spirit for its substance or its style and get a full measure of both. Spirit interiors, in particular, are better equipped and appointed than those in many other small cars."   - 1981 AMC Spirit

1981 AMC Eagle 4-door

1981 AMC Eagle 2-door

Press Kit: "The 1981 Eagle 2-dr. and 4-dr. sedan offer a combination of luxury and the convenience of a compact with the superior traction and handling of four-wheel drive. For 1981, American Motors leads the U.S. auto industry with another first and exclusive. All Eagle models utilize 100 percent one-side galvanized steel on all exterior body panels. A 2.5 liter 4-cylinder engine is standard, with 4.2 liter 6-cylinder engine optional."

– 1981 AMC Eagle

1981 AMC Eagle SX/4

1981 AMC Eagle Kammback

1981 AMC Eagle Station Wagon

1981 AMC Eagle 4-door & 2-door Sedans

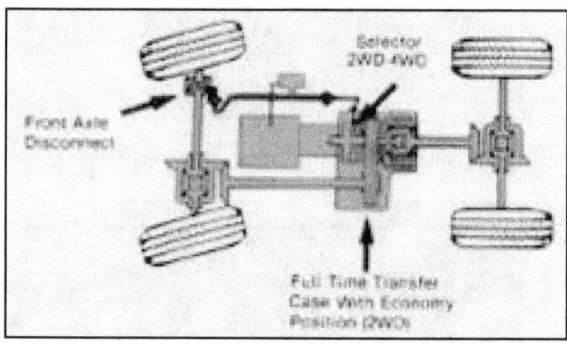

1981 AMC AMX Turbo Pace Car

Press Kit: "The AMX Turbo Pace Car is an exclusive – the personal design of Richard A. Teague, American Motor's Vice President of Automotive Design. This two-passenger, aerodynamically efficient vehicle will be one of four official pace cars in the PPG Indy Car World Series during the 1981 racing season."

– 1981 AMX Turbo

1981 - BUICK

3.8 liter V6 turbo, 4.1 liter V6 & 5.0 liter V8 gas & 5.7 V8 diesel engines

- 1981 Buick Riviera
- Riviera instrument panel
- Available landau top
- Riviera T Type console

- 1981 Buick Electra Park Avenue
- 1981 Buick Electra Limited
- Electra Limited interior
- Electra instrument panel

Electra & LeSabre engines: 3.8 & 4.1 liter V6 & 5.0 liter V8 gas & 5.7 V8 diesel engines

- 1981 Buick LeSabre Limited
- 1981 Buick LeSabre Limited Coupe
- LeSabre Limited interior
- LeSabre instrument panel

From the Brochure: "Classic design, whether traditional or contemporary, whether in buildings or bridges, has an inherent rightness about it. It's an enduring quality that stems both from form and the ingenious use of materials. In short, it brings beauty to function. We submit that in the automotive world, our 1981 Buicks possess these very same elements."

– 1981 Buick

Those '80s Cars

2.5 liter (151 CID) 4-cylinder & 2.8 liter (173 CID) 6-cylinder engines

3.8 liter (231 CID) 6-cylinder & 4.3 liter (265 CID) 8-cylinder engines

- 1981 Buick Skylark Limited
- 1981 Buick Skylark Coupe
- 1981 Buick Skylark Limited & Sport available bucket seats
- Skylark instrument panel

- 1981 Buick Century Limited
- 1981 Buick Century Sedan
- Formal Roofline

- **Refreshed:** 1981 Buick Regal Sport Coupe w/Décor Package
- 1981 Buick Regal Coupe
- 1981 Buick Regal Limited interior
- Regal instrument panel

1981 Buick Century Station Wagon with Designers' Accent Paint (back)
1981 Buick Century Estate Wagon with Woodgrain (front)

1981 Buick LeSabre Estate Wagon

1981 Buick Electra Estate Wagon

1981 - CADILLAC

1981 Cadillac Fleetwood Brougham Coupe

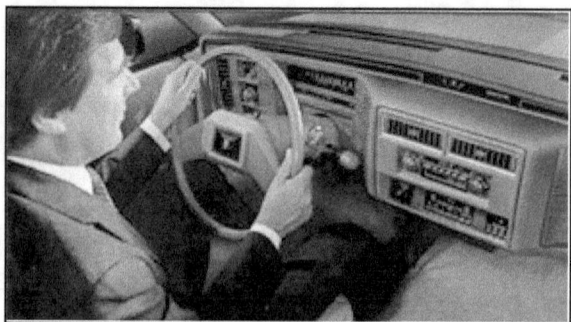
1981 Cadillac deVille interior

1981 Cadillac Sedan deVille

Cadillac introduces this year the V8-6-4 fuel-injected engine as standard equipment. This is a forerunner of today's widely used cylinder deactivation systems by many manufacturers.

1981 Cadillac Seville Elegante

ALL THESE ENGINEERING ADVANCEMENTS ARE AVAILABLE ON ONLY SIX CARS IN 1981.

New V8-6-4 Fuel Injection.
Cadillac is the first carmaker anywhere to offer an engine that automatically goes from 8 to 6 to 4 cylinders and back again as you drive.

It's the exclusive V8-6-4 fuel injected engine offered only by Cadillac in 1981. And it's the standard gasoline engine for all 1981 Cadillacs.

An engine without a carburetor.
Because there is no carburetor with new V8-6-4 Fuel Injection, no carburetor maintenance or adjustments are ever required. Instead, electronically controlled injectors meter a precise mixture of fuel and air to the engine with digital accuracy.

Memory Seat—with "His and Her" settings.
Simply adjust the 6-way power seat to a comfortable driving position, press the "set" button and then one of the two numbered recall buttons. This Cadillac exclusive will store the position you've selected in its memory bank. Then, whenever you touch the appropriate recall button, Memory Seat will automatically return to that same comfortable driving position.

MPG Sentinel.
Push a button and Cadillac's MPG Sentinel (standard with V8-6-4 Fuel Injection) displays how many cylinders are active at that moment. Pushing another button displays average miles per gallon and instantaneous mpg. While touching a third button will

display your estimated driving range. Using this information, you could help yourself become a more efficient driver.

On-Board Computer Diagnostics.
New for DeVilles and Fleetwood Broughams with V8-6-4 Fuel Injection. This system helps take the guesswork out of servicing. It enables a service technician to find and correct possible problem areas quickly — simply by pushing buttons in the car, referring to a code book and making the necessary repairs. A subsequent push of buttons tells him if the problem is properly resolved.

Performance Continuity System.
If a sensor gives an improper signal, the on-board computer automatically substitutes a suitable reading for that sensor.

This allows continued operation of your Cadillac until repairs can be made. Standard with V8-6-4 Fuel Injection. A heritage of innovation and quality lives on with Cadillac 1981.

1981 Cadillac Eldorado instrument panel

1981 Cadillac Seville Elegante interior

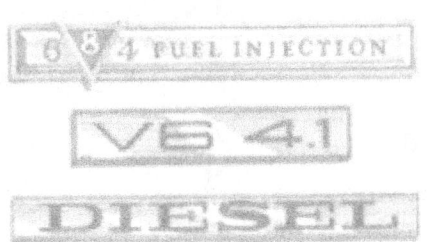

1981 Cadillac Eldorado Biarritz

Those '80s Cars 45

1981 - CHEVROLET

1981 Chevrolet Corvette

1981 Chevrolet Corvette instrument panel

1981 Chevrolet Corvette

3 trim levels: Sport Coupe, Berlinetta & Z28

Last Model Run: 1981 Chevrolet Camaro Sport Coupe with optional Custom interior

14 rubber-cushioned body mounts on a full-perimeter frame

Refreshed: 1981 Chevrolet Monte Carlo Sport Coupe with optional Special Custom interior

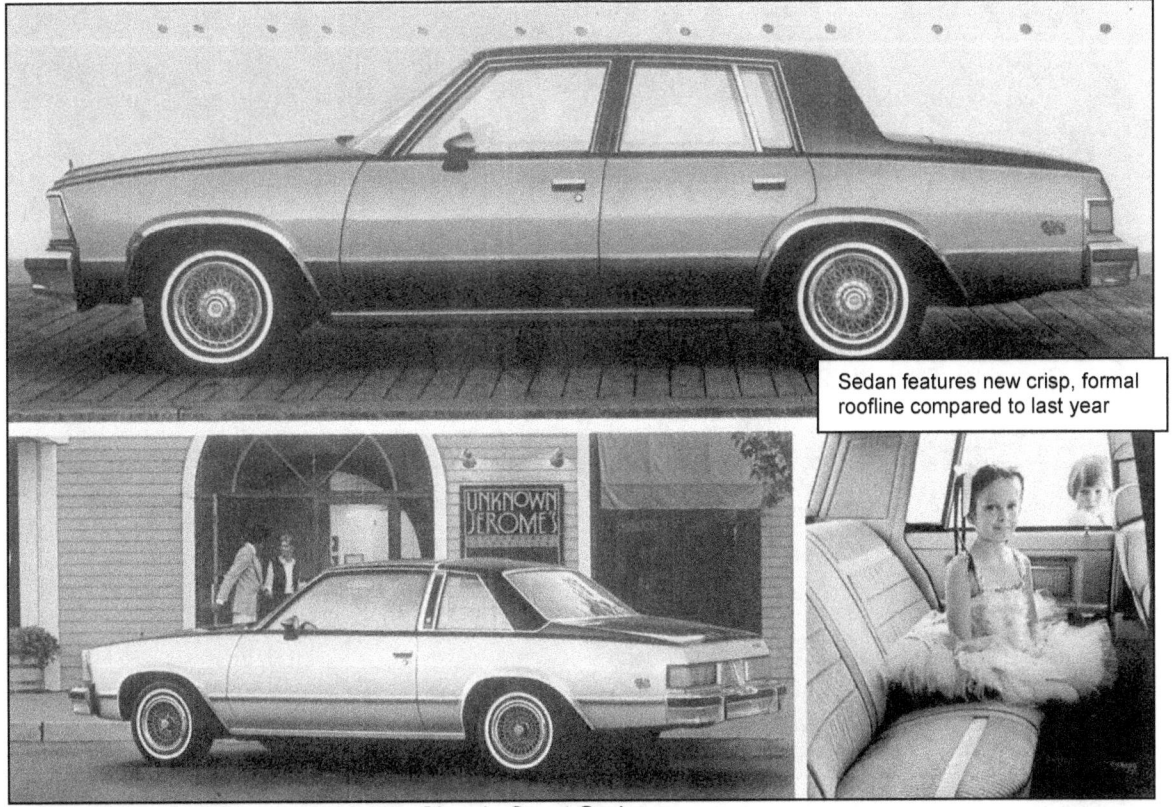

Refreshed: 1981 Chevrolet Malibu Classic Sport Sedan
Last Model Run: 1981 Malibu Classic Landau Coupe Optional Custom interior

Sedan features new crisp, formal roofline compared to last year

Citation X-11 sports a high output 2.8 liter V6

Over 41 cu. ft. of cargo space

1981 Chevrolet Citation X-11 Hatchback Coupe with optional Custom interior
1981 Chevrolet Citation 4-door Hatchback Sedan

Those '80s Cars 47

1.6 liter OHC 4-cylinder

1981 Chevrolet Chevette 2-door Hatchback Coupe with optional Custom interior

CHEVY EL CAMINO

The 1981 Chevy El Camino blends the proven ability of a hardworking truck with the appeal of a thoroughly handsome automobile. A proven combination of rugged beauty, elegance and value. This year there are some significant improvements, too: fresh styling inside and out, important technological refinements, new options, new elegance and more!

1981 Chevrolet El Camino Conquista (car-based truck)

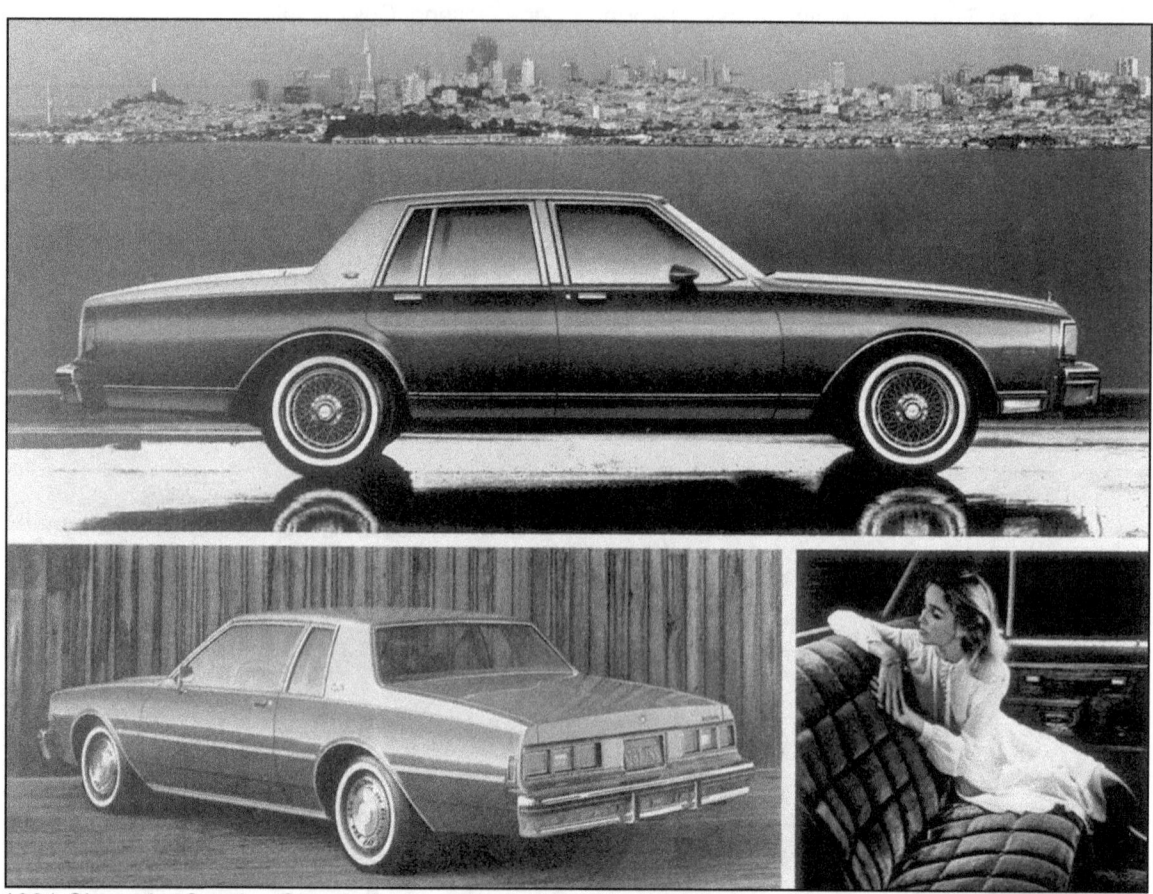

1981 Chevrolet Caprice Classic Sedan with optional Special Custom interior
1981 Chevrolet Impala Sport Coupe

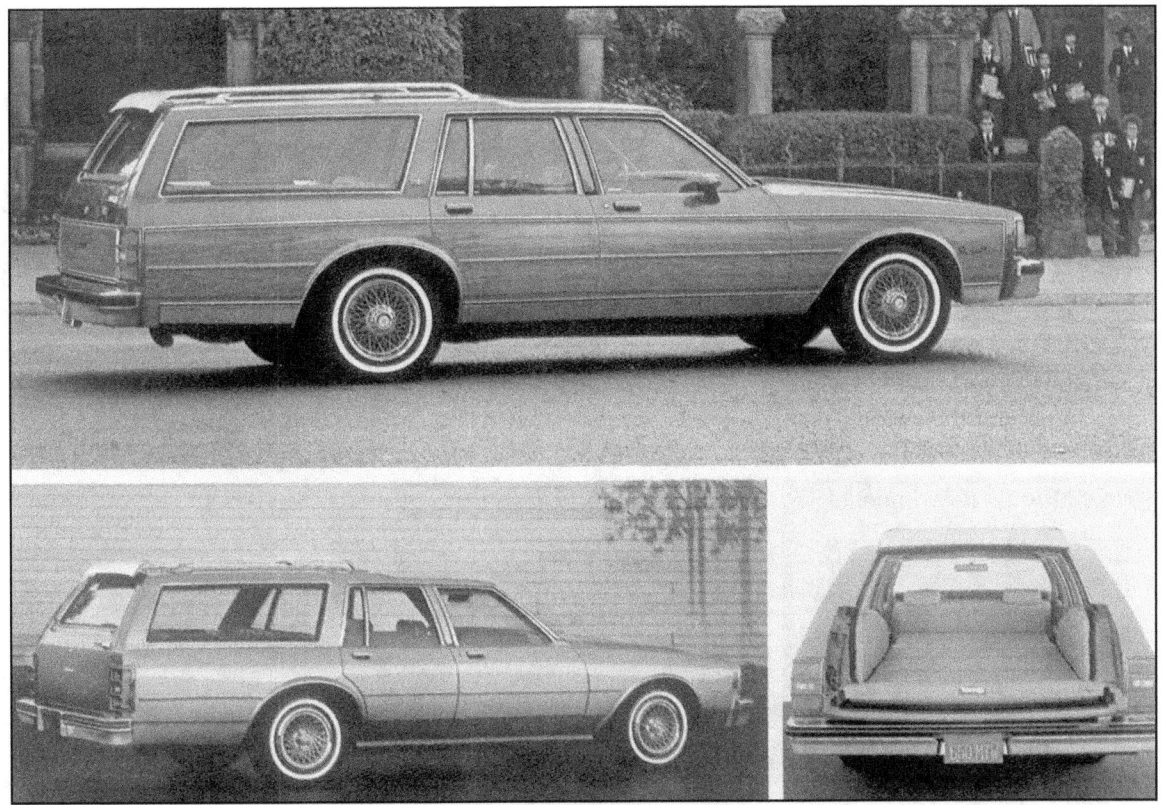
1981 Chevrolet Impala Wagon with more than 87 cu. ft. of cargo space

1981 Chevrolet Malibu Classic Wagon with more than 71 cu. ft. of cargo space

1981 - CHRYSLER / IMPERIAL

5.2 liter V8 with EFI

New Model: 1981 Imperial

9-button trip computer

1981 Imperial instrument panel

1981 Imperial Mark Cross leather interior

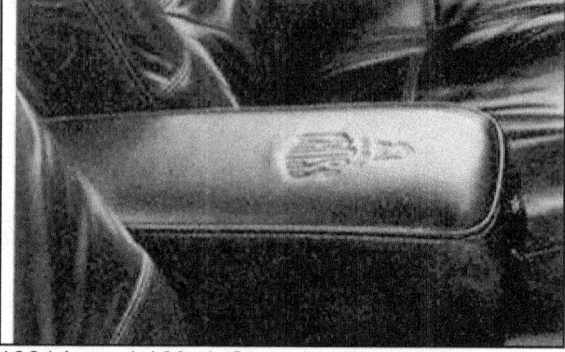

1981 Imperial Mark Cross leather interior

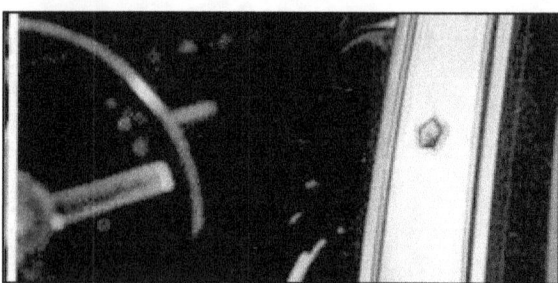

1981 Imperial Cartier Crystal Pentastar

From the Brochure: "No other American automobile offers as complete a list of standard luxury features as Imperial. Including WSW steel-belted radial tires; Goodyear all-weather Arriva or Michelin. A choice of four sophisticated sounds systems. Speed Control. All power assists. Individually adjustable power seats. Sophisticated electronic instrumentation. There is only one extra-cost option: an electrically powered sliding roof. The 1981 Imperial is America's totally equipped personal luxury car."

— 1981 Imperial

Last Model Run: 1981 Chrysler New Yorker

Last Model Run: 1981 Chrysler Newport

1981 Chrysler Newport interior

1981 Chrysler Cordoba Corinthian Package

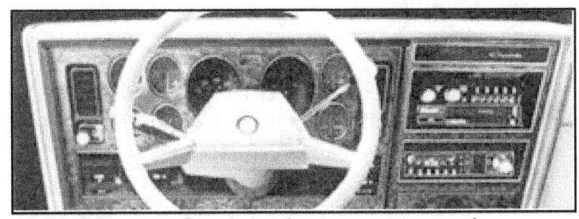
1981 Chrysler Cordoba instrument panel

1981 Chrysler New Yorker interior

1981 Chrysler New Yorker instrument panel

1981 Chrysler Cordoba standard interior

1981 Chrysler Cordoba with optional Cabriolet Roof and two-tone paint treatment

1981 Chrysler Cordoba LS

Last Model Run: 1981 Chrysler LeBaron Medallion 4-door Sedan

1981 Chrysler LeBaron interior

Last Model Run: 1981 Chrysler LeBaron Town & Country Wagon

Last Model Run: 1981 Chrysler LeBaron 2-door

1981 Chrysler LeBaron instrument panel

From the Brochure: "LeBaron for 1981 carries with it an unmistakable air of space-efficient elegance. And LeBaron pairs the promise of its looks with the performance of its Super Six 2-barrel engine, the driving ease and convenience of Torqueflite automatic transmission, power steering, power front disc brakes and a host of other standard features.

Pick your car from LeBaron – a new price class – or LeBaron Medallion. Both categories provide two-door specialty hardtops and four-door sedans. If you have a penchant for station wagons, the LeBaron Town & Country is outstanding."

- 1981 Chrysler LeBaron

1981 - DODGE

Last Model Run: 1981 Dodge St. Regis

1981 Dodge St. Regis instrument panel

1981 Dodge St. Regis standard cloth interior

> **From the Brochure:** "It's a beautiful way to close off the outside world. Just being inside St. Regis is something special – the quiet, the comfort, and the luxury. Quality surrounds you in excellence of design, tasteful selection of materials, careful attention to detail. But most importantly, St. Regis signifies outstanding value, because the 1981 St. Regis offers a higher appointment level and more standard equipment than last year's model."
>
> - 1981 Dodge St. Regis

1981 Dodge Mirada with CMX Package

Chrysler Corporation offers a 30 day, 1,000 mile money-back guarantee

1981 Dodge Mirada

1981 Dodge Mirada with optional leather interior

New Model: 1981 Dodge Aries SE 4-door Wagon

2.2 liter OHC 4-cylinder

New Model: 1981 Dodge Aries SE 4-door

1981 Dodge Aries SE instrument panel

New Model: 1981 Dodge Aries optional Premium cloth bucket seats and console

Those '80s Cars

Last Model Run: 1981 Dodge Diplomat Sport Coupe

73.3 cu. ft. of cargo space

Last Model Run: 1981 Dodge Diplomat Salon Wagon

1981 Dodge Diplomat Salon 2-door optional cloth and vinyl bucket seat interior

1981 Dodge Diplomat Medallion 4-door Sedan

1981 Dodge Colt RS

1981 Dodge Challenger

From the Brochure: "Colt RS: efficiency and a whole lot more. The Colt RS takes the Colt Custom and adds even more sportiness – from the Red and Black two-tone paint to the Yellow and Orange accent stripes. Now, attack any road with a 1.6-liter MCA-JET four-cylinder engine, sure-footed front-wheel-drive and the nimble Rallye Handling Package."

1981 Dodge Omni with Custom Exterior Package

From the Brochure: "Consider our 1981 Dodge Omni for a minute. Its transverse-engine, front-wheel-drive design gives Omni interior room to spare for five adult-size passengers... with four doors to get them in and out with a minimum of fuss, and a convenient rear hatch and folding rear seats to turn back-seat space into cargo space. Omni is built with computers and precise automated welders in one of the country's most modern assembly plants and is powered by one of two four cylinder engines... the standard 1.7 liter or the optional Chrysler-designed-and-built 2.2 liter Trans-4."

– 1981 Dodge Omni

1981 Dodge 024 with Sports Appearance Package

1981 Dodge Omni optional Premium interior

From the Brochure: "Let's take it from the 'top.' The 024's superbly streamlined, aerodynamically designed body actually helps curb wind resistance on the highway, improving gas mileage. From its sleek front end to its roomy cargo area, you'll get an extraordinary ride without overextending your fuel budget."

– 1981 Dodge 024

1981 Dodge Omni Rallye instrument cluster & four spoke steering wheel

1981 - FORD

1981 Ford Fairmont Futura 4-door Sedan

1981 Ford Fairmont 2-door Sedan

1981 Ford Fairmont Interior Luxury Group

1981 Ford Fairmont standard bucket seats

79.5 cu. ft. with rear seat folded

1981 Ford Fairmont Futura Squire Wagon

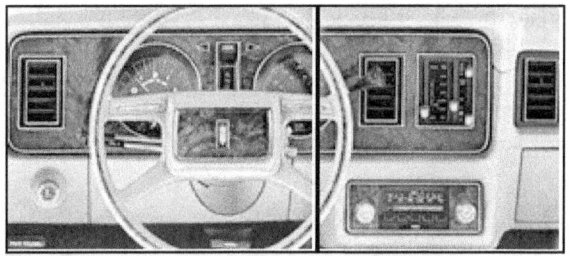
1981 Ford Fairmont instrument panel

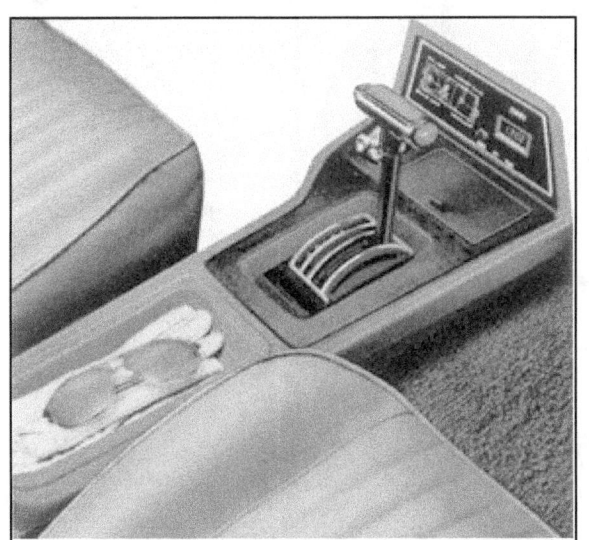

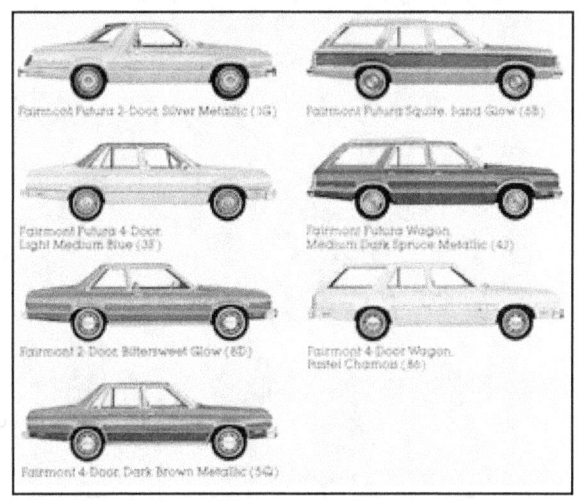

Those '80s Cars   57

1.3 & 1.6 liter 4-cylinder engines

New Model: 1981 Ford Escort GLX 3-Door

New Model: 1981 Ford Escort GLX 4-door

From the Brochure: "Built to take on the world. Top Ford engineers from around the world teamed up to bring together the best of their better ideas. The result: Ford Escort. The new World Car. Escort is engineered for sure-footed traction with front wheel drive. Independent 4-wheel suspension. Rack and pinion steering precision. Plus new all-season steel-belted radial tires."
- 1981 Ford Escort

1981 Ford Escort GLX interior

2.3 liter 4-cylinder, 3.3 liter inline 6 & 4.2 liter V8 engines

New Model: 1981 Ford Granada GLX 2-door & GL 4-door

From the Brochure: "Built for a changing world. Introducing the Ford Granada for 1981, the newest entry in the modern field of American-built touring sedans. This is a totally redesigned Granada." - 1981 Ford Granada

1981 Ford Granada instrument panel

1981 Ford Granada GLX split bench interior

3.3 liter inline 6 is new Thunderbird standard engine

1981 Ford Thunderbird Town Landau

---

58   Those '80s Cars

1981 Ford Thunderbird with optional electronic instrument panel

1981 Ford LTD Crown Victoria 4-door Sedan

1981 Ford Thunderbird & Interior Luxury Group

1981 Ford LTD Crown Victoria interior

> **From the Brochure:**
> "America's most popular sports car. Sporty good looks with sleek, aerodynamic lines and the exciting new T-Roof option."
>
> - 1981 Ford Mustang

1981 Ford Mustang

Ford drops 5.0 liter V8 from Mustang, Granada & Fairmont

1981 Ford Mustang Ghia with new T-Roof option

1981 - LINCOLN

5.8 liter V8 option is dropped

Last Model Run: 1981 Lincoln Town Car 2-door (only the 2-door is discontinued after 1981)

1981 Lincoln Town Car ("Continental" is dropped from the name this year)

1981 Lincoln Town Car 2-door leather interior

1981 Lincoln Town Car standard instrumentation

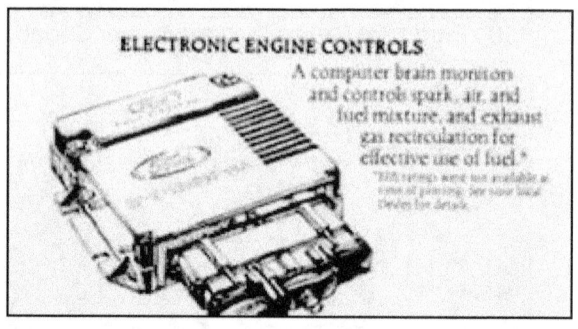

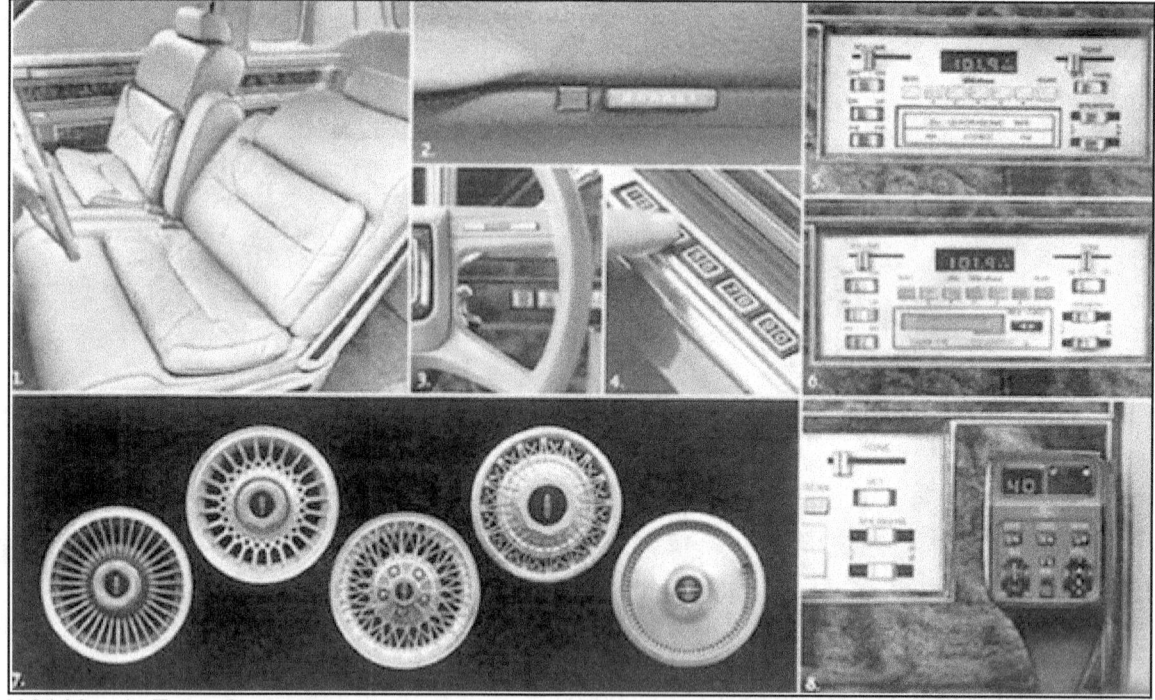

1981 Lincoln Town Car optional features

1981 Lincoln Continental Mark VI 4-door with standard electronic instrument panel

1981 Lincoln Continental Mark VI optional Luxury Group interior features

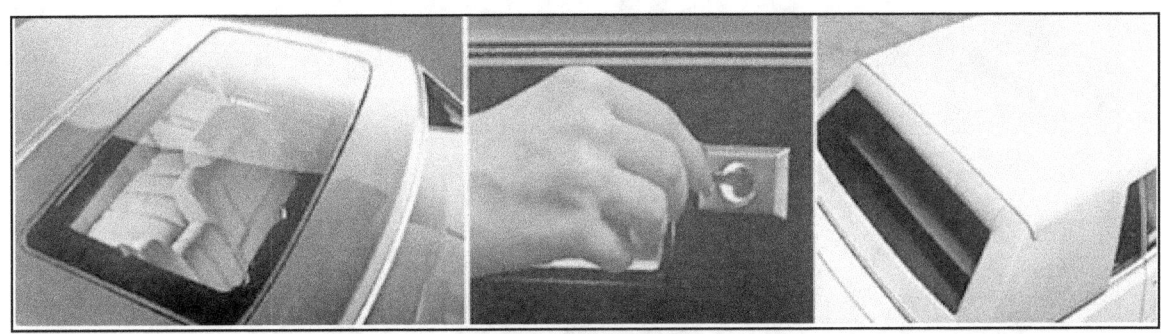

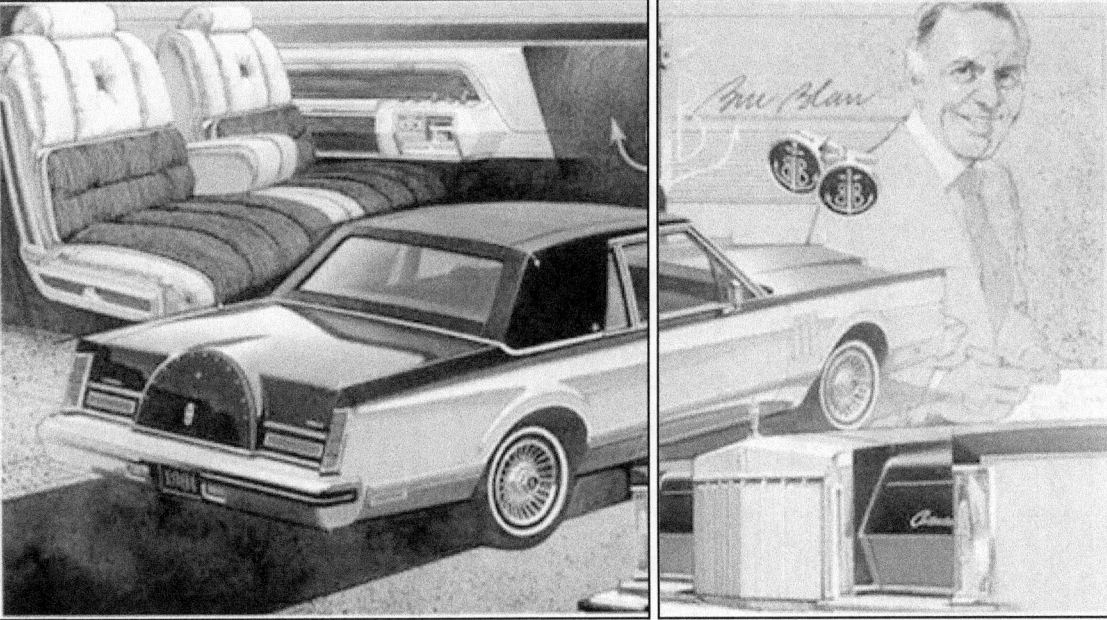

1981 Lincoln Continental Mark VI Bill Blass Designer Series

Those '80s Cars

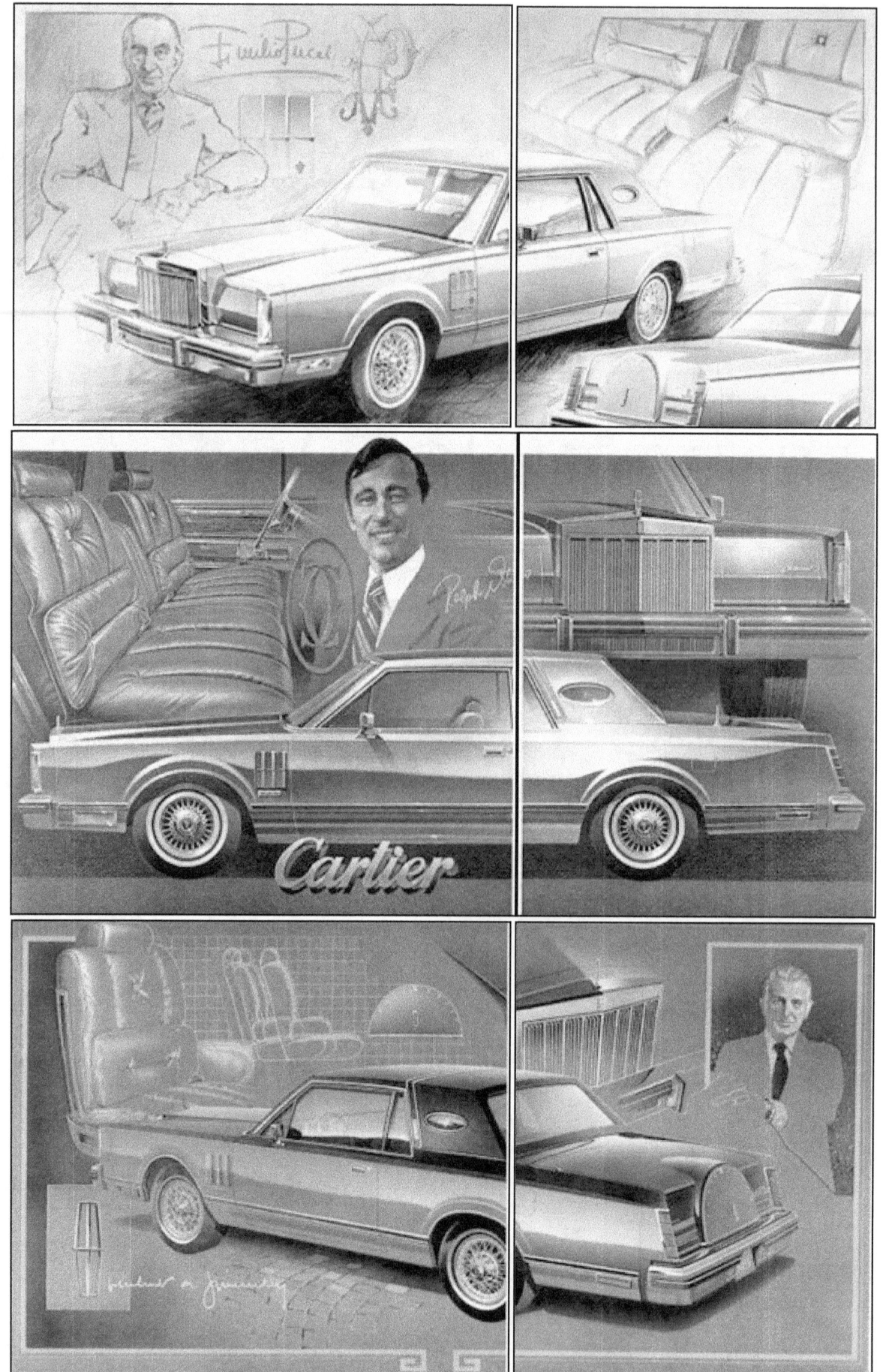

1981 Lincoln Continental Mark VI Pucci(top), Cartier(middle) and Givenchy(bottom) Designer Series

1981 - MERCURY

3.3 liter inline 6 is new Cougar XR-7 standard engine

1981 Mercury Cougar XR-7 GS

1981 Mercury Cougar XR-7 GS optional Recaro seat interior

1981 Mercury Cougar LS 4-door interior with optional leather

2.3 liter 4-cylinder, 3.3 liter inline 6 & 4.2 liter V8 engines

New Model: 1981 Mercury Cougar GS 4-door with optional Tu-Tone paint

New Model: 1981 Mercury Cougar 2-door with optional vinyl roof

1981 Mercury Grand Marquis

Those '80s Cars

1981 Mercury Capri, Black Magic edition shown at right

1981 Mercury Capri optional Black Magic interior

New Model: 1981 Mercury Lynx GS Wagon

New Model: 1981 Mercury Lynx LS

1.3 & 1.6 liter 4-cylinder engines

New Model: 1981 Mercury Lynx GS

1981 Mercury Lynx LS optional interior

Those '80s Cars

1981 - OLDSMOBILE

1981 Oldsmobile Toronado XSC

1981 Oldsmobile Toronado (back)
1981 Oldsmobile Ninety-Eight (left)
1981 Oldsmobile Delta 88 (right)

1981 Oldsmobile Toronado instrument panel

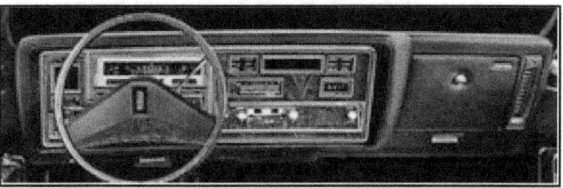
1981 Oldsmobile Ninety-Eight instrument panel

Oldsmobile drops the 5.7 liter V8 engine this year, adds a Buick-sourced 4.1 liter V6 to the Ninety-Eight & Toronado lines, and adds a 4-speed auto on gas V8 engines

1981 Oldsmobile Ninety-Eight LS 4-door

1981 Oldsmobile Ninety-Eight Regency 2-door

1981 Oldsmobile Custom Cruiser

Those '80s Cars

1981 Oldsmobile Delta 88 Royale Brougham 4-door and 2-door Sedans

1981 Oldsmobile Delta 88 Holiday Coupe

1981 Oldsmobile Delta 88 2-door & 4-door

1981 Oldsmobile Delta 88 Royale 2-door Sedan

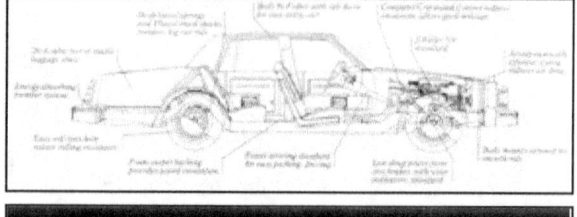

1981 Oldsmobile Delta 88 instrument panel

1981 Oldsmobile Delta 88 Royale 4-door Sedan

Those '80s Cars

Refreshed: 1981 Oldsmobile Cutlass Supreme Coupe (front)
1981 Cutlass Brougham Sedan (back left)
1981 Cutlass Cruiser Brougham (back right)

Cutlass engine options: 3.8 liter V6 gas, 4.3 & 5.0 liter V8 gas (5.0 Cruiser only), 5.7 liter diesel

1981 Oldsmobile Cutlass instrument panel

Oldsmobile drops the fastback/aero Cutlass after 1980

Refreshed: 1981 Oldsmobile Cutlass Calais

1981 Oldsmobile Cutlass Supreme interior

1981 Oldsmobile Cutlass Supreme Brougham interior

Refreshed: 1981 Oldsmobile Cutlass Supreme Brougham

Those '80s Cars

1981 Oldsmobile Omega Brougham 4-door & 2-door Sedans

1981 Oldsmobile Sport Omega

1981 Oldsmobile Omega instrument panel

1981 Oldsmobile Omega ES

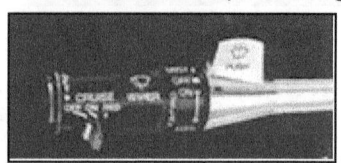
Multi-function lever

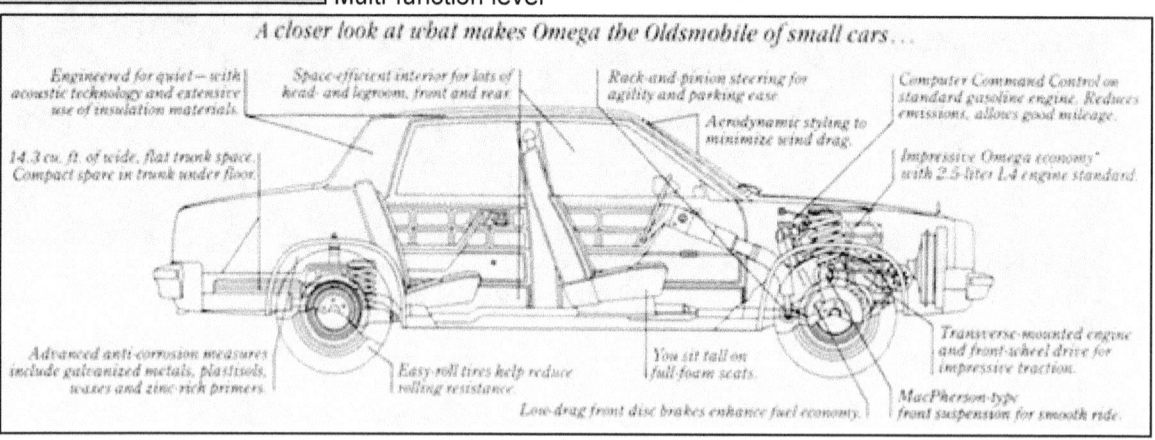

Those '80s Cars

1981 - PLYMOUTH

New Model: 1981 Plymouth Reliant SE 4-door

2.2 liter OHC 4-cylinder

New Model: 1981 Plymouth Reliant SE 2-door

New Model: 1981 Plymouth Reliant SE Wagon

1981 Plymouth Reliant SE instrument panel

1981 Plymouth Sapporo

Sapporo interior: durable cord velour cloth-and-vinyl reclining bucket seats with integral, adjustable headrests and driver side lumbar adjust

Last Model Run: 1981 Plymouth Gran Fury

1981 Plymouth Gran Fury interior

1981 Plymouth Reliant SE standard bench seat

1981 Plymouth Sapporo interior

Those '80s Cars

1.7 liter 4-cylinder w/4-speed manual

1981 Plymouth TC3 with Sport Two-Tone Package

1981 Plymouth TC3 with Custom Exterior Package

1.4 liter 4-cylinder w/4-speed manual. EPA estimated 37 MPG, 50 hwy

1981 Plymouth Champ Custom with LS Package

From the Brochure: "Engineered and built with care by Mitsubishi Motors Corporation in Japan, the 1981 front-wheel drive Plymouth Champ lineup offers three ways to go! Beginning with the basic, highest-mileage Champ, Champ Deluxe and Champ Custom, there's a Champ that's just right for you."
  - 1981 Plymouth Champ

Euro-Sedan: black-out exterior trim, wide tires, cast-aluminum road wheels, Sport Interior, Rallye instruments

1981 Plymouth Horizon Euro-Sedan

1981 Plymouth Horizon with Custom Exterior

From the Brochure: "Meet the highest mileage, lowest priced Horizon for 1981. (Not available in California.) It offers the same front-wheel-drive technology, full five-passenger seating, folding rear seat and handy rear hatch design shared by all our 1981 Horizons. Plus a specially calibrated version of our standard 1.7-liter four-cylinder engine and a special 2.69 overall top gear ratio with standard four-speed manual transaxle."
  - 1981 Plymouth Horizon

1981 - PONTIAC

Refreshed: 1981 Pontiac Grand Prix LJ

1981 Pontiac Grand Prix LJ available leather bucket seats

Grand Prix engines: 3.8 V6, 4.3 V8 & new 5.7 V8 diesel

1981 Pontiac Grand LeMans interior

MORE PONTIAC KNOW-HOW TO THE GALLON

LeMans engines: 3.8 V6 & 4.3 V8

Refreshed: 1981 Pontiac Grand LeMans

Last Model Run: 1981 Pontiac LeMans Coupe and standard interior

Those '80s Cars

1981 Pontiac Grand LeMans Safari & Bonneville Safari Wagons

Last Model Run: 1981 Pontiac Bonneville Brougham 4-door Sedan (will be downsized & renamed in 1982 on the Grand LeMans body)

3.8 V6, 4.3 V8, 5.0 V8 & new 5.7 V8 diesel

Last Model Run: 1981 Pontiac Bonneville Coupe

1981 Pontiac Bonneville Brougham interior

1981 Pontiac Bonneville Coupe available bucket seat interior

Last Model Run: 1981 Pontiac Catalina

1981 Pontiac Phoenix Coupe and 5-Door Hatchback

1981 Pontiac Phoenix LJ interior

New Model: 1981 Pontiac T1000 (Capitalizing on the success of the Chevrolet Chevette, Pontiac gets its version of the subcompact.)

1981 Pontiac Firebird Esprit

1981 Pontiac Formula

1981 Pontiac Firebird interior

Those '80s Cars

1982

1982 - Facts at Glance

News Headlines

- Falkland war ignites
- USA Today launched
- Disney's EPCOT center opens
- 1st artificial heart transplanted
- Vietnam Veterans Memorial dedicated

Tops in Pop Culture

Music
- Physical, Olivia Newton-John

Movies
- ET: The Extra-Terrestrial

TV Show
- 60 Minutes

Sports Champions

Basketball
- L.A. Lakers

Football
- San Francisco 49ers

Baseball
- St. Louis Cardinals

Motor Trend – Car of the Year

Chevrolet Camaro Z28

1982 - AMC / EAGLE

1982 AMC Concord DL 4-door Sedan and Concord Limited 2-door Sedan

2.5 liter (151 CID) 4-cylinder & 4.2 liter (258 CID) 6-cylinder engines

1982 AMC Spirit G.T. Liftback

Manual 5-speed transmission with gauge package

1982 AMC Eagle SX/4, Wagon & 4-door Sedan

1982 Concord DL Wagons

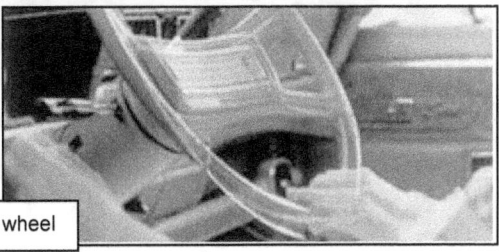

Tilt steering wheel

Those '80s Cars

1982 AMC Eagle 4-door Sedan & 2-door Coupe

AMC Concord & Eagle Limited interior (top)
AMC Spirit & Eagle SX/4 DL interior (bottom)

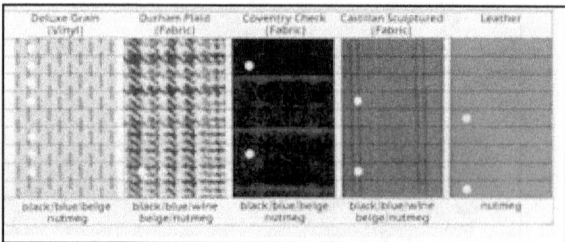

1982 AMC & Eagle upholstery options

1982 AMC & Eagle wheel & cover choices

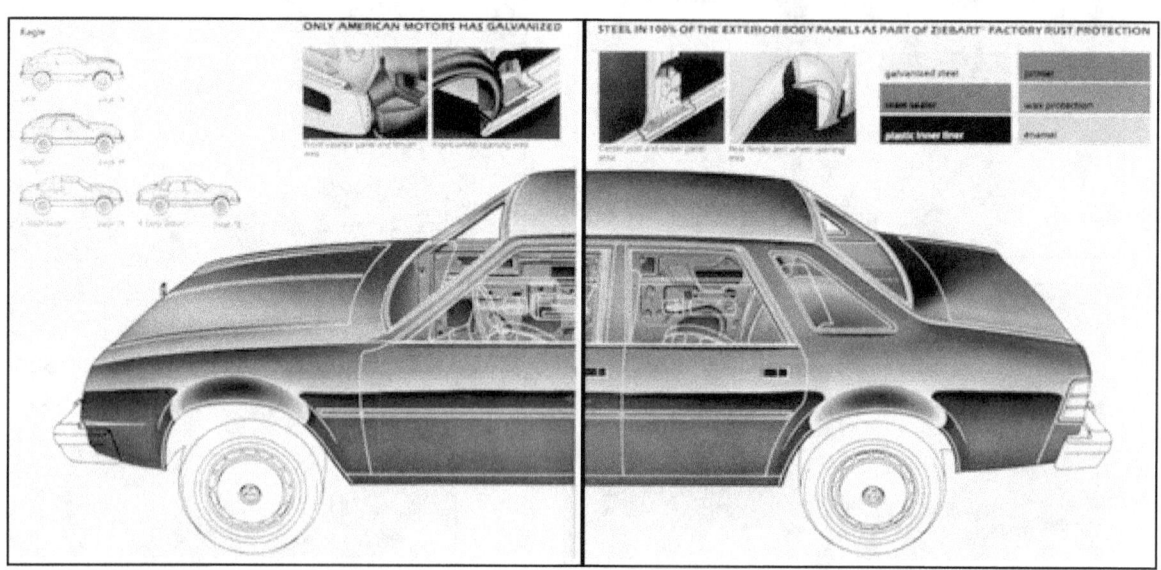

1982 - BUICK

2.5 liter 4-cylinder & 3.0 liter 6-cylinder gas engines

New Model: 1982 Buick Century Sedans

New Model: 1982 Buick Skyhawk 4-door

Front-wheel drive and 1.8 liter 4-cylinder OHV

New Model: 1982 Buick Skyhawk 2-door

1982 Buick Riviera with optional vinyl roof

1982 Buick Riviera

Optional Gran Touring suspension with quicker steering

1982 Buick Riviera interior

Those '80s Cars 77

1982 Buick Electra Limited Coupe

1982 Buick LeSabre Custom Coupe

1982 Buick Electra Park Avenue Coupe

1982 Buick LeSabre Limited Coupe

Available Memory Seat on Electra & Riviera

1982 Buick Electra Park Avenue interior

1982 Buick LeSabre Limited interior

Courtesy & convenience lights now standard

1982 Buick Electra Park Avenue 4-door Sedan

1982 Buick LeSabre Limited 4-door Sedan

1982 Buick Regal Limited Sedan (called Century last year)

1982 Buick Skylark Sedan

New comforts: ETR stereo w/tape, Twilight Sentinel & Electronic Touch Climate Control

3 series: Skylark, Limited & Sport; 2 body styles: 2 & 4 door sedans

1982 Buick Regal Sport Coupe

1982 Buick Skylark Sport Coupe

1982 Buick Regal Limited interior

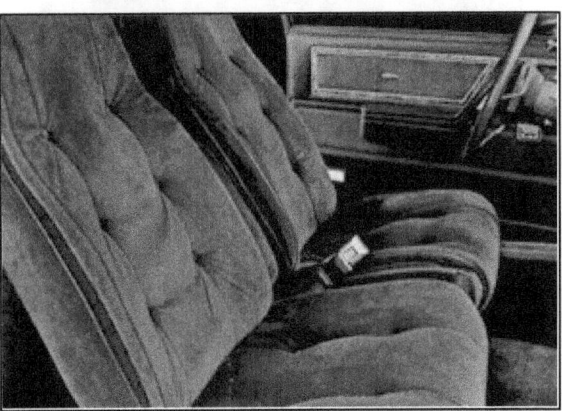
1982 Buick Skylark interior

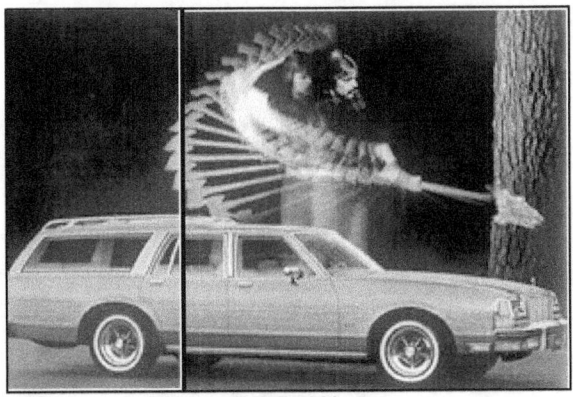
1982 Buick Electra Estate Wagon

1982 Buick Regal Estate Wagon

Those '80s Cars

1982 - CADILLAC

1982 Cadillac deVille

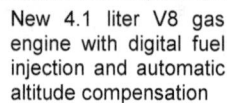

New 4.1 liter V8 gas engine with digital fuel injection and automatic altitude compensation

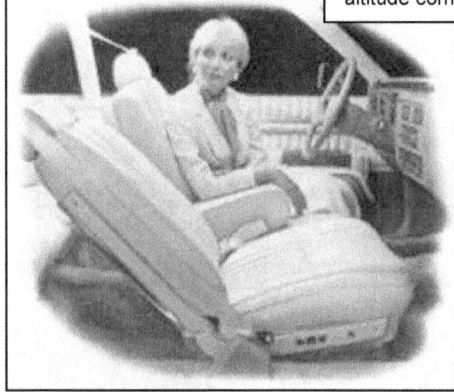

1982 Cadillac Fleetwood Brougham

New Model: 1982 Cadillac Cimarron

1982 Cadillac Seville Elegante

1982 Cadillac Eldorado Biarritz

Eldorado: 15 years of front-wheel drive.

1982 Cadillac Eldorado Touring Coupe

The new HT 4100 Power System.

1982 - CHEVROLET

New Model: 1982 Chevrolet Camaro Z28

New Model: 1982 Chevrolet Camaro Z28

Last Model Run: 1982 Chevrolet Corvette; Collector Edition (shown)

1982 Chevrolet Camaro Berlinetta interior

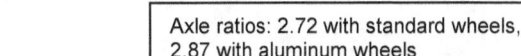
Axle ratios: 2.72 with standard wheels, 2.87 with aluminum wheels

1982 Chevrolet Corvette interior

Camaro engine options: 2.5 liter L4, 2.8 liter V6, 5.0 liter V8 with 4-speed manual or 3-speed auto transmissions

Those '80s Cars 81

1982 Chevrolet Impala 4-door Sedan

1982 Chevrolet Caprice Classic Sedan

1982 Chevrolet Caprice Classic Special Custom

1982 Chevrolet Caprice Classic instrument panel

Locking Wire Wheel Covers

2.5 liter L4 adds EFI for 1982

1982 Chevrolet Citation 3-Door Hatchback

1982 Chevrolet Citation Sport Cloth bucket seats

1982 Chevrolet Citation instrument panel

1982 Chevrolet Citation Special Instrumentation

1982 Chevrolet Citation 4-door Hatchback

1982 Chevrolet Malibu Classic Wagon

New for Malibu in 1982: 4.3 V6 & 5.7 V8 diesel options

1982 Chevrolet Malibu Classic 4-door Sedan

1982 Chevrolet Malibu Classic interior

1982 Chevrolet Monte Carlo

1982 Chevrolet Monte Carlo instrument panel

Those '80s Cars

New Model: 1982 Chevrolet Cavalier 4-door Sedan and 3-Door Hatchback

1.8 & 2.0 liter L4 engines

New Model: 1982 Chevrolet Cavalier 2-door Coupe & 5-Door Wagon

New Model: 1982 Chevrolet Celebrity 4-door & 2-door Sedans

1982 Chevrolet Celebrity interior

2.5 L4 & 2.8 V6 engines

New Model: 1982 Chevrolet Celebrity

1982 Chevrolet Chevette

1982 Chevrolet Chevette

1982 - CHRYSLER / IMPERIAL

New Model: 1982 Chrysler Town & Country

New Model: 1982 Chrysler LeBaron Medallion 2-door Coupe

LeBaron: now front-wheel drive with 2.2 liter (135 CID) standard and a Mitsubishi-built 2.6 liter (156 CID) optional

New Model: 1982 Chrysler LeBaron Mark Cross convertible

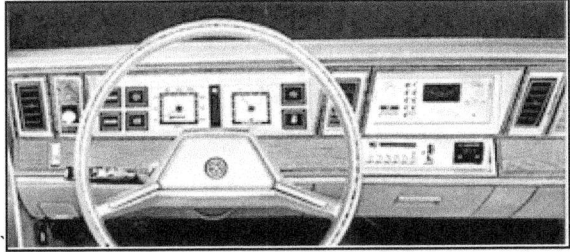

1982 Chrysler LeBaron instrument panel

1982 Chrysler LeBaron Medallion interior

99.9" wheelbase, 179.7" length weighing just under 2,500 lbs

New Model: 1982 Chrysler LeBaron Medallion 4-door Sedan

Those '80s Cars

1982 Chrysler Cordoba

1982 Chrysler Cordoba instrument panel

1982 Chrysler Cordoba cloth interior

1982 Imperial instrument panel

1982 Imperial cloth interior

New Model: 1982 Chrysler New Yorker

1981's LeBaron is re-styled and re-branded as 1982's replacement for the New Yorker

1982 Chrysler New Yorker cloth interior

1982 Chrysler New Yorker instrument panel

New Series: 1982 Imperial FS (Frank Sinatra)

Those '80s Cars

1982 - DODGE

New Model: 1982 Dodge 400 LS 2-door Coupe

Front-wheel drive with 2.2 liter, optional Mitsubishi-built 2.6 liter

New Model: 1982 Dodge 400 LS 4-door Sedan

1982 Dodge Omni

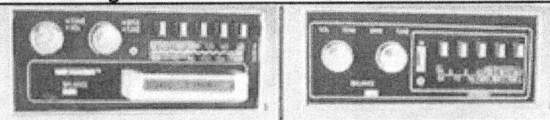

26 EPA estimated MPG
41 MPG highway

1982 Dodge Aries SE 4-door Sedan, Aries Custom 2-door Sedan, Aries SE Wagon

New Model: 1982 Dodge 400 Convertible

Those '80s Cars

Challenger 2.6 liter & 5-speed manual transmission standard

1982 Dodge imports: Challenger, Colt RS, Colt Custom 4-door Hatchback

1982 Dodge Charger 2.2

2.2 liter w/4-speed manual or 3-speed auto

New Model: 1982 Dodge Rampage

1982 Dodge Diplomat

1,145 lb payload

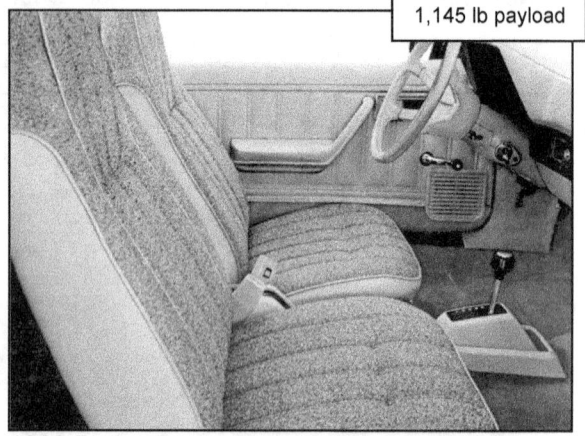

1982 Dodge Rampage optional cloth interior

16.7 cu. ft. trunk, 18-gallon fuel tank

1982 Dodge Mirada with T-Bar Roof

Those '80s Cars

1982 - FORD

1982 Ford Mustang GLX Coupe
5.0 high output V8 optional

Last Model Run: 1982 Ford Thunderbird Heritage Series

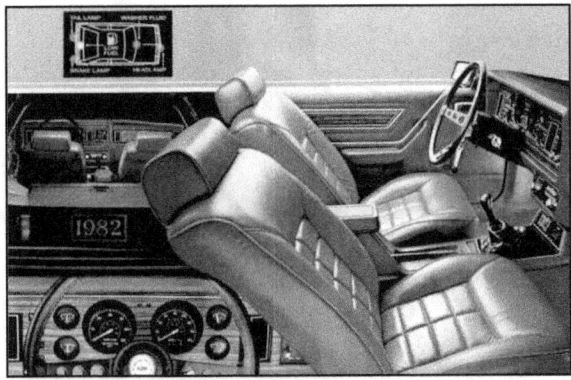

1982 Ford Mustang GLX interior

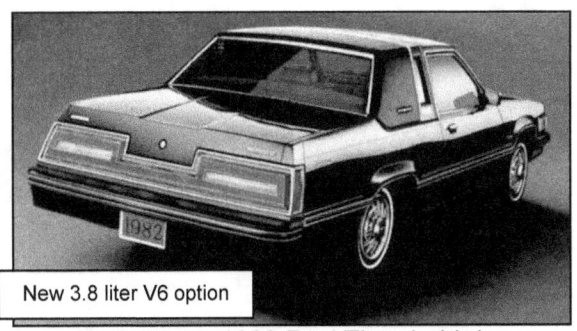

New 3.8 liter V6 option

Last Model Run: 1982 Ford Thunderbird Heritage Series

1982 Ford Fairmont 2-door Coupe & interior

1982 Ford Thunderbird optional digital dash

1982 Ford Fairmont Futura 2-door Coupe

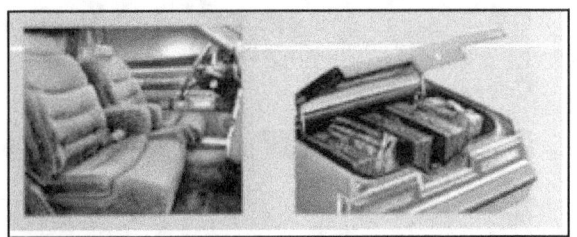

1982 Ford Thunderbird Heritage interior and deep-well trunk

1982 Ford Fairmont Futura Interior Luxury Group

1982 Ford Fairmont Futura 4-door Sedan

1982 Ford Escort 4-door GL Wagon (top left)
New Model & **Last Model Run:** 1982 Ford Granada GL Wagon (top right)
1982 Ford LTD Country Squire (bottom)

Last Model Run: 1982 Ford Granada GL 2-door Coupe

New 3.8 liter V6 option

New Model & **Last Model Run:** 1982 Ford Granada GL Wagon with Squire Option

1982 Ford Granada GL interior

Last Model Run: 1982 Ford Granada L 4-door Sedan

From the Brochure: "Quality is Job 1. At Ford Division, we believe our 1982 automobiles are the finest we have ever produced. This lineup of cars, from the sporty EXP to the elegant Thunderbird, with brand-new Escort 4-door Hatchback and Granada Wagon models, represents the latest in technology and Ford engineering achievement."
— 1982 Ford

1982 Ford Granada GLX instrument panel

5.8 liter V8 option is dropped

1982 Ford LTD Crown Victoria 4-door Sedan

LTD: 4-speed automatic overdrive transmission is standard

1982 Ford LTD Crown Victoria 2-door Coupe

LTD has over 22 cu. ft. of cargo space in its deep-well trunk

New Model: 1982 Ford Escort GL 4-door Hatchback

Escort outsold all import car lines in its first year

1982 Ford Escort GLX 2-door Hatchback

New Model: 1982 Ford EXP

1.6 liter 4-cylinder w/4-speed manual overdrive transaxle

New Model: 1982 Ford EXP

1982 Ford EXP optional shearling & leather

1982 - LINCOLN

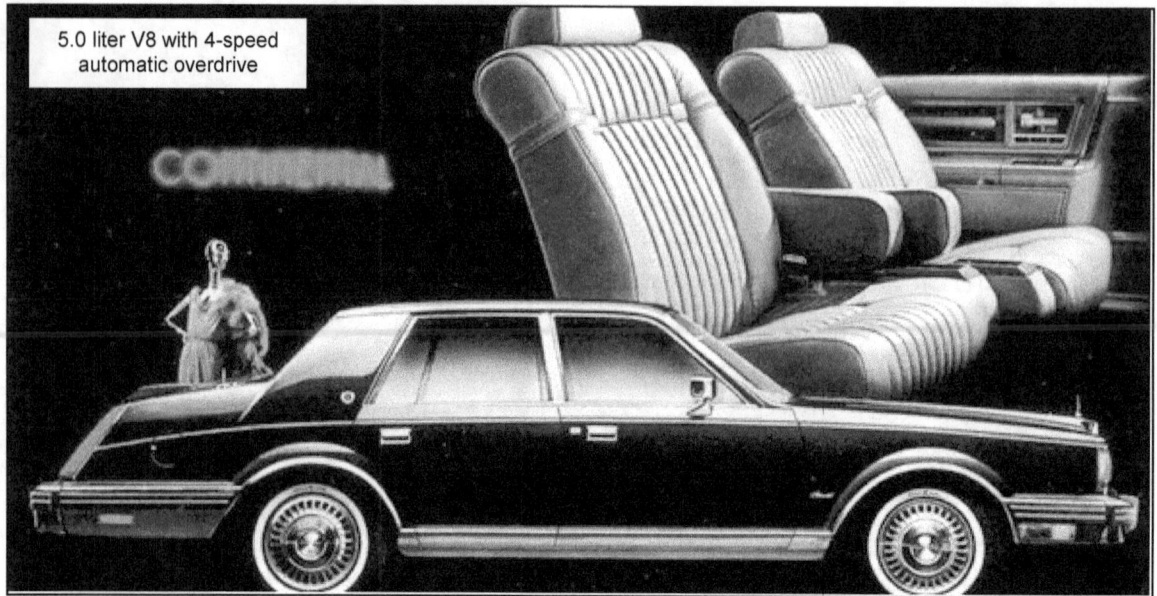
5.0 liter V8 with 4-speed automatic overdrive

New Model: 1982 Lincoln Continental

New Model: 1982 Lincoln Continental Givenchy Designer Series

New Model: 1982 Lincoln Continental Signature

1982 Lincoln Continental Givenchy Designer Series cloth interior

1982 Lincoln Continental instrument panel

From the Brochure: "Presenting the most original Continental since the original Continental. The new Continental for 1982. New in size, new in design, new in spirit, new in splendor. The most elegant Continental ever fashioned. But for all its contemporary character, Continental draws upon the rich traditions of the past… as in its formal rear-deck treatment."
 - 1982 Lincoln Continental

1982 Lincoln Continental Mark VI Signature Series 2-door

1982 Lincoln Town Car Signature Series

1982 Lincoln Continental Mark VI Signature Series 4-door

1982 Lincoln Town Car Signature Series cloth interior

Lincoln Continental Mark VI Signature Series

From the Brochure: "Electronic Instrument Panel and Message Center. The stylish, easy-to-read Electronic Instrument Panel includes electronic digital speedometer, electronic graphic fuel gauge, month/day/date electronic clock. The Message Center includes trip log, warning messages and instantaneous fuel economy."

- 1982 Lincoln Town Car

1982 Lincoln Town Car dash with optional electronic instrument panel with message center

1982 Lincoln Town Car Signature Series

Those '80s Cars

1982 - MERCURY

New 3.8 liter V6 option
5.0 liter V8 dropped

Last Model Run: 1982 Mercury Cougar XR-7 (GS trim level shown)

1982 Mercury Cougar XR-7 GS instrument panel

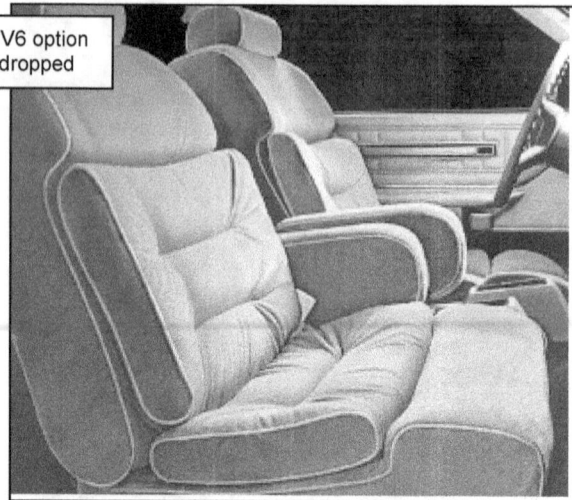

1982 Mercury Cougar XR-7 GS interior

New Model: 1982 Mercury Lynx LS 5-Door

1982 Mercury Lynx GL 3-Door

1982 Mercury Lynx LS interior

58.3 cu. ft. cargo space

1982 Mercury Lynx GS Wagon with Villager option (front) and GL Wagon (back)

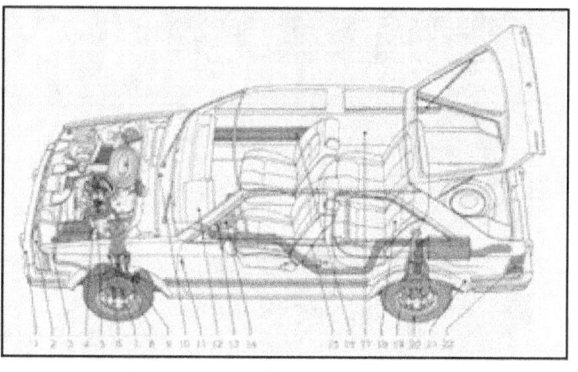

1.6 liter 4-cylinder w/4-speed manual overdrive transaxle

New Model: 1982 Mercury LN7

New Model: 1982 Mercury LN7

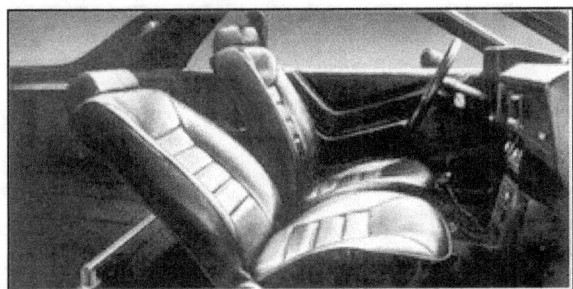

1982 Mercury LN7 interior

New Model: 1982 Mercury LN7

1982 Mercury LN7 instrument panel

5.0 high output V8 optional

1982 Mercury Capri RS with T-Roof

1982 Mercury Capri optional Recaro interior

From the Brochure: "LN7. Starting today, there is something beyond the fuel-efficient automobile. Come drive a road you've never traveled before. The new two-seater Mercury LN7 will change forever your ideas about what 'economy' means. It has 29 EPA estimated MPG, 46 estimated highway… along with stunning good looks and the best aerodynamic ratings of any standard-equipped American-built car. Engineered with some of the most advanced technology of our times… including front-wheel drive and a four-wheel independent suspension specially tuned for sport handling. And that translates into something that's been on the endangered species list until now, the fun driving. LN7: high style and high mileage… in a real driver's car."   – 1982 Mercury LN7

Those '80s Cars

1982 Mercury Zephyr Z-7 GS

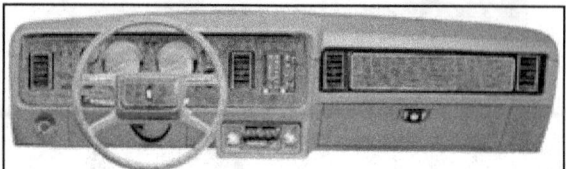
1982 Mercury Zephyr instrument panel

1982 Mercury Zephyr Z-7 GS interior

AM/FM Stereo 8-Track Tape Player

Last Model Run: 1982 Mercury Cougar LS 4-door Sedan

1982 Mercury Cougar LS interior

5.8 liter V8 option is dropped

1982 Mercury Grand Marquis 4-door Sedan

1982 Mercury Grand Marquis interior

1982 Mercury Zephyr GS 4-door Sedan

Those '80s Cars

1982 - OLDSMOBILE

1982 Oldsmobile Toronado Brougham, Ninety Eight Regency Brougham & Delta 88 Royale Brougham

1982 Oldsmobile Ninety-Eight Regency Coupe

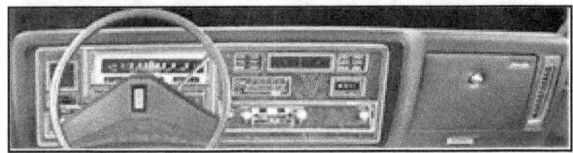
1982 Oldsmobile Ninety-Eight instrument panel

New Brougham pillow seats

1982 Oldsmobile Ninety-Eight Regency Brougham interior

Available new Memory Seats on Toronado

1982 Oldsmobile Toronado Brougham interior

1982 Oldsmobile Toronado instrument panel

1982 Oldsmobile Delta 88 Royale Brougham Coupe & interior (below)

New Model: 1982 Oldsmobile Cutlass Ciera

Cutlass Ciera engine choices: Pontiac-sourced 2.5 EFI 4-cylinder gas, Buick-sourced 3.0 liter V6 gas, Oldsmobile 4.3 liter V6 diesel

Cutlass Supreme adds 4.3 liter V6 diesel option

1982 Oldsmobile Cutlass Supreme

1982 Oldsmobile Cutlass Ciera interior with optional bucket seats

1982 Oldsmobile Cutlass Supreme dash panel

87.2 cu. ft. cargo room

1982 Oldsmobile Custom Cruiser

71.8 cu. ft. cargo room

1982 Oldsmobile Cutlass Cruiser

1982 Oldsmobile Custom Cruiser interior

1982 Oldsmobile Supreme interior

New Omega ES series delivers a high output version of the 2.8 liter V6

1982 Oldsmobile Omega

1982 Oldsmobile Omega instrument panel

1982 Oldsmobile Omega Brougham interior

Firenza powered by Chevy-source 1.8 & 2.0 liter 4-cylinder and choice of 4-speed manual or 3-speed automatic

New Model: 1982 Oldsmobile Firenza

New Model: 1982 Oldsmobile Firenza

From the Brochure: "Firenza. The new small Olds with so much to like. Want a sporty, fun-to-drive car that's easy on gas? Firenza comes through with an economical 4-cylinder. Want front-wheel drive, MacPherson strut front suspension, rack-and-pinion steering? They're yours."

- 1982 Oldsmobile Firenza

Those '80s Cars

1982 - PLYMOUTH

3.7 liter 2-bbl Slant Six w/3-speed auto are standard

New Model: 1982 Plymouth Gran Fury (based on stable-mate design, Dodge Diplomat)

New Model: 1982 Plymouth Gran Fury

1982 Plymouth Gran Fury interior

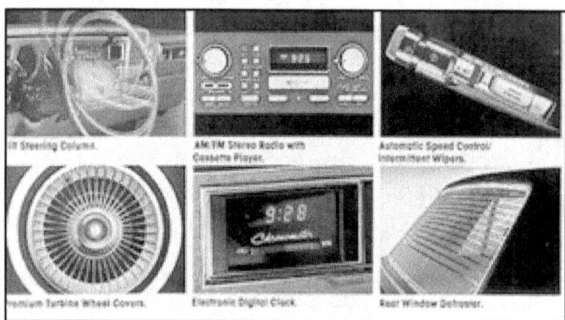

1982 Plymouth Gran Fury options

33.9 cu. ft. cargo space

1982 Plymouth Turismo

2.6 liter 4-cylinder w/5-speed manual

1982 Plymouth Sapporo

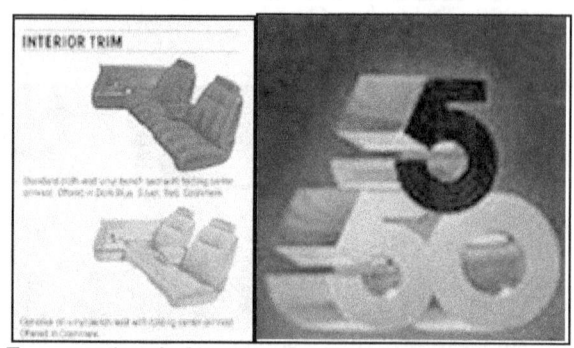

Fury seating & Chrysler Corporation's 5/50 Protection Plan

1982 Plymouth Reliant SE 2-door Coupe

1982 Plymouth Reliant SE interior

1982 Plymouth Reliant SE Wagon

1982 Plymouth Reliant Custom 4-door Sedan

1982 Plymouth Horizon Custom

1982 Plymouth Champ Custom with LS Package

From the Brochure: "What are Americans demanding in a car today? Fuel economy, high-quality design and construction and reliability... in a word: value. We think they'll find it all in one American car: the well-built 1982 Plymouth Reliant that's rated at 26 EPA est MPG, 41 estimated highway."
- 1982 Plymouth Reliant

Those '80s Cars

1982 - PONTIAC

New Model: 1982 Pontiac Firebird S/E

Firebird engine options: 2.5 liter L4, 2.8 liter V6, 5.0 liter V8 with 4-speed manual or 3-speed auto transmissions

1982 Pontiac Firebird optional leather interior

New Model: 1982 Pontiac Firebird Trans Am

From the Brochure: "Drivers get ready! Pontiac's totally new Firebird's here. And like the magnificent "Birds" of the past, it's a road machine that will fire up a generation!"
- 1982 Pontiac Firebird

Grand Prix replaces 4.3 V8 with 4.1 V6

1982 Pontiac Grand Prix Brougham (and available Landau Package in back)

1982 Pontiac Grand Prix Landau interior

1982 Pontiac Grand Prix LJ instrument panel

New Model: 1982 Pontiac 6000 Coupe

2.5 4-cylinder & 2.8 V6 gas engines, 4.3 liter V6 diesel

New Model: 1982 Pontiac 6000 LE 4-door Sedan

From the Brochure: "Introducing a bold new challenger to the world's great road cars. Pontiac 6000 LE. This totally new Pontiac brilliantly merges impressive riding comfort with responsive handling.

Here's a road car with everything you want. Front-wheel drive. MacPherson strut front suspension. First-class fit and finish. A generous interior that comfortably seats five adults. And deluxe acoustical insulation.

Pontiac 6000 LE also offers an exclusive Pontiac-tuned suspension that rides as well as it handles."

- 1982 Pontiac 6000

1982 Pontiac 6000 optional bucket seat interior

1982 Pontiac 6000 instrument panel

Those '80s Cars

1982 Pontiac Bonneville Model G Sedan
(re-badged from 1981's Grand LeMans)

3.8 & 4.1 liter V6 gas engines
& 5.7 liter V8 diesel

1982 Pontiac Bonneville Brougham interior

1982 Pontiac Bonneville instrument panel

1982 Pontiac Bonneville Model G Wagon

1982 Pontiac Phoenix SJ Coupe

1982 Pontiac Phoenix Hatchback

1982 Pontiac Phoenix instrument panel

J2000 standard power: 1.8 liter 4-cylinder, 4-speed

1982 Pontiac Phoenix LJ interior

New Model: 1982 Pontiac J2000 LE 2-door Coupe

1.6 liter 4-cylinder

1982 Pontiac T1000 5-Door & 3-Door models

1982 Pontiac T1000 instrument panel

1982 Pontiac T1000 optional cloth interior

New Model: 1982 Pontiac J2000 LE Wagon

New Model: 1982 Pontiac J2000 LE 4-door Sedan

1982 Pontiac J2000 LE interior

New Model: 1982 Pontiac J2000 SE Hatchback

1983

1983 - Facts at Glance

News Headlines

- Motorola introduces mobile phones in the United States
- Sally Ride becomes 1st American woamn in space
- IBM introduces PC XT
- MS Word & Lotus 1-2-3 are released
- Cabbage Patch Doll is introduced

Tops in Pop Culture

Music
- Every Breath You Take, The Police

Movies
- Star Wars Episode VI: Return of the Jedi

TV Show
- Dallas

Sports Champions

Basketball
- Philadelphia 76ers

Football
- Washington Redskins

Baseball
- Baltimore Orioles

Motor Trend – Car of the Year

AMC/Renault Alliance

1983 - AMC / EAGLE

1983 AMC Spirit DL Liftback & Concord Limited Wagon

1983 AMC Concord DL Sedan and Concord DL Wagon

1983 AMC Spirit GT Liftback

1983 AMC Spirit GT Liftback

1983 AMC / Eagle & Renault

1983 Eagle SX/4

1983 Eagle Sedan & Wagon

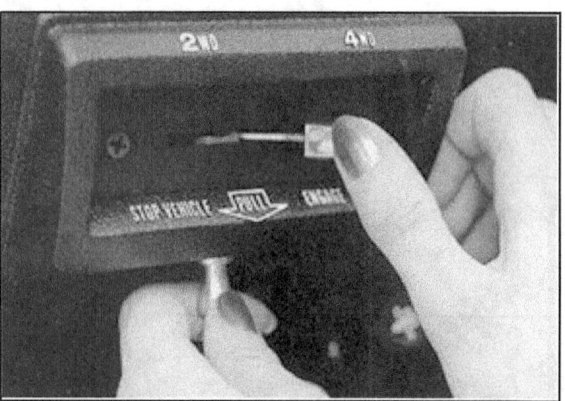
1983 Eagle

1983 AMC / Eagle options

1983 Renault Alliance sold at AMC Dealers
(Renault purchased AMC / Eagle / Jeep)

1983 Renault Fuego sold at AMC dealers

1983 - BUICK

3.0 liter V6, 110 hp, 145 lb/ft torque

1983 Buick Century T Type

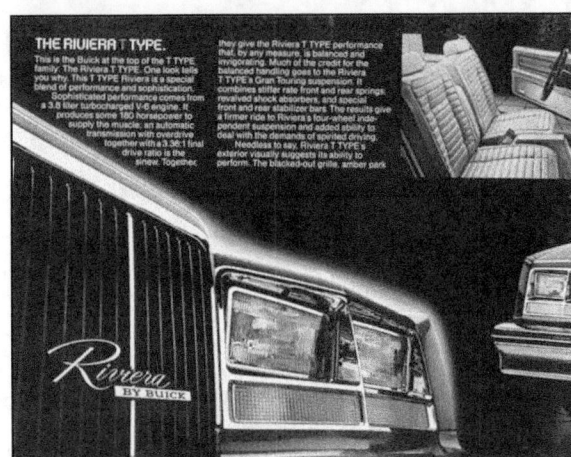

1983 Buick Riviera T Type

3.8 liter V6 4-bbl turbo, 180 hp, 290 lb/ft torque

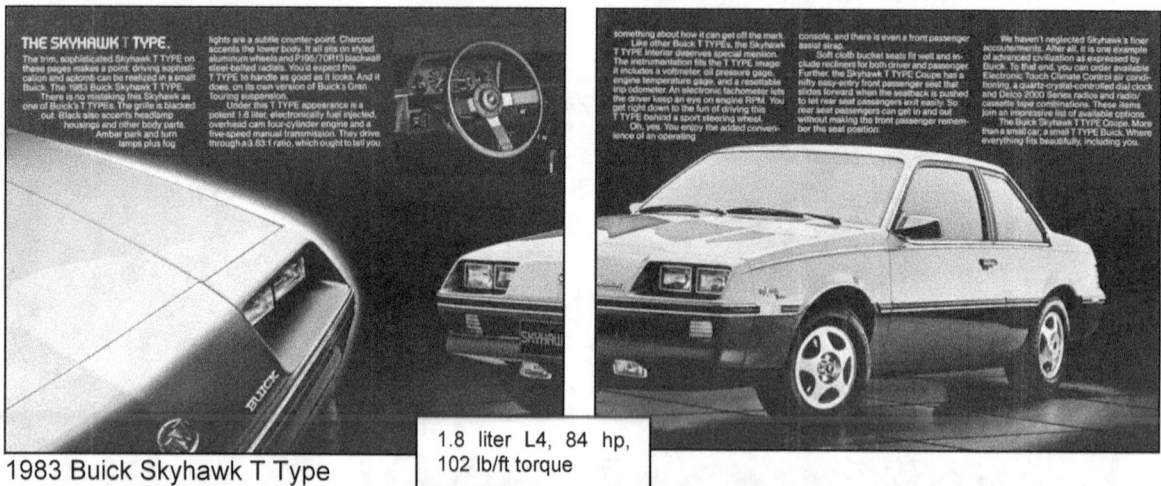

1983 Buick Skyhawk T Type — 1.8 liter L4, 84 hp, 102 lb/ft torque

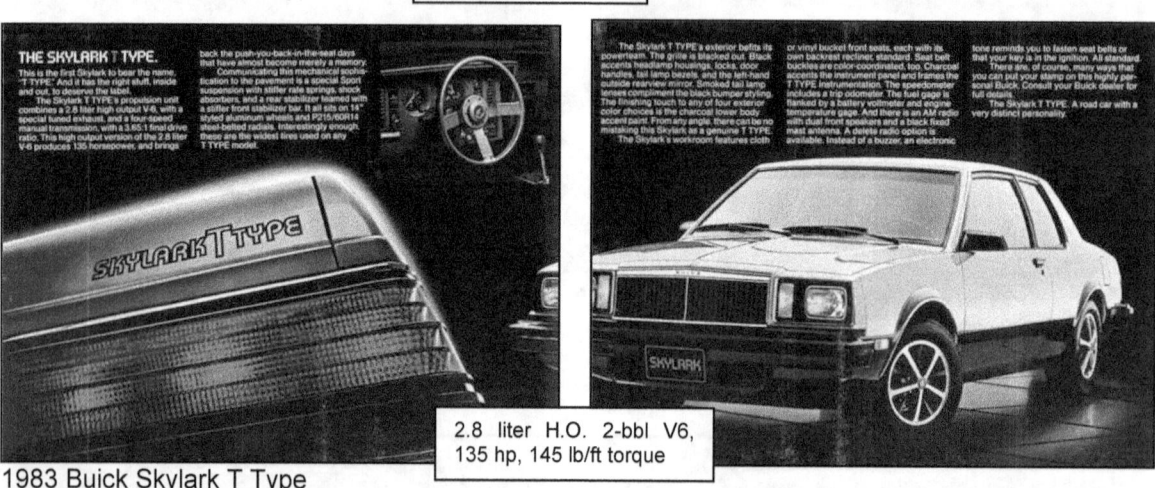

1983 Buick Skylark T Type — 2.8 liter H.O. 2-bbl V6, 135 hp, 145 lb/ft torque

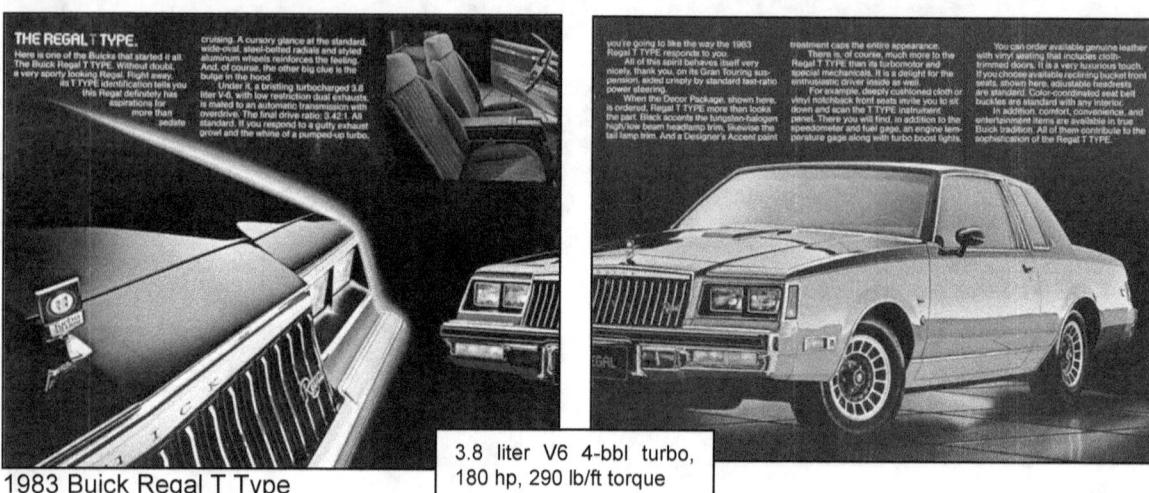

1983 Buick Regal T Type — 3.8 liter V6 4-bbl turbo, 180 hp, 290 lb/ft torque

From the Brochure: "The Buick T Types. Buicks that test the driver in you. Here is a series of five highly individual Buicks that are styled differently from other Buicks, and are endowed with technical sophistication to make them distinctive and appealing.

The T Type Buicks include the Riviera T Type, the Regal T Type, the Century T Type, Skylark T Type and Skyhawk T Type. Each is intended to redefine the concepts of performance and style. The results happily speak for themselves."

- 1983 Buick

1983 Buick LeSabre Estate Wagon

1983 Buick Electra Estate Wagon

1983 Buick Electra Park Avenue

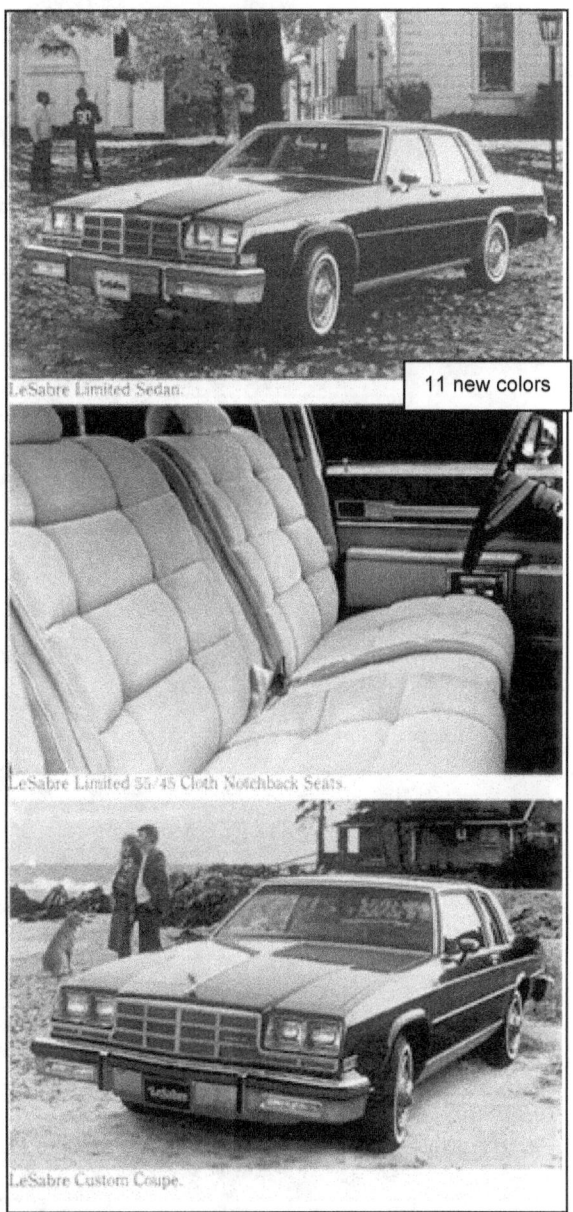
1983 Buick LeSabre Limited Sedan & Custom Coupe

1983 - CADILLAC

1983 Cadillac Cimarron

New 2.0 EFI 4-cylinder with new 5-speed manual transmission are standard

1983 Cadillac Cimarron

1983 Cadillac Cimarron interior and trunk

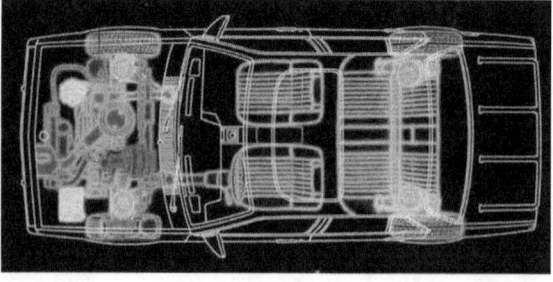

1983 Cadillac Coupe deVille

1983 Cadillac Seville

1983 Cadillac Coupe deVille interior

Sierra Grain leather & Tampico carpeting

1983 Cadillac Seville Elegante interior

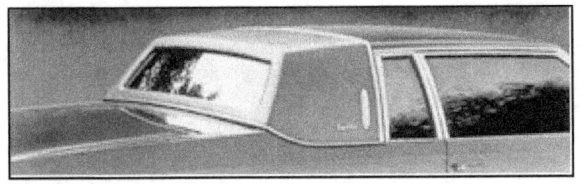

From the Brochure: "In 1983, the pursuit of excellence continues. You can see it in the subtle refinements of the Cadillac grille. Hear it in the clean, full sound of Cadillac's radios. Feel it in the smooth, quiet Cadillac ride."
- 1983 Cadillac

Those '80s Cars

1983 Cadillac Fleetwood Brougham Sedan

1983 Cadillac Eldorado

1983 Cadillac Fleetwood Brougham interior

1983 Cadillac Eldorado Touring Coupe & Biarritz interiors

From the Brochure: "What makes a Cadillac a Cadillac? It can be summed up in a single word: excellence. For over 80 years, the Cadillac name has stood for excellence in its many forms. Innovative engineering. Solid comfort. Quality that endures. The Cadillac name has been a synonym with integrity. And, in doing so, the Cadillac wreath and crest has become a symbol of excellence the world over." - 1983

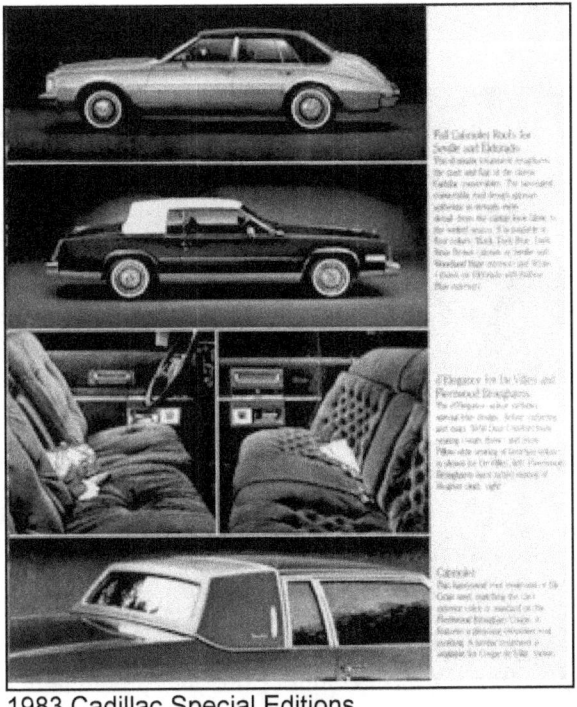
1983 Cadillac Special Editions

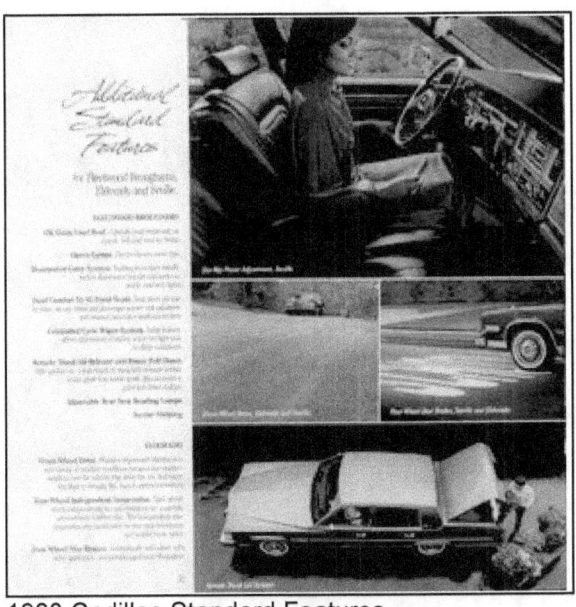
1983 Cadillac Standard Features

1983 Cadillac Fleetwood Limousine

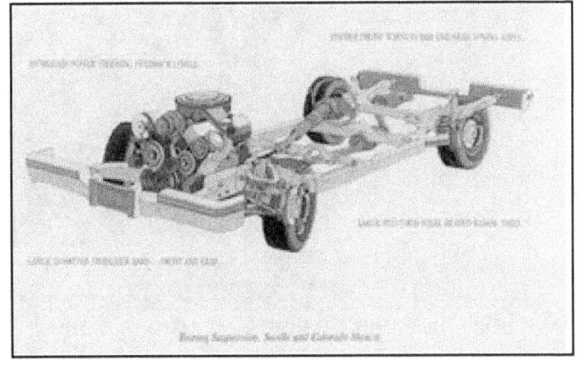

Those '80s Cars

1983 - CHEVROLET

1983 Chevrolet Monte Carlo

Monte Carlo CL Special Custom interior

1983 Chevrolet Monte Carlo with removable glass roof panels

1983 Chevrolet Monte Carlo instrument panel

1983 Chevrolet Caprice Classic interior

21 cu. ft. trunk space

1983 Chevrolet Caprice Classic Estate Wagon
1983 Chevrolet Impala Sedan (bottom)

1983 Chevrolet Citation CL Custom interior

Over 1,000,000 sold in previous 3 years

1983 Chevrolet Citation Hatchback Coupe

1983 Chevrolet Camaro Sport Coupe & Berlinetta Coupe

New 5-speed manual transmission

1983 Chevrolet Camaro instrument panel

1983 Chevrolet Chevette

New 2.0 EFI and New 5-speed manual transmission

1983 Chevrolet Cavalier

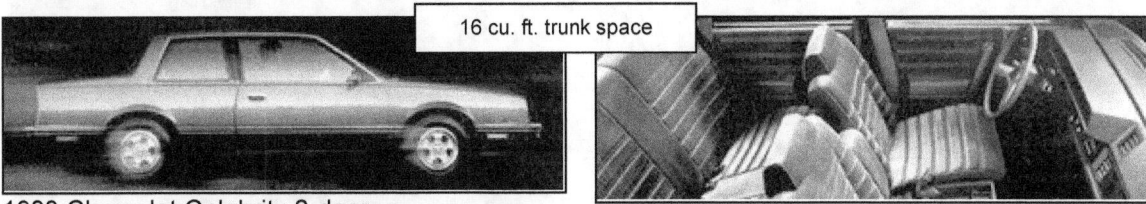

16 cu. ft. trunk space

1983 Chevrolet Celebrity 2-door

1983 Chevrolet Celebrity interior

Last Model Run: 1983 Chevrolet Malibu Classic Wagon

1983 Chevrolet Malibu Classic interior

Those '80s Cars

1983 - CHRYSLER / IMPERIAL

1983 Imperial optional leather interior

Last Model Run: 1983 Imperial

1983 Imperial instrument panel

1983 Imperial features

Last Model Run: 1983 Imperial

1983 Chrysler New Yorker Fifth Avenue

1982's New Yorker is re-branded as 1983 New Yorker Fifth Avenue to make room for a new front-drive New Yorker

1983 Chrysler New Yorker Fifth Avenue optional leather interior

1983 Chrysler New Yorker Fifth Avenue instrument panel

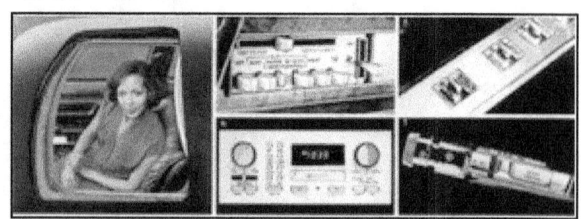
1983 Chrysler New Yorker Fifth Avenue features

1983 Chrysler E Class instrument panel & optional interior (standard on New Yorker)

2.2 liter (135 CID) standard and a Mitsubishi-built 2.6 liter (156 CID) is optional on both E Class & New Yorker

From the Brochure: "Chrysler's largest front-wheel drive sedan. Chrysler E Class, America's newest front-wheel drive automobile, offers a highly desirable combination of six-passenger room, outstanding ride and handling, and superb styling – all in an efficient, contemporary size."
- 1983 Chrysler E Class

New Model: 1983 Chrysler Executive Sedan

1983 Chrysler Cordoba interior

New Model: 1983 Chrysler E Class

E Class & New Yorker have a 3" longer wheelbase than LeBaron

New Model: 1983 Chrysler New Yorker

Last Model Run: 1983 Chrysler Cordoba with Cabriolet Roof Package

1983 Chrysler Cordoba instrument panel

From the Brochure: "We've re-engineered the American luxury car. Compromise will never be part of the lifestyle of the people who are going places. They know that when they step out of a Chrysler Cordoba, they step out in style. They tell the world that individuality and common sense still exist."
- 1983 Chrysler Cordoba

Those '80s Cars

1983 Chrysler LeBaron convertible with Mark Cross Package

1983 Chrysler LeBaron 4-door Sedan

From the Brochure: "Like no other cars in America, Europe or Japan. The Chrysler LeBarons have restored a feeling about an American car that's been missing for some time. The feeling: pride. The Chrysler Corporation is proud to build the LeBarons as the latest example of advanced automotive technology. We've focused a lot of our engineering expertise on making the LeBarons handsome, efficient front-wheel drive cars that are technically sound and luxurious." – 1983 Chrysler LeBaron

1983 Chrysler Town & Country

LeBaron instrumentation changes after 1982

1983 Chrysler LeBaron 2-door Coupe

1983 - DODGE

1983 Dodge 400 Convertible

1983 Dodge 400 2-door

1983 Dodge 400 4-door

From the Brochure: "Owning one is like owning the road. Since its wheels first touched pavement last year, it has been obvious that Dodge 400 is an automobile with a singular purpose… to rekindle the pure enjoyment of driving.

Today Dodge 400 lineup offers a choice of three sporty front-wheel drive models, all designed with a canny awareness of energy economy.

For 1983, Dodge 400 offers, a four-passenger convertible and distinctive two- and four-door models."

- 1983 Dodge 400

New Model: 1983 Dodge 600 ES Sedan

Front-wheel drive, 2.2 liter 4-cylinder, 3-speed automatic, 103" wheelbase, 17 cu. ft. trunk, 24 estimated MPG, 32 MPG estimated highway

New Model: 1983 Dodge 600 Sedan

1983 Dodge 600 standard interior

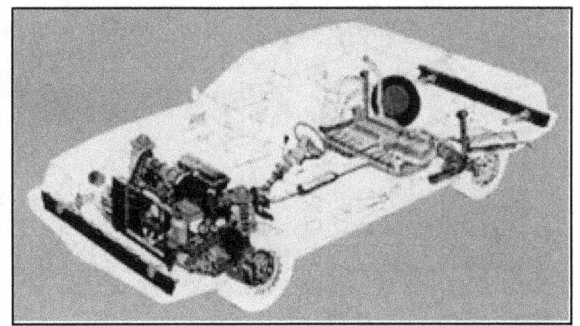

Those '80s Cars

121

1983 Dodge Charger — New 1.6 liter 4-cylinder engine introduced mid-year

1983 Dodge Aries SE 2-door — 2.2 liter 4-cylinder now standard

1983 Dodge Charger 2.2 — New front storage and shift console. Sport suspension, 5-speed manual, & 14" Rallye wheels are standard

1983 Dodge Aries Wagon with Aries Sedan

1983 Dodge Charger instrument panel

New heater for improved distribution
1983 Dodge Aries SE interior

New Model: 1983 Dodge Shelby Charger

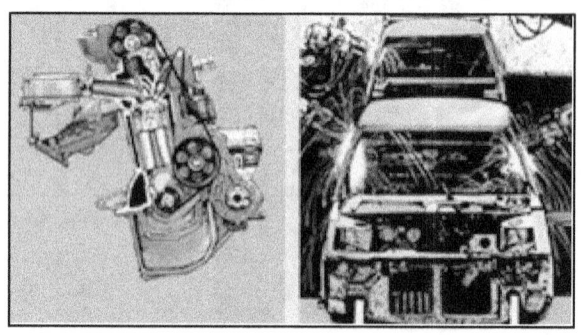

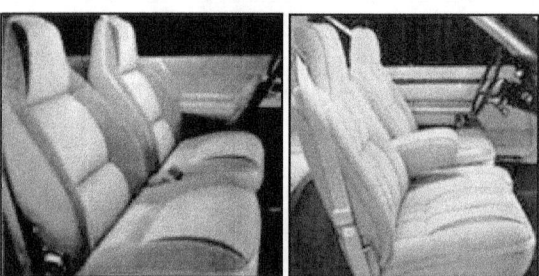
1983 Dodge Charger & Mirada interiors

Last Year Model: 1983 Dodge Mirada CMX

1983 Dodge Diplomat Salon

1983 Dodge Omni

New 1.6 liter 4-cylinder engine introduced mid-year

1.4 liter 4-cylinder engine & 4-speed manual are standard

1983 Dodge Colt Custom

1983 Dodge Omni Custom

Colt offers 4 trim levels: base, Deluxe, Custom and RS

1983 Dodge Colt Custom RS

1983 Dodge Omni Custom interior

1983 Dodge Rampage 2.2

1983 Dodge Challenger Technica

From the Brochure: "At Dodge, driving excellence is engineered in. Design has a lot to do with the sophisticated formula that makes front-wheel drive technology work so well in the 1983 Dodge car lines. Not just make-it-look-nice styling, but aerodynamic styling that uses the flow of the air to hold the car to the road while maximizing engine power and fuel efficiency."
- 1983 Dodge

Rampage standard & deluxe interiors

Those '80s Cars

1983 - FORD

1983 Ford product line-up
New Model: 1983 Ford LTD sedan (2nd from top)

New Model: 1983 Ford LTD Wagon

LTD engines: 2.3 liter 4-cylinder, 3.3 inline 6 & 3.8 liter V6

1983 Ford LTD interior

New options: EFI, 5-speed manual, TR-type wheels, handling suspension

1983 Ford Escort GT

1983 Ford LTD Crown Victoria 2-door Coupe

1983 Ford LTD Country Squire

1983 Ford LTD Country Squire

1983 Ford LTD Crown Victoria 2-door Coupe

1983 Ford Escort Wagon

New Model: 1983 Ford Thunderbird

Standard 3.8 liter V6
Optional 5.0 liter V8
.35 drag coefficient
New Model: 1983 Ford Thunderbird

1983 Ford Thunderbird interior

Refreshed: 1983 Ford Mustang GT

1983 Ford EXP

Refreshed: 1983 Ford Mustang GLX

Fairmont: the choice of over 1.3 million owners
Last Model Run: 1983 Ford Fairmont Futura

New: Mustang convertible
Refreshed: 1983 Ford Mustang line

1983 Ford Fairmont Futura interior

Last Model Run: 1983 Ford Fairmont Futura

Those '80s Cars

1983 - LINCOLN

1983 Lincoln Town Car Signature Series

Mark VI Signature Series interior

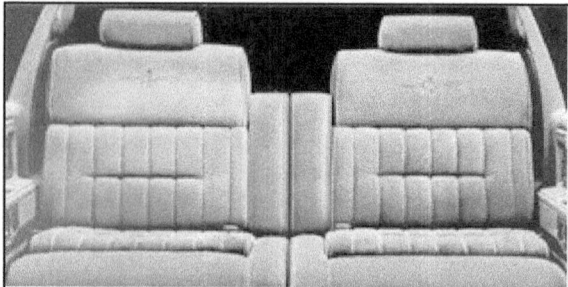
1983 Lincoln Town Car Signature Series interior

Last Model Run: 1983 Lincoln Continental Mark VI Signature Series 2-door Coupe

1983 Lincoln Continental

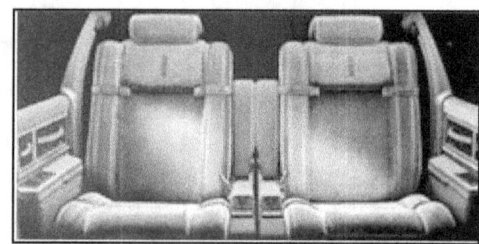

1983 - MERCURY

New Model: 1983 Mercury Cougar

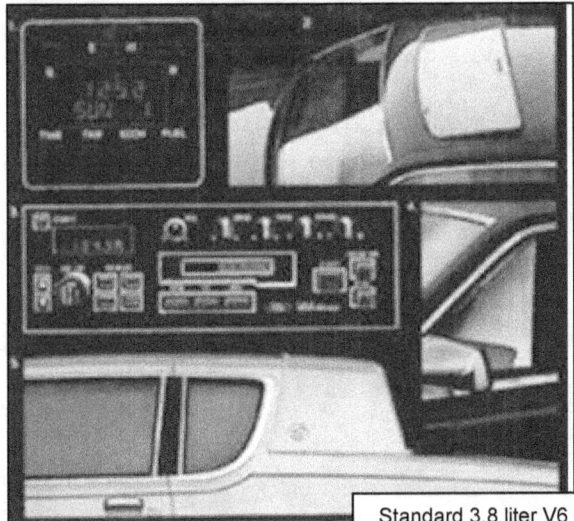

1983 Mercury Cougar options

Standard 3.8 liter V6
5.0 liter V8 optional

1983 Mercury Cougar LS interior

1983 Mercury Capri Black Magic, Capri L & GS

1983 Mercury Grand Marquis 4-door Sedan

With introduction of intermediate Marquis, all full-size models are now branded Grand Marquis

1983 Mercury Grand Marquis standard cloth interior

1983 Mercury Grand Marquis Colony Park Wagon

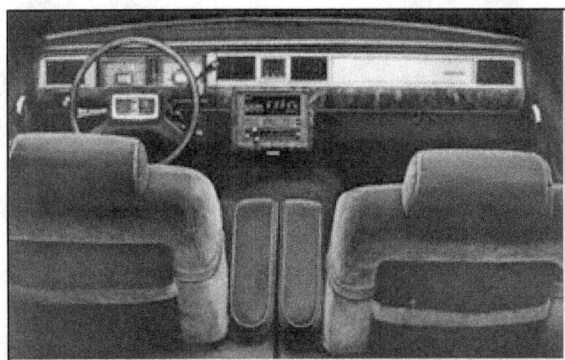

1983 Mercury Grand Marquis LS interior

Those '80s Cars

105.6" wheelbase
New Model: 1983 Mercury Marquis

New Model: 1983 Mercury Marquis Wagons

1983 Mercury Marquis optional interior

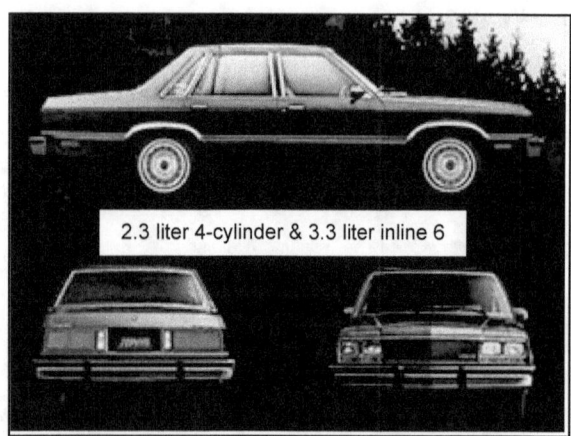
2.3 liter 4-cylinder & 3.3 liter inline 6
Last Model Run: 1983 Mercury Zephyr

1983 Mercury Lynx LS 5-Door

1983 Mercury Lynx GS 3-Door

1983 Mercury Lynx RS – 1.6 liter EFI 4-cylinder engine with 5-speed manual transmission and performance handling suspension are all standard equipment.

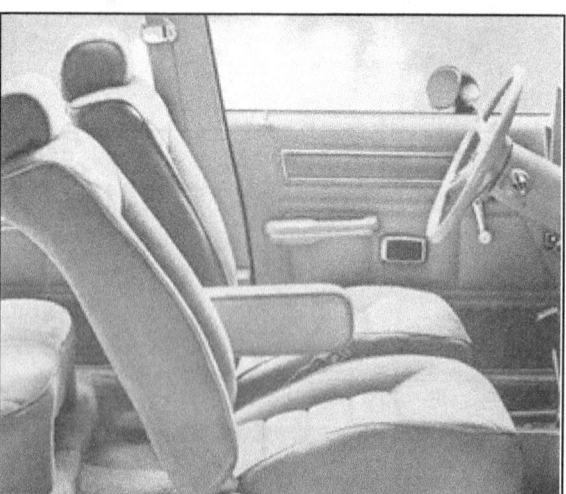
1983 Mercury Lynx LS interior

1983 Mercury LN7

128

Those '80s Cars

1983 - OLDSMOBILE

1983 Oldsmobile Cutlass Ciera Brougham Sedan

1983 Oldsmobile Cutlass Ciera LS Coupe

New Ciera ES series introduced in addition to the previous LS and Brougham series

Ciera coupes get a wider b-pillar this year

1983 Oldsmobile Cutlass Ciera Brougham Sedan interior

1983 Oldsmobile Cutlass Ciera instrument panel

1983 Oldsmobile Cutlass Supreme Brougham

1983 Oldsmobile Cutlass Supreme Brougham Coupe

1983 Oldsmobile Cutlass Supreme dash panel

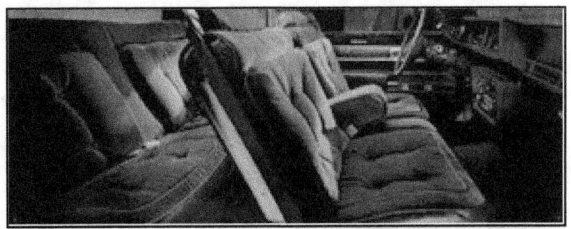
1983 Oldsmobile Supreme Brougham interior

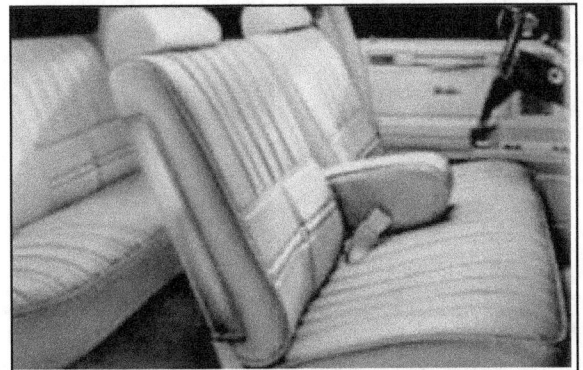
1983 Oldsmobile Cutlass Cruiser interior

1983 Oldsmobile Cutlass Cruiser

Those '80s Cars

1983 Oldsmobile Toronado Brougham Coupe interior

1983 Oldsmobile Ninety-Eight Regency Coupe

1983 Oldsmobile Ninety-Eight Regency Sedan

1983 Oldsmobile Ninety-Eight Regency Coupe optional leather interior

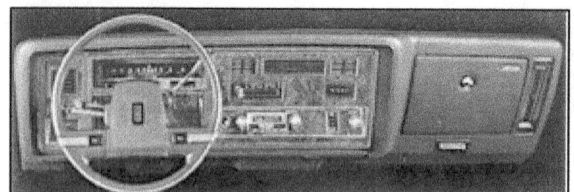
1983 Oldsmobile Ninety-Eight instrument panel

1983 Oldsmobile Toronado Brougham Coupe

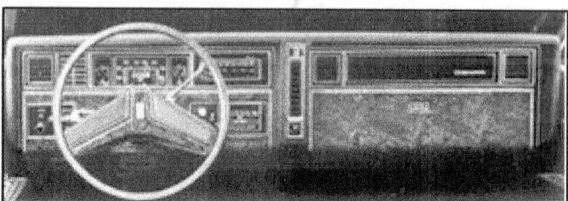
1983 Oldsmobile Toronado instrument panel

1983 Oldsmobile Delta 88 Royale Coupe

1983 Oldsmobile Delta 88 Royal interior

20.8 cu. ft. trunk
1983 Oldsmobile Delta 88 Sedan

1983 Oldsmobile Firenza Hatchback

1983 Oldsmobile Custom Cruiser interior

1983 Oldsmobile Omega Brougham Sedan

1983 Oldsmobile Custom Cruiser

1983 - PLYMOUTH

1983 Plymouth Gran Fury

1983 Plymouth Gran Fury instrument panel

1983 Plymouth Gran Fury interior

New 1.6 liter 4-cylinder engine introduced mid-year; 2.2 liter 4-cylinder optional

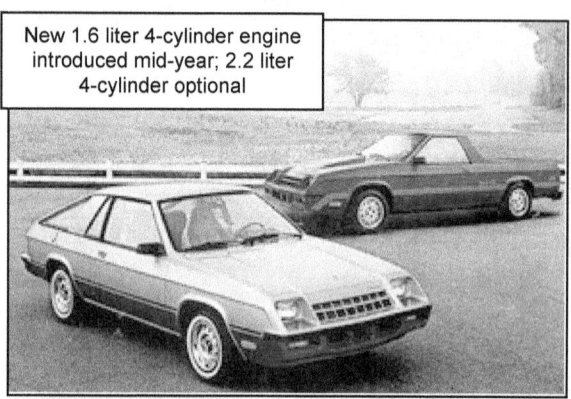
1983 Plymouth Turismo 2.2 & Scamp GT (back)

1983 Plymouth Turismo 2.2 interior

From the Brochure: "Zip on by the pump. The dashing good looks of a sporty car... the carry-all utility of a small truck... excellent performance... and equally excellent fuel economy. Put them all together and you get the all-new 1983 Plymouth Scamp."
- **New Model:** 1983 Plymouth Scamp

1983 Plymouth Turismo 2.2 interior

1983 Plymouth Scamp interior

From the Brochure: "Turismo steps out with front-wheel drive efficiency that's packaged in sleek, distinctive sporty styling. The smart, spacious interior has room for five and standard front cloth-and-vinyl sport type high bucket seats for comfort and support."
- 1983 Plymouth Turismo

1983 Plymouth Reliant Special Edition 4-door Sedan

1983 Plymouth Reliant Special Edition interior

1983 Plymouth Reliant Special Edition Wagon

1983 Plymouth Special Edition 2-door Coupe

1983 Plymouth Horizon

New 1.6 liter 4-cylinder engine introduced mid-year

Last year's Champ is renamed Colt in 1983

1983 Plymouth Colt Custom RS 3-Door

1983 Plymouth Horizon Custom instrument panel

1983 Plymouth Sapporo Technica

New Technica Package with digital gauges

1983 Plymouth Horizon standard interior

1983 Plymouth Sapporo Technica dash panel

Those '80s Cars

1983 - PONTIAC

1983 Pontiac Firebird S/E & standard coupes

1983 Pontiac Firebird Trans Am interior

1983 Pontiac Firebird Trans Am instrument panel

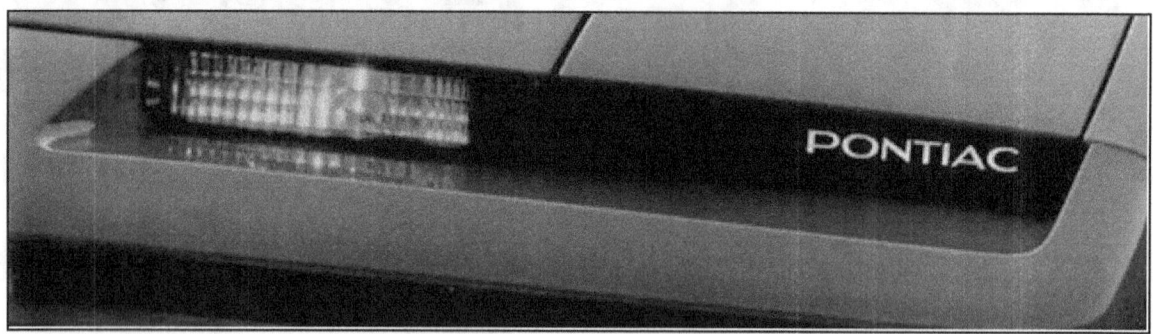

1983 Pontiac 6000 2-door Coupe & 6000 LE 4-door Sedan

From the Brochure: "Special Touring Edition. Our most exciting high-performance front-wheel-drive sedan is an eloquent rebuttal to those who think drivers' sedans are the private domain of Europe. The subtle but striking tone-on-tone paint highlights the STE's sophisticated character. Four halogen headlamps, two inboard-mounted driving lamps and the front air dam contribute to its serious stance. The Goodyear Eagle GT's are mounted on ventilated cast aluminum wheels. An STE exclusive, these new wheels minimize unsprung weight and aid in braking cooling. Shock absorbers, springs, front and rear stabilizers and the power rack and pinion steering were tuned to take advantage of the tire capabilities and extract an impressive combination of ride and handling. There's also a refined 2.8 liter High Output V-6 that combines with a three-speed automatic to impart smooth effortless response."

- 1983 Pontiac 6000 STE

1983 Pontiac 6000 STE instrument panel

1983 Pontiac 6000 STE interior

Those '80s Cars

1982's 4.1 V6 option is dropped and replaced by a 5.0 V8 on Grand Prix & Bonneville

1983 Pontiac Grand Prix LJ

1983 Pontiac Bonneville Brougham Sedan

1983 Pontiac Grand Prix optional bucket seats

1983 Pontiac Bonneville Brougham interior

Last Model Run: 1983 Pontiac Bonneville Wagon

1983 Pontiac Bonneville instrument panel

1983 Pontiac Grand Prix instrument panel

Note lower dash bezel trim differences

Those '80s Cars

New Model: 1983 Pontiac Parisienne

1983 Pontiac Phoenix LJ 5-Door Hatchback

Pontiac drops the "J" off last year's J2000 & adds a 2.0 liter 4-cylinder option

1983 Pontiac 2000 Coupe & Convertible

1983 Pontiac Phoenix instrument panel

1983 Pontiac 2000 SE/LE interior

1983 Pontiac Phoenix LJ interior

Pontiac 2000 instrument panel & rally gauges

1983 Pontiac 1000 (The "T" is dropped from last year's T1000 moniker)

1983 Pontiac T1000 interior with optional cloth

1983 Pontiac T1000 gauges

Those '80s Cars

1984

1984 - Facts at Glance

News Headlines

- Indria Ghandi is assassinated
- Summer Olympics held in LA
- French identify AIDS virus
- AT&T is broken up
- Apple Macintosh goes on sale
- CD players are introduced
- Michael Jackson's Thriller sells over 37 million copies

Tops in Pop Culture

Music
- When Doves Cry, Prince

Movies
- Ghost Busters

TV Show
- Dynasty

Sports Champions

Basketball
- Boston Celtics

Football
- L.A. Raiders

Baseball
- Detroit Tigers

Motor Trend – Car of the Year

Chevrolet Corvette

1984 - AMC / EAGLE

Luxury. Security. Unbeatable 4-Wheel Drive.

American Eagle is an automobile with the comfort and luxury of a fine road car, plus the capability to let you "shift-on-the-fly" to the confidence of 4-wheel drive. It's a well-appointed and equipped vehicle that's ready to take you and your family almost anywhere—in style and comfort—no matter what the road conditions.

Eagle has a powerful 4.2 liter, 6-cylinder engine with 5-speed manual transmission standard. But it's Eagle's luxurious interior that makes this elegant vehicle a pleasure to drive. There are individually reclining front seats in a choice of Deluxe grain vinyl or Highland Check fabric and conveniently positioned instruments and controls set in a color-keyed, woodgrain-accented instrument panel. In addition, there's a large selection of optional equipment and trim levels available in Eagle, offering the **feel** of a luxurious touring car.

With Eagle Limited, luxury is standard. There are reclining seats in supple leather, dual remote control mirrors, plush carpeting, wire wheel covers, and more.

So whichever Eagle model you select, 4-door Sedan, 4-door Eagle Wagon Sport or Wagon Limited, you'll find you have a vehicle that's roomy, comfortable, dependable and secure.

Enter the world of luxury 4-wheel drive with American Eagle.

1984 - BUICK

Last Model Run: 1984 Buick Regal Limited Sedan Buick Regal T Type with Designers' Package

Tach & turbo boost gauges are standard on T Type

1984 Buick Regal Limited interior 1984 Buick Skylark Limited interior

Standard rack-and-pinion steering, MacPherson-strut front suspension and trailing-axle coil spring rear suspension

1984 Buick Skylark T Type Buick Skylark Custom Coupe

Automatic level control is optional

1984 Buick Century T Type Sedan 1984 Buick Century Custom Coupe

1984 Buick Century Limited interior

1984 Buick Skyhawk Limited interior

Skyhawk T Type has new 150-horsepower turbo 1.8 liter 4-cylinder OHC engine

1984 Buick Skyhawk Custom Coupe   1984 Buick Skyhawk Limited Sedan

1984 Buick Riviera T Type   1984 Buick Riviera Convertible

Last Model Run: 1984 Buick Electra Limited Coupe   1984 Buick Electra Park Avenue Sedan

1984 Buick Electra Park Avenue interior

1984 Buick LeSabre Limited

Those '80s Cars

1984 - CADILLAC

1984 Cadillac Fleetwood Brougham Coupe

1984 Cadillac Fleetwood Brougham Sedan

Dual Comfort front seats, both 6-way powered, and rear seat adjustable reading lamps standard

1984 Cadillac Fleetwood Brougham optional leather interior

Last Model Run: 1984 Cadillac Coupe deVille

Last Model Run: 1984 Cadillac Sedan deVille

1984 Cadillac deVille interior

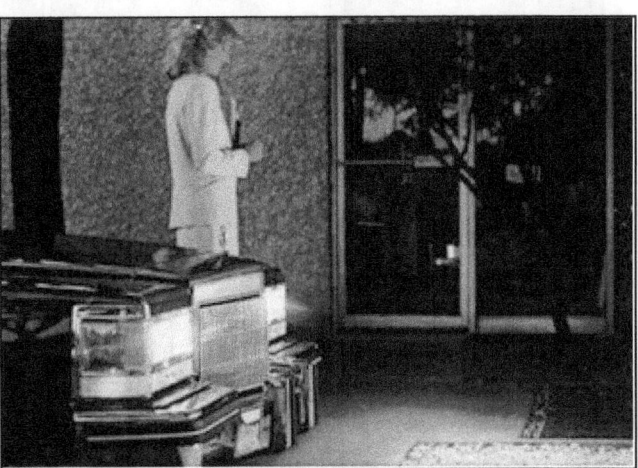

Those '80s Cars

1984 Cadillac Seville

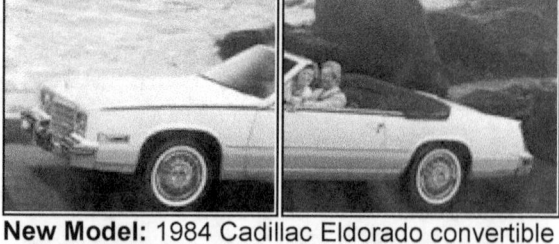
New Model: 1984 Cadillac Eldorado convertible

1984 Cadillac Seville Elegante

1984 Cadillac Eldorado Touring Coupe

1984 Cadillac Seville instrument panel

1984 Cadillac Eldorado Touring Coupe interior

1984 Cadillac Cimarron

Those '80s Cars

1984 - CHEVROLET

1984 Chevrolet Camaro Z28

1984 Chevrolet Camaro Berlinetta interior

1984 Chevrolet Cavalier Type 10 Hatchback

1984 Chevrolet Cavalier CS Sedan

0-100-0 in 22.4 seconds

5.7 V8 Cross-Fire Injection

New Model: 1984 Chevrolet Corvette

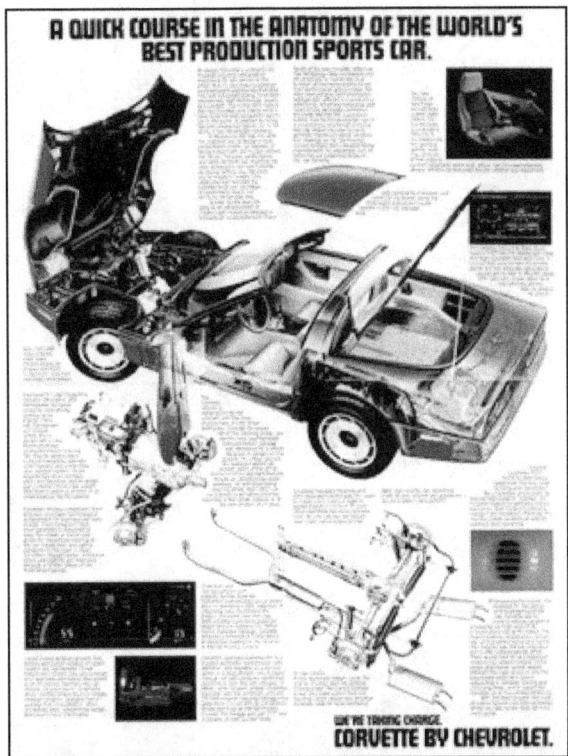

1984 Chevrolet Cavalier instrument panel

1984 Chevrolet Cavalier Type 10 Coupe

Those '80s Cars

1984 Chevrolet Citation II 4-door Hatchback

1984 Chevrolet Citation II 4-door Hatchback

Last year's Citation is re-branded as the Citation II

1984 Chevrolet Citation II CL Custom interior

1984 Chevrolet Citation II X-11 instrument panel

1984 Chevrolet Monte Carlo SS

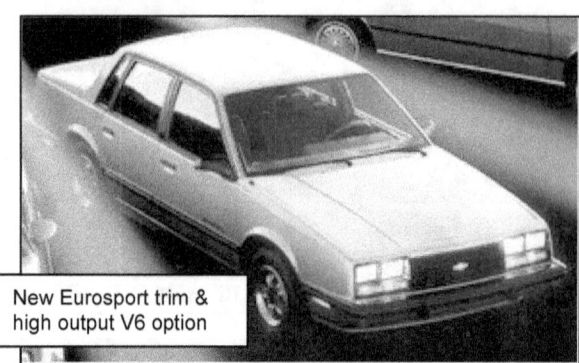

New Eurosport trim & high output V6 option

1984 Chevrolet Celebrity Eurosport

1984 Chevrolet Monte Carlo interior

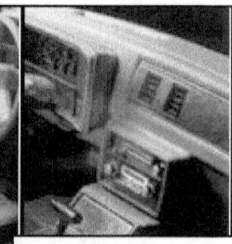

New 5.0 V8 with 4-speed auto overdrive option

1984 Chevrolet Celebrity CL Custom interior

Over 110 billion owner-driven miles

1984 Chevrolet Chevette

Those '80s Cars

1984 Chevrolet Caprice Classic Sedan

From the Brochure: "Sure we made Caprice crisp and stylish on the outside, but you're going to spend most of your time on the inside. With that fact in mind, Chevrolet engineers made Caprice's interior the way real cars were meant to be. For your comfort, there's an even richer standard front bench seat in sedan and coupe for 1984, with fold-down center armrest, large door armrests and door pull straps, all standard.

Caprice uses extensive acoustical insulation to help quiet your world. Even the door bottoms have sealers to hush harsh pavement noise." – 1984 Chevrolet Caprice Classic

1984 Chevrolet Caprice Classic instrument panel

1984 Chevrolet Caprice Classic interior

1984 Chevrolet Impala interior

1984 Chevrolet Impala

Those '80s Cars

1984 - CHRYSLER

1984 Chrysler Fifth Avenue

"New Yorker" name is dropped from the Fifth Avenue model in 1984 & the 5.2 liter (318 CID) V8 becomes standard

1984 Chrysler Fifth Avenue instrument panel

1984 Chrysler Fifth Avenue optional leather

New Model: 1984 Chrysler Laser XE Turbo

2.2 liter 4-cylinder is standard with a new optional turbocharger available

1984 Chrysler Laser interior

1984 Chrysler Laser XE instrument panel

2.2 liter 4-cylinder rated at 99 hp
2.2 turbo rated at 142 hp

1984 Chrysler LeBaron electronic instruments

New on convertible: rear side windows and top

1984 Chrysler LeBaron Town & Country Wagon & Convertible with woodgrain paneling
1984 Chrysler LeBaron Coupe, Sedan and Convertible

1984 Chrysler LeBaron Mark Cross interior

1984 Chrysler Executive Sedan

Limousine/Executive Sedan rear seat

Executive Sedan and Limousine have 40.2" of rear legroom

Limousine is 210.4" long with a 131" wheelbase

Executive Sedan is 203.4" long with a 124" wheelbase

Last Model Run: 1984 Chrysler E Class

E Class replaced in 1985 with Plymouth Caravelle

1984 Chrysler E Class split bench interior

1984 Chrysler New Yorker instrument panel

New digital instrumentation is standard on New Yorker in 1984

Refreshed: 1984 Chrysler New Yorker

Those '80s Cars

1984 - DODGE

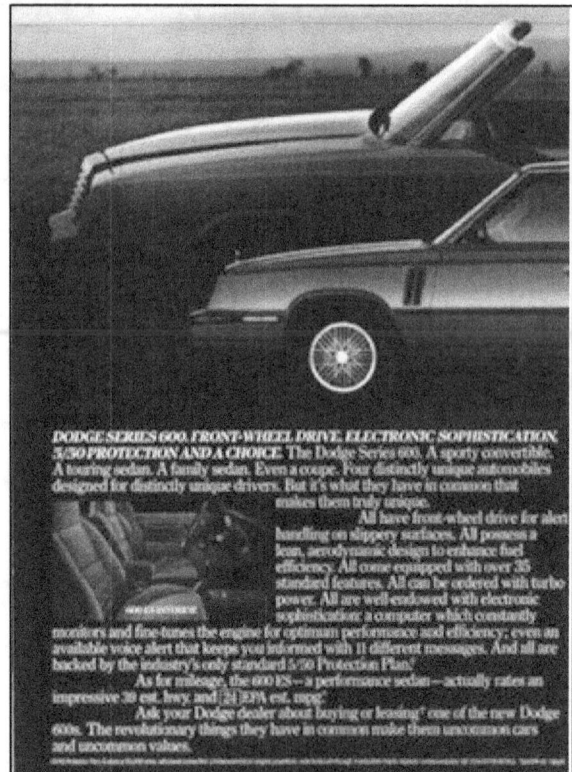

1984 Dodge 600 (last year's 400 Coupe & Convertible are re-badged as 600 this year)

Dodge Caravan, Daytona & 600 Convertible

New Model: 1984 Dodge Caravan

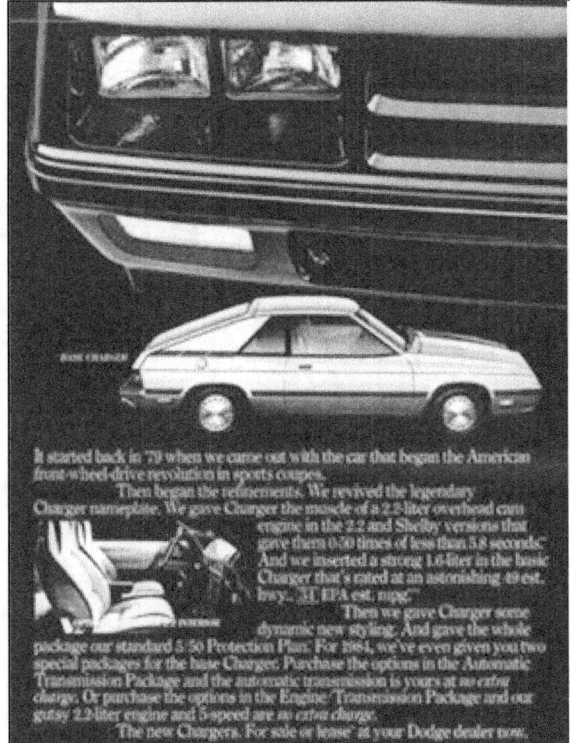
1984 Dodge Charger advertisement

New Model: 1984 Dodge Colt Vista Wagon

1.6 liter turbo 4-cylinder EFI, 102 hp

1984 Dodge Turbo Colt

1984 Dodge Diplomat SE interior

New Model: 1984 Dodge Conquest

1984 Dodge Conquest instrument panel

1984 Dodge Diplomat SE

1984 Dodge Aries SE 4-door Sedan

Those '80s Cars

New Model: 1984 Dodge Daytona

New Trim Series: 1984 Dodge Omni GLH

1984 - FORD

2.3 liter EFI turbo, 145 hp at 4,600 RPM

1984 Ford Thunderbird Turbo Coupe

2.3 liter EFI turbo

New Series: 1984 Ford Mustang SVO

1984 Ford Thunderbird Turbo Coupe interior with optional leather

1984 Ford Mustang SVO interior

Thunderbird trim series: base, élan, FILA and Turbo Coupe

1984 Ford Thunderbird Turbo Coupe instrument panel

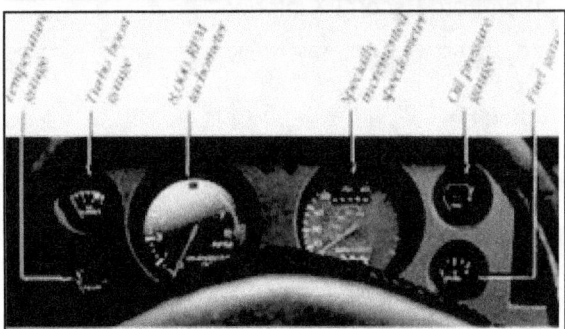

1984 Ford Mustang SVO instrument panel

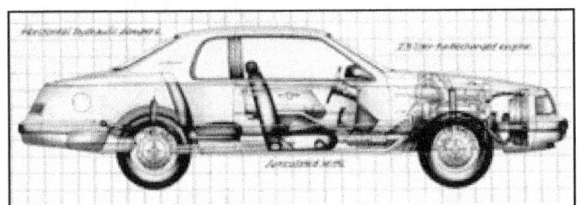

Those '80s Cars

1984 Ford Escort LX Wagon

1984 Ford Escort GT instrument panel

1984 Ford Escort LX interior

1984 Ford Escort GL 4-door Hatchback

1.6 liter EFI turbo, 5-speed manual

1984 Ford Escort GT 2-door Hatchback

Standard 2.3 liter 4-cylinder

New Model: 1984 Ford Tempo GL 4-door Sedan

1984 Ford Tempo instrument panel

1984 Ford Tempo GL interior

2.0 liter diesel optional

New Model: 1984 Ford Tempo L 2-door Coupe

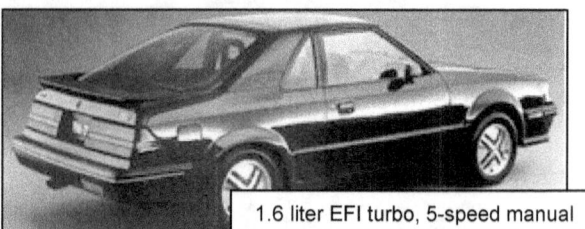
1.6 liter EFI turbo, 5-speed manual

1984 Ford EXP Turbo Coupe

1984 Ford EXP instrument panel

Those '80s Cars

1984 Ford LTD Wagon with optional bumper guards (left)
1984 LTD 4-door Sedan with optional styled road wheels (right)

1984 Ford LTD Crown Victoria interior with optional Interior Luxury Group leather seating surfaces and special sew style

1984 Ford LTD Brougham interior with optional leather seating surfaces and thick carpeting. Brougham comes standard with electronic digital clock, auto parking brake release, illuminated entry, dual illuminated vanity mirrors and Light Group.

LTD Crown Victoria wagons offers optional Dual Facing Rear Seats for 8-passenger seating and a standard 3-Way Magic Doorgate

1984 Ford LTD Country Squire Wagon

1984 Ford LTD Crown Victoria 4-door Sedan

1984 Ford LTD Crown Victoria 2-door Coupe

1984 Ford LTD Crown Victoria

Those '80s Cars

1984 - LINCOLN

1984 Lincoln Town Car

New Model: 1984 Lincoln VII LSC

Standard 5.0 liter EFI V8 with 4-speed automatic overdrive
2.4 liter turbocharged diesel, sourced by BMW, is optional

1984 Lincoln Town Car Cartier

New Model: 1984 Lincoln VII LSC

1984 Lincoln Town Car Cartier interior

1984 Lincoln VII LSC interior

1984 Lincoln Town Car

.38 drag coefficient

New Model: 1984 Lincoln VII

Those '80s Cars

Refreshed: 1984 Lincoln Continental

Refreshed: 1984 Lincoln Continental

Standard 5.0 liter EFI V8 with 4-speed automatic overdrive
2.4 liter turbocharged diesel, sourced by BMW, is optional

Refreshed: 1984 Lincoln Continental Valentino

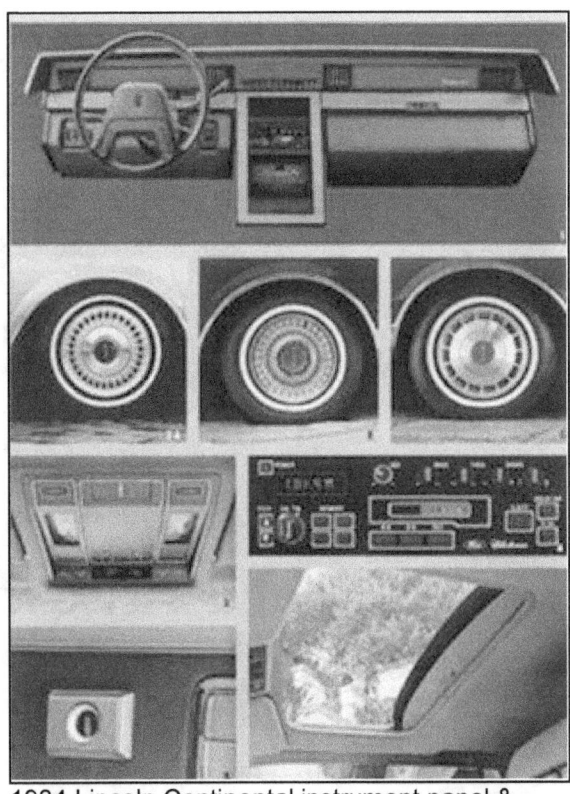
1984 Lincoln Continental instrument panel & features

1984 Lincoln Continental interior

Refreshed: 1984 Lincoln Continental Givenchy

Those '80s Cars

1984 - MERCURY

1984 Mercury Cougar XR-7 Turbo instruments

1984 Mercury Marquis Brougham

1984 Mercury Capri Turbo RS

1984 Mercury Capri Turbo RS interior

1984 Mercury Cougar XR-7 Turbo

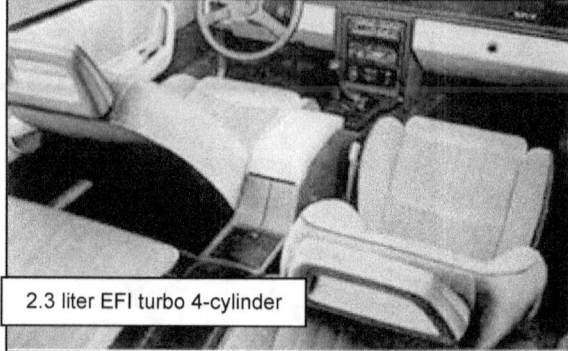
2.3 liter EFI turbo 4-cylinder
1984 Mercury Cougar XR-7 Turbo interior

1984 Mercury Grand Marquis

1984 Mercury Capri GS

1984 Mercury Capri roof options

AM/FM Stereo Cassette

1.6 liter EFI turbo, 5-speed manual

1984 Mercury Lynx LTS 4-door Hatchback

1984 Mercury Lynx GS interior

1984 Mercury Lynx Villager Wagon

1984 Mercury Lynx instrument panel

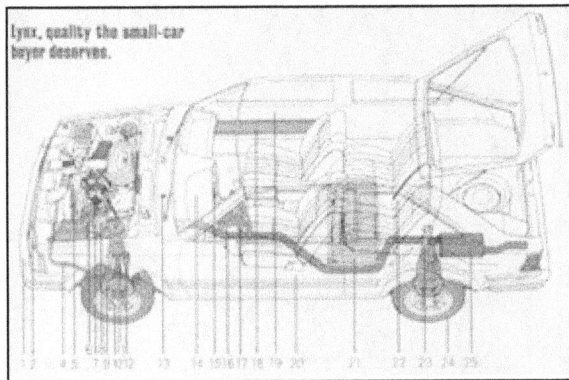

New Model: 1984 Mercury Topaz LS 4-door

Standard 2.3 liter 4-cylinder
Optional 2.0 liter 4-cylinder diesel

New Model: 1984 Mercury Topaz Sport 2-door

From the Brochure: "A more enlightened approach. There is a new kind of driver beginning to make an impact on the American scene. This more enlightened person shuns mere styling unsupported by substantial engineering. Mercury understands the message."
– 1984 Mercury Topaz

New Model: 1984 Mercury Topaz

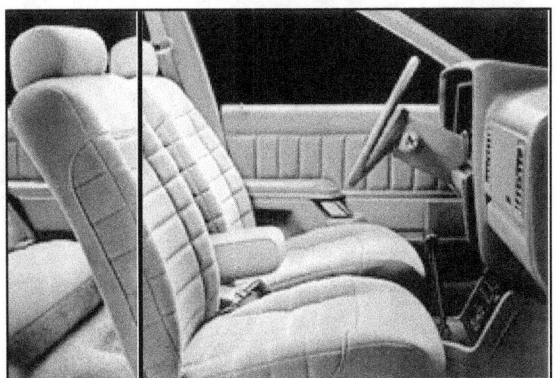

1984 Mercury Topaz LS interior

Those '80s Cars

1984 - OLDSMOBILE

5.0 liter V8 standard

Last Model Run: 1984 Oldsmobile Ninety-Eight Regency Brougham

From the Brochure: "There is something very special that goes along with the ownership of an Oldsmobile automobile. It's more than stylish good looks which win so many glances of approval. It's more than the luxurious interiors so pleasing to the senses."
—1984 Oldsmobile

160

Those '80s Cars

1984 Oldsmobile Toronado Brougham

From the Brochure: "That special feeling goes beyond the tangible and the visible. Most notably, it is a feeling of *pride*, the pride you feel inside. The feeling of *confidence*. The sense of *well being*. You invested wisely and well and you feel very good about it."
-1984 Oldsmobile

Cutlass Ciera adds a Holiday Coupe trim model & a 3.8 liter V6 to the options list

New Model: Cutlass Cruiser moves from the Supreme's platform to the Ciera's

Those '80s Cars

Last Model Run: 1984 Oldsmobile Omega

3 trim series:
Omega
Omega Brougham
Omega ES

6 trim series:
Firenza
Firenza S
Firenza LX
Firenza ES
Firenza SX
Firenza GT

1984 - PLYMOUTH

1984 Plymouth Gran Fury 4-door Sedan

1984 Plymouth full product line
New Models: Voyager & Colt Vista Wagon

1984 Plymouth Gran Fury interiors (standard bench above & optional 60/40 split bench)

1984 Plymouth Turismo

1984 Plymouth Horizon

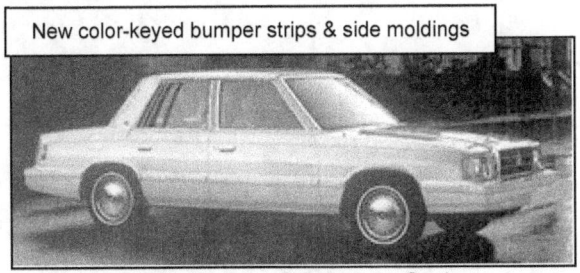
New color-keyed bumper strips & side moldings
1984 Plymouth Reliant SE 4-door Sedan

1984 Plymouth Reliant SE Wagon

1984 - PONTIAC

New Model: 1984 Pontiac Fiero SE

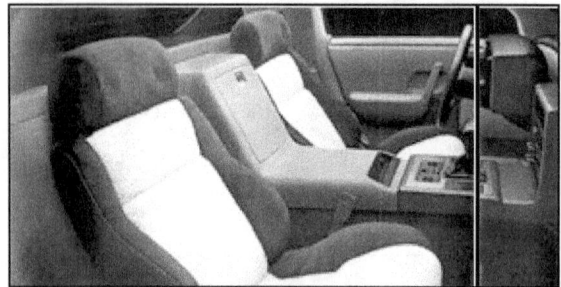
1984 Pontiac Fiero SE interior - fleece & suede

1984 Pontiac Fiero instrument cluster

1984 Pontiac Grand Prix & Bonneville LE interior

1984 Pontiac Firebird S/E

1984 Pontiac Firebird Lear Siegler seat and S/E & Trans Am instrument panel

From the Brochure: "The overall look of Fiero emphasizes its clean, uncluttered shape, a calculated departure from the sharp edges of the 'folded paper' school of automotive design.

Fiero is powered by a mid-mounted 2.5 liter 4-cylinder engine with electronic fuel injection. A performance-geared 4-speed manual transmission is standard on Fiero." - 1984 Pontiac Fiero

1984 Pontiac Grand Prix LE

1984 Pontiac Grand Prix & Bonneville dash

1984 Pontiac Bonneville LE

1984 Pontiac 6000 LE 4-door Sedan

1984 Pontiac 6000 LE Wagons

1984 Pontiac 6000 LE Coupe with optional Landau roof

1984 Pontiac 6000 instrument panel

1984 Pontiac 6000 STE electronic instruments

1984 Pontiac 6000 LE interior

1984 Pontiac Parisienne Brougham

1984 Pontiac Parisienne Brougham interior

1984 Pontiac Parisienne instrument panel with available gauge package

1984 Pontiac Parisienne Wagon

Those '80s Cars

1984 Pontiac 2000 Sunbird Wagon — "Sunbird" added to the 2000 name

1984 Pontiac 2000 Sunbird S/E Hatchback with Turbo/EFI (1.8 liter OHC EFI turbo 4-cylinder)

1984 Pontiac 1000 3-Door & 5-Door Hatchbacks

1984 Pontiac 1000 instrument panel

1984 Pontiac 1000 interior with optional cloth

1984 Pontiac 2000 Sunbird Coupe & LE Sedan

1984 Pontiac 2000 Sunbird instrument panel

Last Model Run: 1984 Pontiac Phoenix SE Coupe

Last Model Run: 1984 Pontiac Phoenix LE 5-Door Hatchback

1984 Pontiac Phoenix instrument panel

1984 Pontiac Phoenix LE interior

1985

1985 - Facts at Glance

News Headlines

- Live Aid concert raises $50 million for famine relief in Ethiopia
- 8.1 earthquake hits Mexico City
- Boris Becker becomes the youngest player to win Wimbledon, at 17 years old

Tops in Pop Culture

Music
- Careless Whisper, Wham! Featuring George Michael

Movies
- Back to the Future

TV Show
- The Cosby Show

Sports Champions

Basketball
- L.A. Lakers

Football
- San Francisco 49ers

Baseball
- Kansas City Royals

Motor Trend – Car of the Year

Volkswagen GTI

Those '80s Cars

1985 - AMC / EAGLE

4.2 liter 6-cylinder engine with 5-speed manual transmission is standard equipment

1985 AMC Eagle Wagon

1985 - BUICK

New Model: 1985 Buick Electra Park Avenue

New Model: 1985 Buick Somerset Regal Limited

Basic power team is a 3.0 liter V-6 with 4-speed automatic overdrive transmission and front-wheel drive

3.8 V6 gas & 4.3 V6 diesel engine options

1985 Buick Electra Park Avenue interior

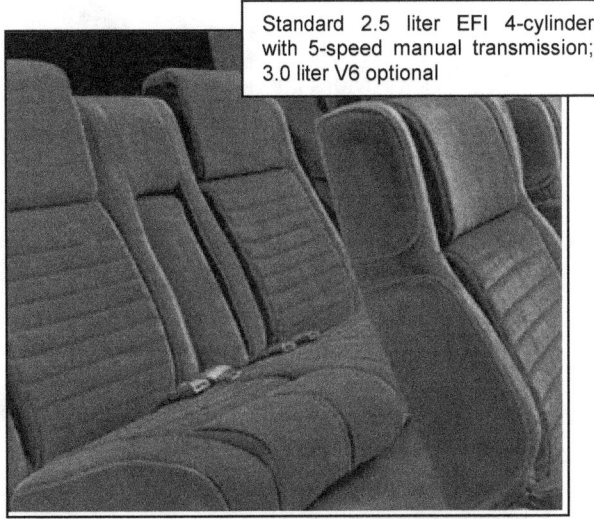

Standard 2.5 liter EFI 4-cylinder with 5-speed manual transmission; 3.0 liter V6 optional

1985 Buick Somerset Regal Limited interior

1985 Buick Somerset Regal instrument panel

1985 Buick Riviera Convertible

189.1" overall length
104.9" wheelbase

1985 Buick Century Custom Sedan

Those '80s Cars

1985 Buick Riviera interior

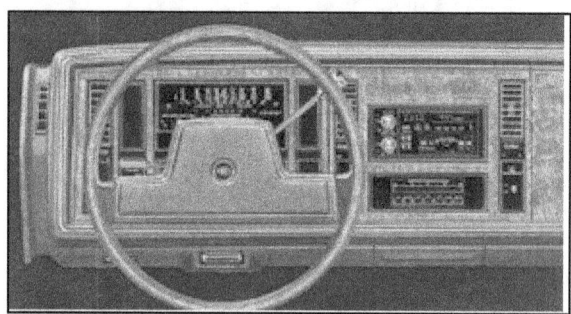
1985 Buick Riviera instrument panel

1985 Buick Regal Limited

1985 Buick Regal Limited interior

1985 Buick Century Limited interior & dash

1985 Buick Skyhawk T Type Coupe

1985 Buick Skyhawk Limited interior

170   Those '80s Cars

1985 Buick Regal Limited instrument panel

200hp, turbo 3.8 V6
New Series: 1985 Buick Regal Grand National

Last Model Run: 1985 Buick LeSabre Limited 4-door Sedan

1985 Buick LeSabre Limited interior

1985 Buick LeSabre instrument panel

1985 Buick Skyhawk instrument panel

1985 Buick Skyhawk Wagon

Last Model Run: 1985 Buick Skylark Limited 4-door Sedan

1985 Buick Skylark instrument panel

1985 Buick Skylark Limited interior

Those '80s Cars

1985 - CADILLAC

Down-sized and now front-wheel drive

New Model: 1985 Cadillac Fleetwood Sedan

New Model: 1985 Cadillac Coupe deVille

1985 Cadillac Fleetwood d'Elegance interior

1985 Cadillac deVille cloth interior

4.1 liter V8 gas & 4.3 liter V6 diesel engines

New Model: 1985 Cadillac Fleetwood Coupe

New Model: 1985 Cadillac Sedan deVille

1985 Cadillac Fleetwood leather interior

1985 Cadillac deVille instrument panel with two-tier design

172

Those '80s Cars

Last Model Run: 1985 Cadillac Eldorado

Last Model Run: 1985 Cadillac Eldorado Biarritz convertible

Last Model Run: 1985 Cadillac Eldorado Touring Coupe

1985 Cadillac Eldorado Biarritz leather interior

1985 Cadillac Eldorado digital instrument cluster

1985 Cadillac Eldorado Touring Coupe leather interior

1985 Cadillac Cimarron

1985 Cadillac Fleetwood Brougham Sedan

Those '80s Cars

Last Model Run: 1985 Cadillac Seville

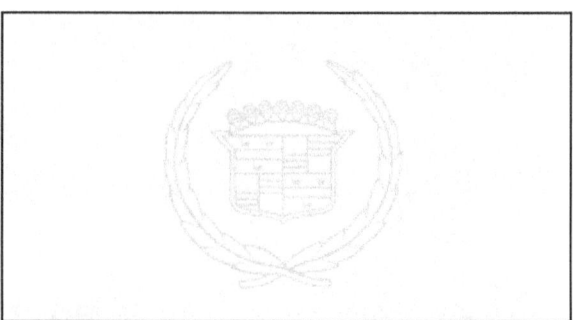

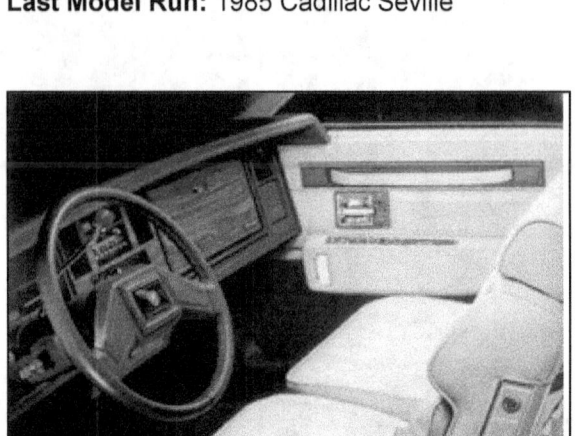
1985 Cadillac Seville leather interior

1985 Cadillac Fleetwood Brougham Coupe

1985 Cadillac Fleetwood Brougham instrument panel

Last Model Run: 1985 Cadillac Seville Elegante

1985 Cadillac Fleetwood Brougham standard cloth interior

1985 Cadillac Seville Elegante leather interior

New Model: 1985 Cadillac Fleetwood Seventy Five Limousine

1985 - CHEVROLET

1985 Chevrolet Camaro

1985 Chevrolet Camaro electronic instruments

New 2.8 V6 Multi-Port Fuel Injection (MFI) available for Cavalier, Citation II, Celebrity & Camaro Sport Coupe

1985 Chevrolet Impala

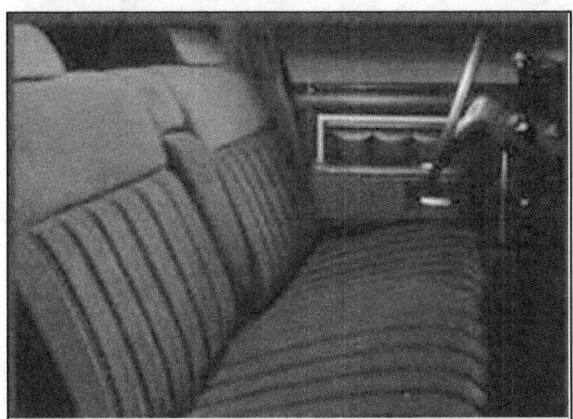
1985 Chevrolet Impala interior

1985 Chevrolet Corvette

New for Corvette: Tuned-Port Fuel Injected 5.7 liter V8. Z51 models are 2 seconds a lap faster than '84.

1985 Chevrolet Caprice Classic Wagon

1985 Chevrolet Caprice Classic interior

1985 Chevrolet Celebrity Eurosport Wagon

Those '80s Cars

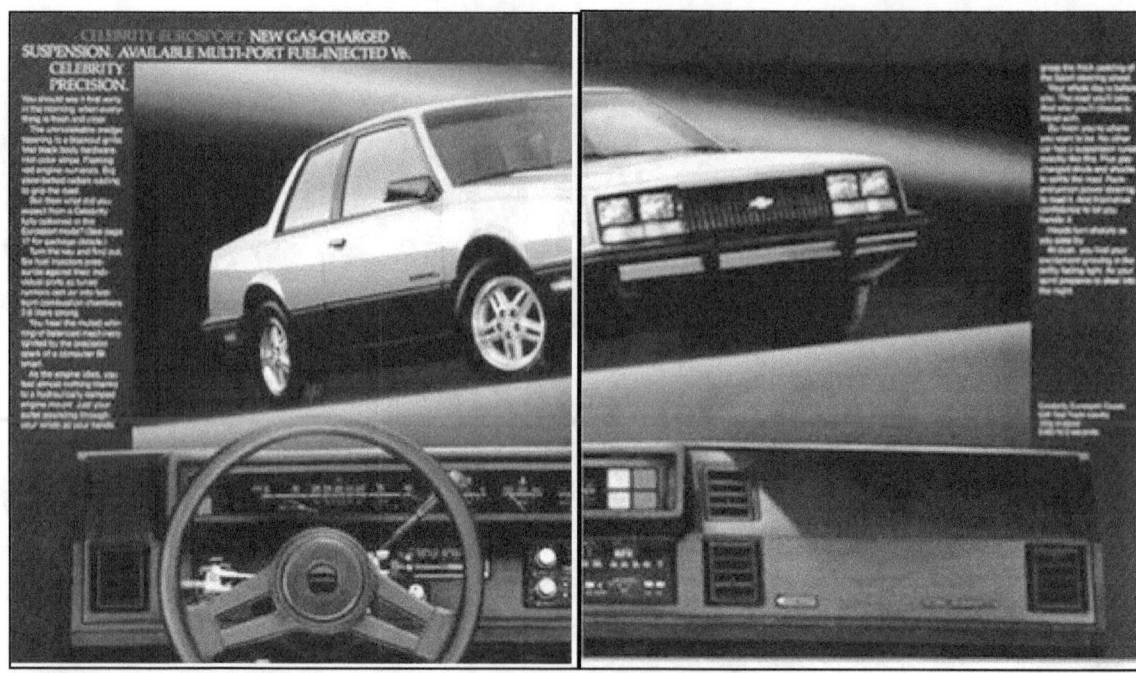
1985 Chevrolet Celebrity Eurosport 2-door Coupe & instrument panel

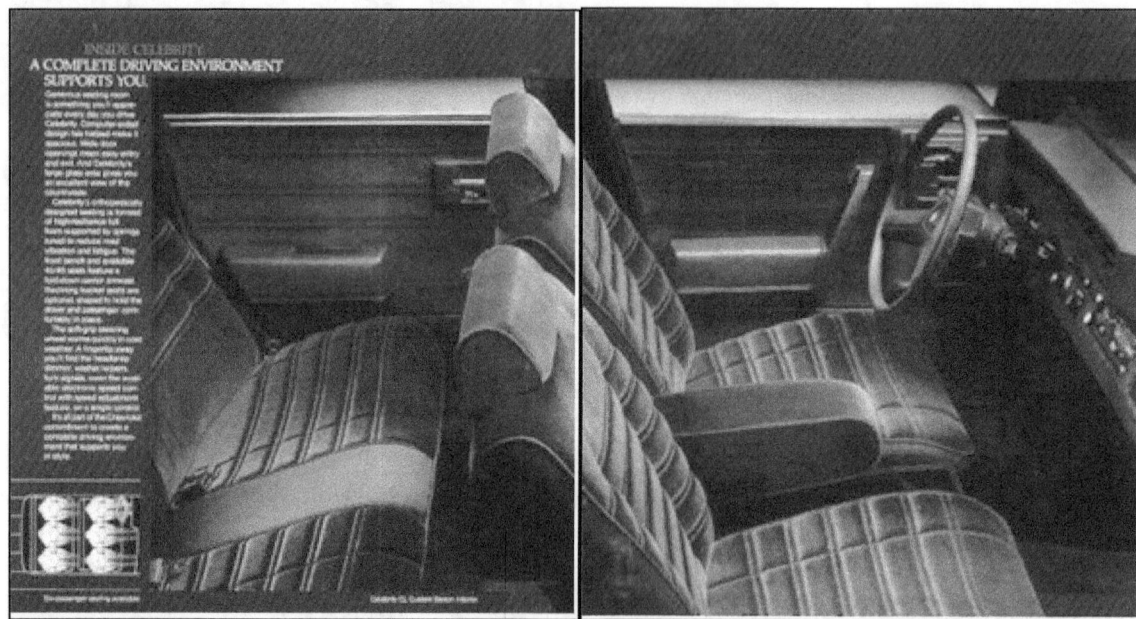
1985 Chevrolet Celebrity CL Custom interior

1985 Chevrolet Cavalier Type 10 Coupe

1985 Chevrolet Cavalier CL Custom interior

Last Model Run: 1985 Chevrolet Citation II

1985 Chevrolet Citation CL Custom interior

96.3% of Chevettes registered in the past 8 years are still on the road

1985 Chevrolet Chevette

1.5 L4 & 1.5 L4 Turbo engines

1.0 L3 engine

New Model: 1985 Chevrolet Sprint

New Model: 1985 Chevrolet Spectrum

1985 Chevrolet Monte Carlo

Those '80s Cars

177

1985 - CHRYSLER

1985 Chrysler Fifth Avenue

Over 50 standard features on the Fifth Avenue

1985 Chrysler Fifth Avenue instrument panel

1985 Chrysler LeBaron Coupe, Convertible Sedan and Town & Country Wagon

LeBaron sports a revised grille. The 2.2 turbo engine gains 4 hp over last year's model.

1985 Chrysler LeBaron standard interior

1985 Chrysler New Yorker

1985 Chrysler New Yorker instrument panel

New push-button climate control introduced this year

1985 Chrysler New Yorker leather interior

1985 Chrysler LeBaron instrument Panel

1985 Chrysler Laser XE Turbo

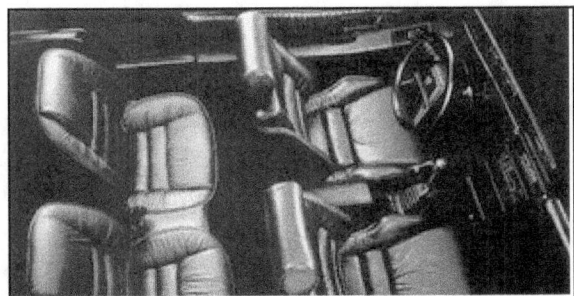
1985 Chrysler Laser optional leather interior

1985 Chrysler Laser instrument panel

New Model: 1985 Chrysler LeBaron GTS

1985 Chrysler Limousine

Those '80s Cars

1985 - DODGE

New Model: 1985 Dodge Lancer ES

2.2 liter OHC multi-point EFI 4-cylinder 99hp
2.2 liter OHC multi-point EFI 4-cylinder turbo 146hp
with 5-speed manual or 3-speed auto

1985 Dodge 600 4-door Sedan

1985 Dodge 600 Club Coupe

1985 Dodge Aries SE Wagon

Those '80s Cars

1985 Dodge Diplomat SE 4-door Sedan

3 trim series: Omni, Omni SE, Omni GLH

1985 Dodge Omni

3 trim series: Daytona, Daytona Turbo & Daytona Turbo Z
Turbo Z: 0-50 in 5.51 seconds

1985 Dodge Daytona Turbo Z

145hp 2.6 liter turbo 4

1985 Dodge Conquest

1985 Dodge Colt E 5-Door & 3-Door Hatchbacks

2.0 liter 4-cylinder

1985 Dodge Colt Vista Wagon

1985 Dodge Colt Premier 4-door Sedan

1985 - FORD

1985 Ford Mustang GT

Standard new articulated seats on the GT series

1985 Ford Mustang GT interior

1985 Ford Mustang instrument panel

Mustang 3.8 liter V6 optional on LX 2- & 3-door models; standard on LX convertible

Mustang LX, in 2-door, 3-door and convertible models, is packed with extra value standard equipment. The 2-door also comes with a very attractive price.

Mustang LX Convertible combines the fine points of the 2-door with a power retractable top for true open air cruising.

Mustang GT 3-door and **GT Convertible** are excellent performers on all fronts. They have quick acceleration and firm suspensions for solid road holding capability.

1985½ Mustang SVO was developed by Ford Special Vehicle Operations group to set new standard in affordable grand touring cars. Higher performance and aero-designed headlamps head the list of new SVO features. For availability of the 1985½ SVO, see your Ford Dealer.

1985 Ford Tempo GLX interior

1985 Ford Tempo instrument panel

Tempo: New standard EFI on 2.3 liter 4-cylinder engine

Tempo GLX is available in standard and Luxury packages, each equipped with numerous comfort and convenience features.

Tempo GL comes in four new equipment packages: standard, Select, Luxury and Sport. So anyone can enjoy GL's outstanding value.

Tempo L adds electronic fuel injection, new side window demisters and integral instrument panel storage shelf to its impressive list of features.

1985 Ford EXP Luxury Coupe

1985 Ford Thunderbird FILA

New Thunderbird instrument panel for 1985

1985 Ford Thunderbird Turbo Coupe instruments

1985 Ford Thunderbird Turbo Coupe interior

1985 Ford LTD Crown Victoria 4-door Sedan

1985 Ford LTD Crown Victoria instrument panel

1985 Ford LTD Wagon with Squire Option

1985 Ford LTD Brougham instrument panel

1985 Ford LTD Brougham interior

1985 Ford LTD Brougham 4-door Sedan

New LTD LX model comes with 5.0 HO & modified handling

1985 Ford Escort LX 4-door Hatchback

1985 - LINCOLN

Last year for diesel option

1985 Lincoln Mark VII LSC

From the Brochure: "The luxury line that offers the luxury of choice. In today's world, it is not enough for a luxury car to offer a plush interior and a quiet ride. Real-world driving conditions dictate that the modern luxury automobile provide other 'luxuries' as well. Safe and responsive handling, poise under the worst conditions, and a passenger compartment that is not only elegant, but also spacious, functional and convenient – these are necessities in today's luxury automobile. There are certain intangible luxuries, too: quality workmanship, value, and not the least, the sheer joy of driving." – 1985 Lincoln

1985 Lincoln Continental

New grille & tail lamps

1985 Lincoln Town Car

Those '80s Cars

1985 - MERCURY

1985 Mercury Capri interior

1985 Mercury Capri RS

Capri RS: standard 5.0 liter High-Output V8, 4-bbl carburetor and 5-speed overdrive manual gearbox

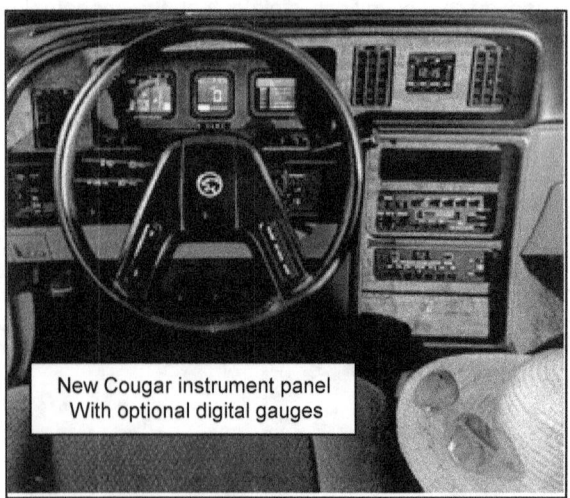

New Cougar instrument panel With optional digital gauges

1985 Mercury Cougar digital instrument panel

2.3 liter turbo 4-cylinder standard on XR-7 series

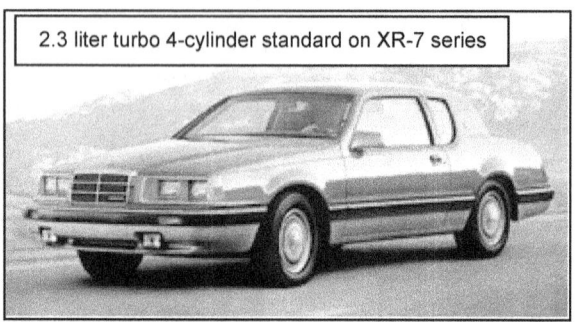
1985 Mercury Cougar XR-7

Engine choices: 3.8 V6 & 5.0 V8

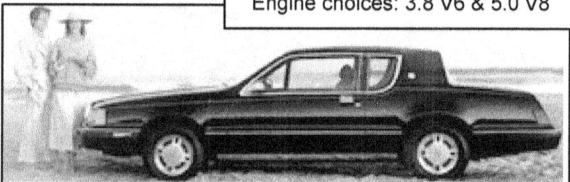
1985 Mercury Cougar LS

1985 Mercury Grand Marquis & Colony Park

1985 Mercury Grand Marquis LS 4-door Sedan

1985 Mercury Grand Marquis LS interior

1985 Mercury Topaz LS

1985 Mercury Lynx Wagon

New standard EFI on 2.3 liter

1985 Mercury Topaz LS interior

1985 Mercury Lynx GS interior

1985 Mercury Lynx GS 4-door Hatchback

1985 Mercury Marquis Brougham

1985 Mercury Marquis Wagons

1985 Mercury Marquis interior

1985 - MERKUR

.33 drag coefficient

New Model: 1985 Merkur XR4Ti

2.3 liter OHC turbocharged 4-cylinder engine with 5-speed overdrive manual transmission are standard

New Model: 1985 Merkur XR4Ti

1985 Merkur XR4Ti instrument panel

1985 Merkur XR4Ti interior

175 horsepower
200 lb. ft. torque

MERKUR XR4TI FROM GERMANY. PERFORMANCE THAT GOES BEYOND MERE STATISTICS.

1985 - OLDSMOBILE

New Model: 1985 Oldsmobile Ninety-Eight Regency Brougham Coupe

New Model: 1985 Oldsmobile Ninety-Eight Regency Brougham Sedan

1985 Oldsmobile Ninety-Eight Regency Brougham

In 1985, the Ninety-Eight is down-sized and now has front-wheel drive with 3.0 & 3.8 liter V6 gas and a 4.3 liter V6 diesel engine choices and a 4-speed automatic overdrive

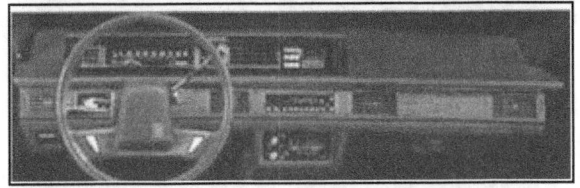

1985 Oldsmobile Ninety-Eight instrument panel

1985 Oldsmobile Wagons

1985 Oldsmobile Firenza

Those '80s Cars

Last Model Run: 1985 Oldsmobile Toronado Caliente

1985 Oldsmobile Cutlass Sierra Coupe & Cutlass Supreme Sedan

1985 Oldsmobile Cutlass Ciera ES interior

1985 Oldsmobile Cutlass Ciera instrument panel & optional electronic instruments

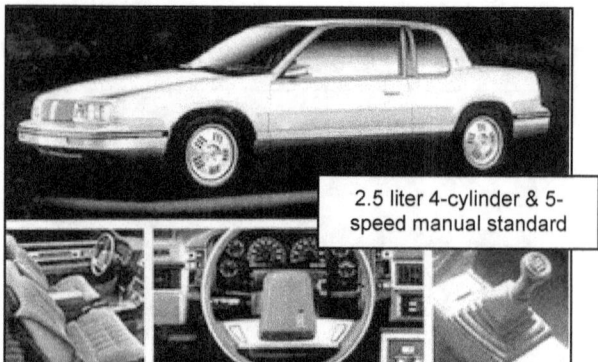

2.5 liter 4-cylinder & 5-speed manual standard

New Model: 1985 Oldsmobile Calais

New Model: 1985 Oldsmobile Calais 500

1985 Oldsmobile Cutlass Supreme Coupe, Cutlass Ciera Sedan & Cutlass Cruiser

1985 Oldsmobile Cutlass Salon interior

1985 Oldsmobile Cutlass Supreme instrument panel & optional Rallye gauge cluster

1985 - PLYMOUTH

1985 Plymouth model line

1985 Plymouth Voyager LE

1985 Plymouth Horizon

1985 Plymouth Turismo Duster

1985 Plymouth Reliant LE Coupe & Sedan

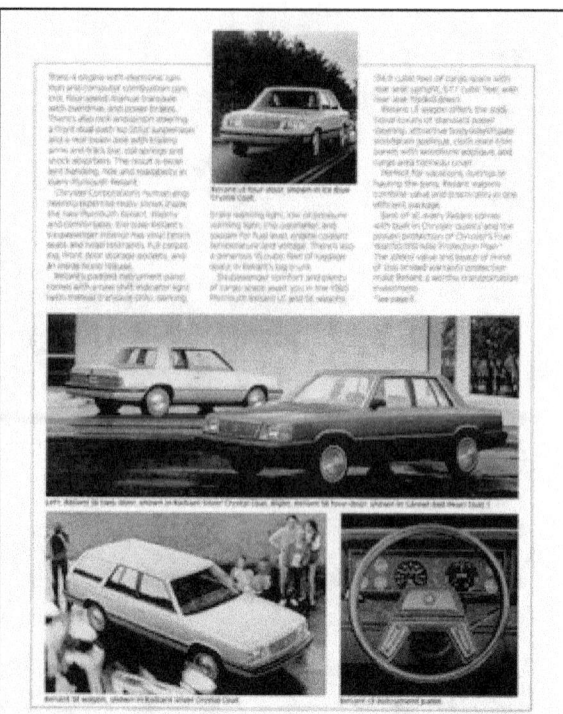
1985 Plymouth Reliant Coupe, Sedan, Wagon

1985 Plymouth Gran Fury Salon

1985 Plymouth Colt

1985 Plymouth Conquest

1985 Plymouth Caravelle replaces 1984's Chrysler E Class

New Model: 1985 Plymouth Caravelle SE

1985 - PONTIAC

New Model: 1985 Pontiac Grand Am Coupe & Grand Am LE Coupe

Grand Am power choices: 2.5 liter 4-cylinder with 5-speed manual or 3-speed automatic and 3.0 liter V6 with 3-speed automatic

1985 Pontiac Fiero GT

Fiero adds 2.8 liter V6 option w/4-speed manual or 3-speed auto

1985 Pontiac Grand Am Rally instrumentation

1985 Pontiac Fiero instrument panel

1985 Pontiac Gram LE interior

1985 Pontiac 1000 3-Door & 5-Door Hatchbacks

1985 Pontiac Fiero SE interior

1985 Pontiac Sunbird S/E Turbo

Those '80s Cars

1985 Pontiac Firebird Trans Am

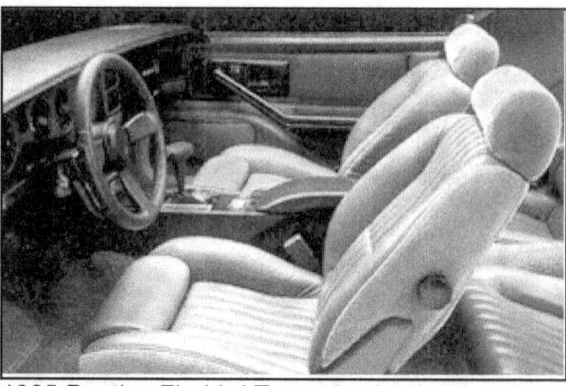
1985 Pontiac Firebird Trans Am leather interior

1985 Pontiac Firebird full gauge package

Diesel option dropped on Grand Prix & Bonneville

1985 Pontiac Grand Prix Brougham

1985 Pontiac Bonneville Brougham

"2000" dropped from name & 2.0 dropped

1985 Pontiac Sunbird Coupe, Sedan & Wagon

1985 Pontiac Bonneville & Grand Prix dash

1985 Pontiac Sunbird LE Convertible

1985 Pontiac Parisienne Brougham Sedan

1985 Pontiac Parisienne Wagon

1985 Pontiac Sunbird S/E instrument panel

1986

1986 - Facts at Glance

News Headlines

- SALT signed
- Chernobyl nuclear accident
- Iran-Contra Affair begins
- Mike Tyson becomes youngest heavyweight champion
- UK & France announce plans for Channel Tunnel
- Shuttle Challenger disaster

Tops in Pop Culture

Music
- That's What Friends Are For, Dionne & Friends

Movies
- Top Gun

TV Show
- The Cosby Show

Sports Champions

Basketball
- Boston Celtics

Football
- Chicago Bears

Baseball
- N.Y. Mets

Motor Trend – Car of the Year

Ford Taurus LX

Those '80s Cars

1986 - AMC / EAGLE

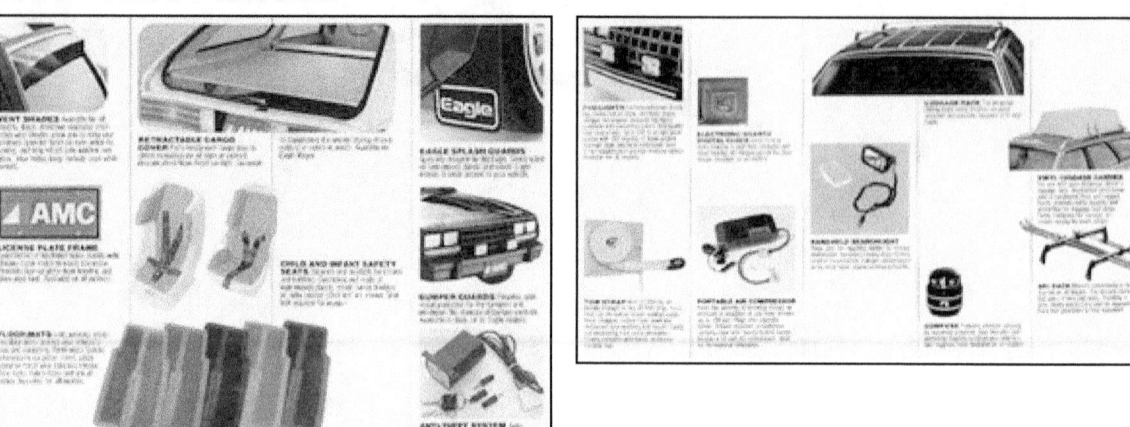

1986 - BUICK

New Model: 1986 Buick Riviera

From the Brochure: "A new kind of Riviera. From the beginning, more than 20 years ago, Riviera has represented a special kind of Buick. Highly advanced in design. Extraordinarily well appointed. An automobile that makes a distinctive personal statement.

In 1986, a new Riviera will takes its place in the long line of these legendary Buicks. It will have a degree of electronic sophistication unprecedented in Riviera's history. All at the fingertip command of its owner."

- 1986 Buick Riviera

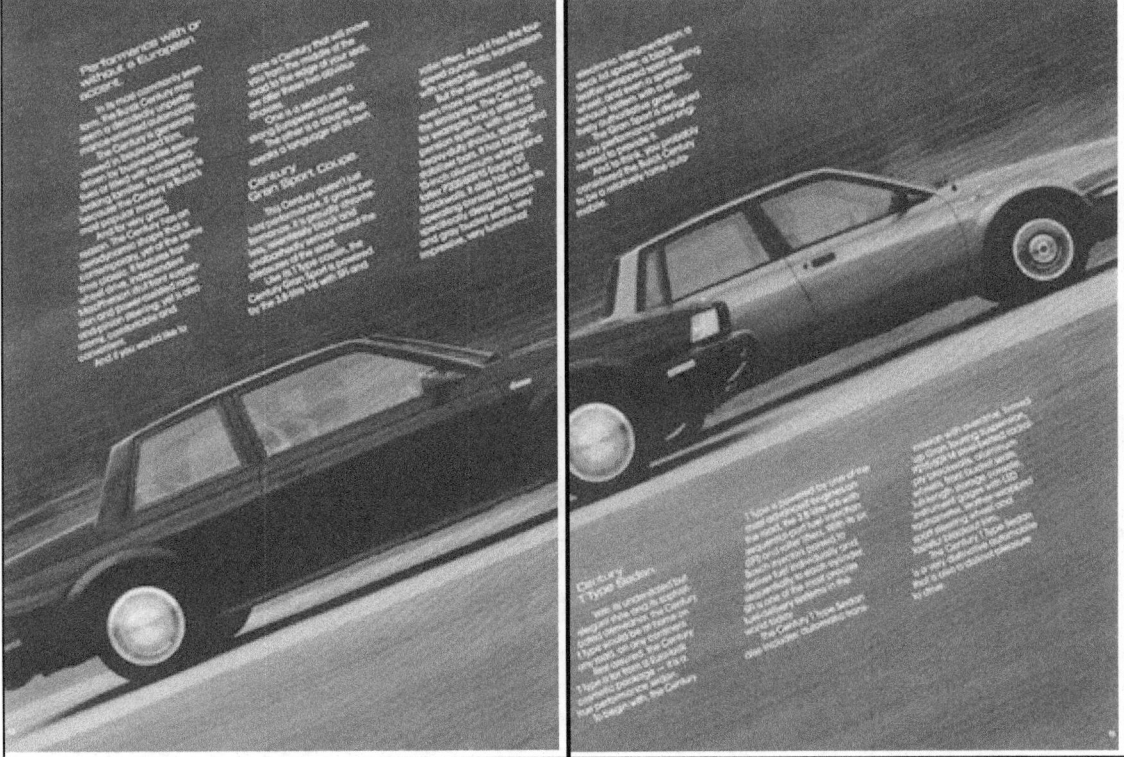

1986 Buick Century T Type

Those '80s Cars

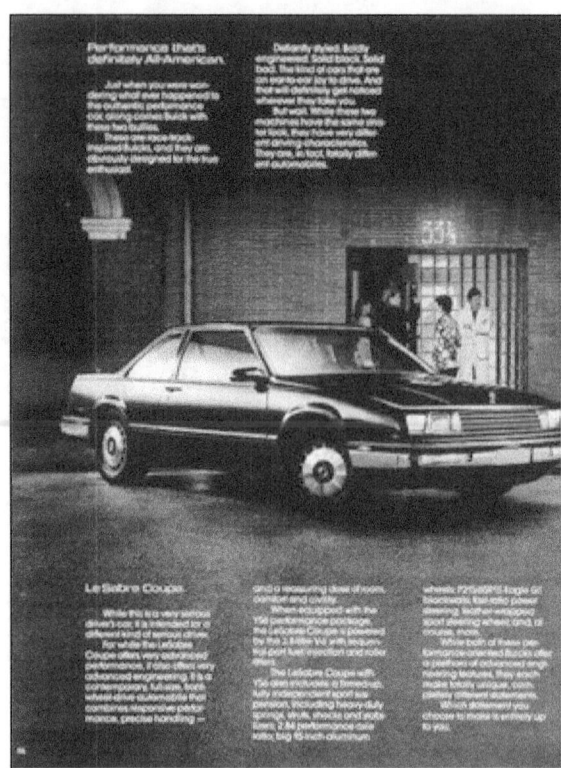
New Model: 1986 Buick LeSabre Coupe

1986 Buick Regal Grand National

1986 Buick Electra T Type Sedan

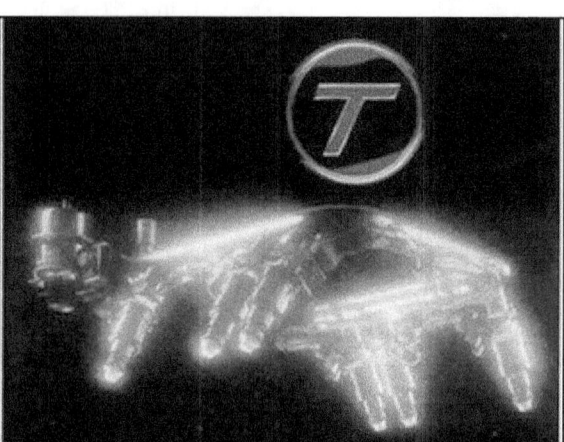
1986 Buick sequential-port fuel injection

1986 Buick Skyhawk T Type

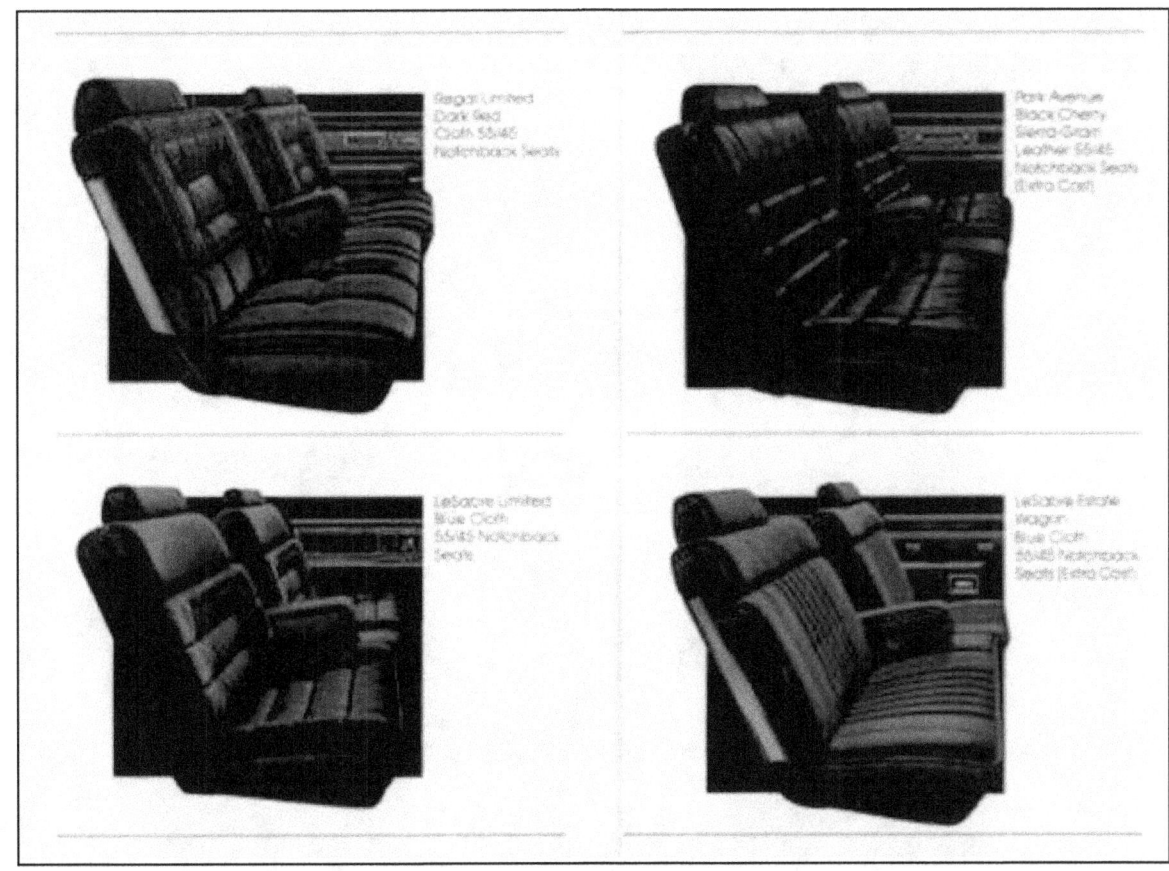

1986 Buick Skylark Sedan

1986 Buick Skylark interior

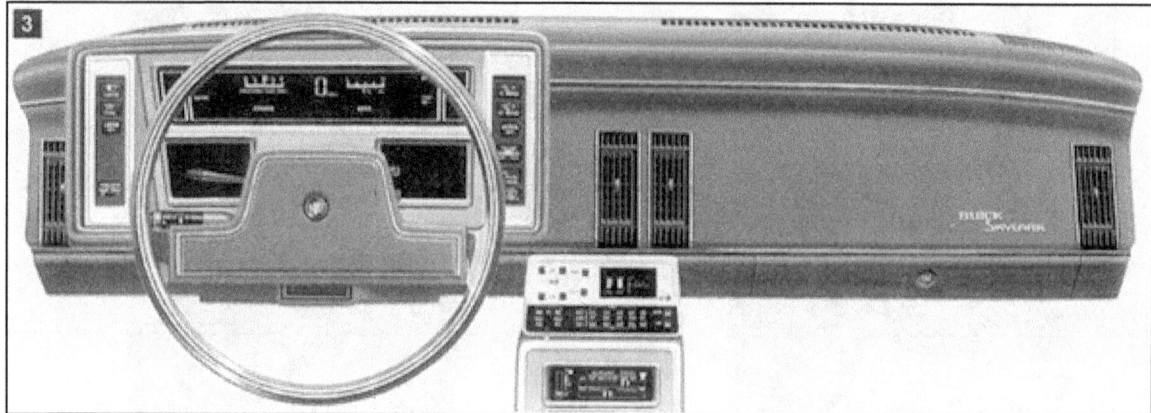
1986 Buick Skylark instrument panel

> **From the Brochure:** "For drivers that seek family or business transportation that lies just below the Century in size, two new sedans have joined the proud Buick line: the Skylark Custom and the Skylark Limited. Both offer Buick value and ride comfort in a car engineered to provide a rewarding experience for driver and passengers alike. The Skylark delivers a feel and a capability that embody traditional Buick Quality."
>
> - 1986 Buick Skylark

Wouldn't you really rather have a Buick?

1986 - CADILLAC

1986 Cadillac Sedan deVille

1986 Cadillac deVille instrument panel

New elegant seat trim design for 1986

1986 Cadillac deVille interior

From the Brochure: "Contemporary design. Advanced technology. Cadillac luxury. A car that offers optimum traction and responsive power from a front-wheel-drive, transverse-mounted V8 engine."
 - 1986 Cadillac Sedan deVille

1986 Cadillac Coupe deVille

Those '80s Cars

1986 Cadillac Touring Coupe & Sedan

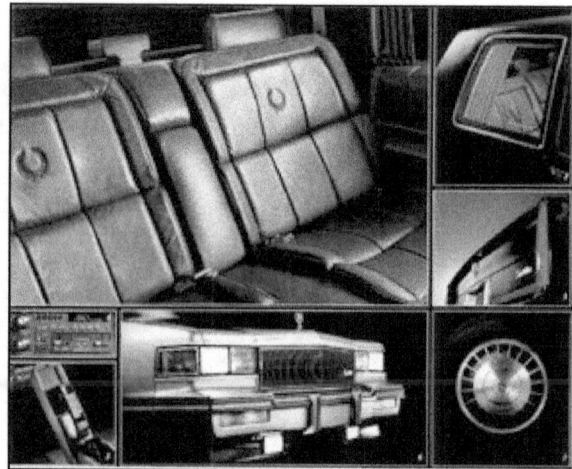
1986 Cadillac Touring Coupe & Sedan

1986 Cadillac Fleetwood Brougham Sedan D'Elegance

New standard Formal Cabriolet roof treatment

1986 Cadillac Fleetwood Sedan

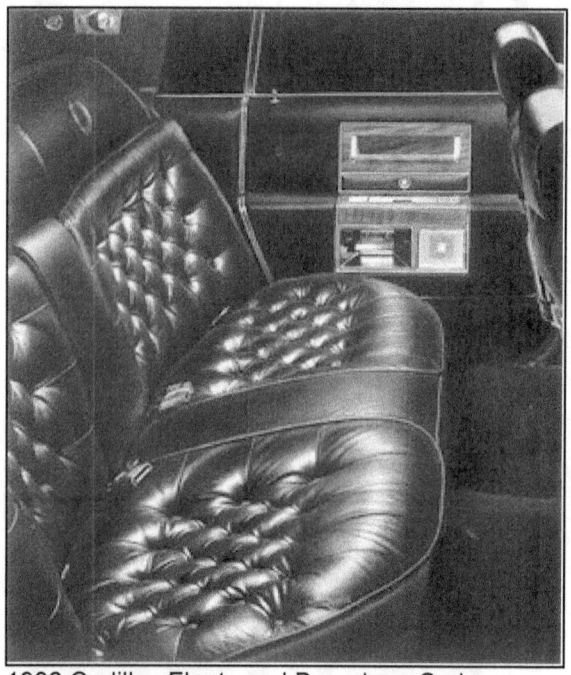
1986 Cadillac Fleetwood Brougham Sedan D'Elegance interior

1986 Cadillac Fleetwood Sedan interior

New size: 108" wheelbase & 188.2" overall length

New Model: 1986 Cadillac Seville

New Model: 1986 Cadillac Eldorado Biarritz

From the Brochure: "Featuring all the advanced engineering of Eldorado – but with the added distinction of a two-tone paint treatment, Cabriolet roof, opera lamps, wire wheel discs, and a wide bodyside molding." - 1986 Cadillac Eldorado Biarritz

1986 Cadillac Seville interior

1986 Cadillac Eldorado Biarritz interior

1986 Cadillac Cimarron interior

1986 Cadillac Cimarron

Those '80s Cars

1986 - CHEVROLET

1986 Chevrolet Corvette
(0-60 in 5.6 seconds)

New Series: 1986 Chevrolet Cavalier Z24 Coupe

1986 Chevrolet Monte Carlo CL interior

1986 Chevrolet Camaro Sport Coupe (top) and Camaro Z28

1986 Chevrolet Cavalier RS Convertible & RS Wagon

1986 Chevrolet Monte Carlo SS

New Series: 1986 Chevrolet Caprice Classic Brougham

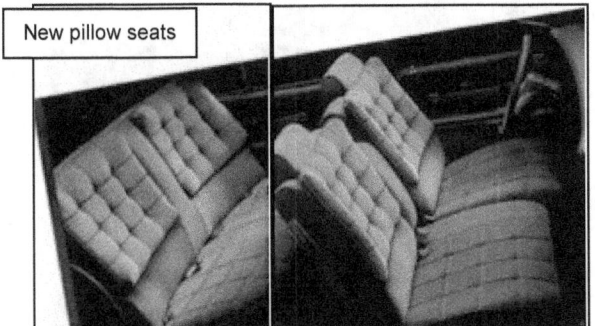
1986 Chevrolet Caprice Classic Brougham interior

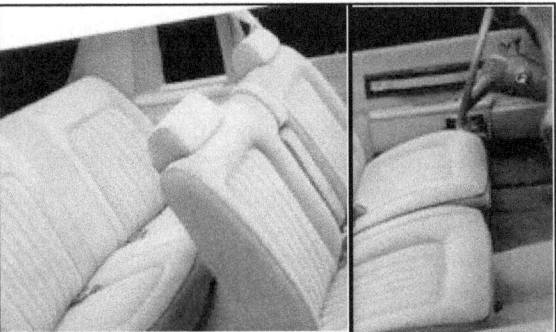
1986 Chevrolet Caprice Classic interior

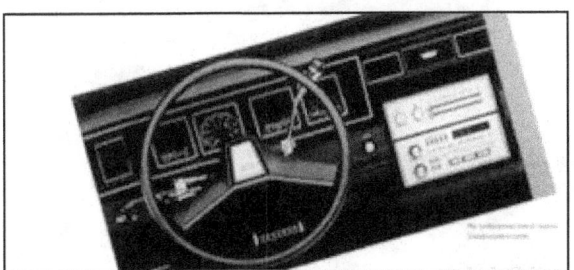
1986 Chevrolet Caprice Classic instrument panel

1986 Chevrolet Caprice Classic Coupe

1986 Chevrolet Caprice Classic Wagon

1986 Chevrolet Celebrity 4-door Sedan, Eurosport Wagon & Eurosport Coupe

1986 Chevrolet Celebrity CL Custom interior

4 & 5 speed manuals & 3 speed automatic transmission options

1986 Chevrolet Chevette S Hatchback Coupe

0-50 in 8.2 seconds

1986 Chevrolet Spectrum 2-door Hatchback

New Model: 1986 Chevrolet Sprint Plus 4-door

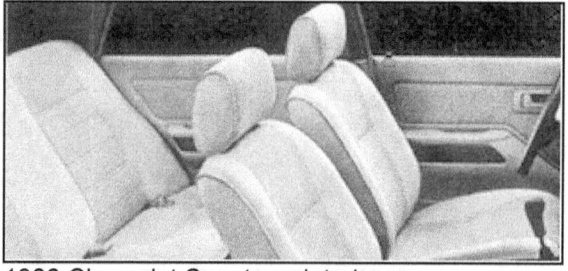

1986 Chevrolet Spectrum interior

1986 Chevrolet Nova CL interior

1.6 OHC L4 with 5-speed manual transmission is standard. 3-speed automatic is optional.

New Model: 1986 Chevrolet Nova Hatchback Sedan (also available in notchback sedan)

1986 - CHRYSLER

1986 Chrysler LeBaron GTS

New 2.5 liter EFI engine
New roof treatment
Refreshed: 1986 Chrysler New Yorker

1986 Chrysler Laser

1986 Chrysler Laser optional leather interior

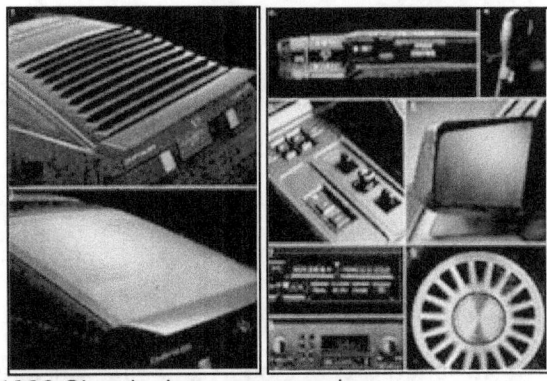
1986 Chrysler Laser accessories

1986 Chrysler New Yorker leather interior

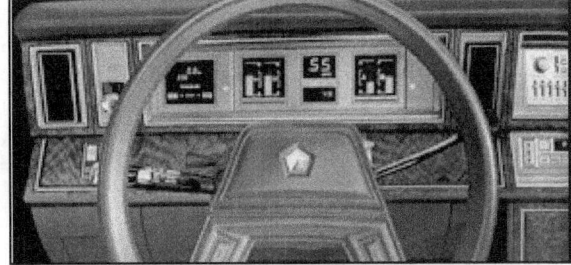
1986 Chrysler New Yorker instrument panel

Those '80s Cars

Refreshed: 1986 Chrysler Town & Country

1986 Town & Country Mark Cross leather interior

Refreshed & Last Model Run: 1986 Chrysler LeBaron Sedan

1986 Chrysler LeBaron instrument panel

Refreshed & Last Model Run: 1986 Chrysler Convertible

New 2.5 liter EFI engine option

Refreshed & Last Model Run: 1986 Chrysler LeBaron Coupe

1986 Chrysler Fifth Avenue

1986 Chrysler LeBaron interior

1986 - DODGE

1986 Dodge Lancer ES

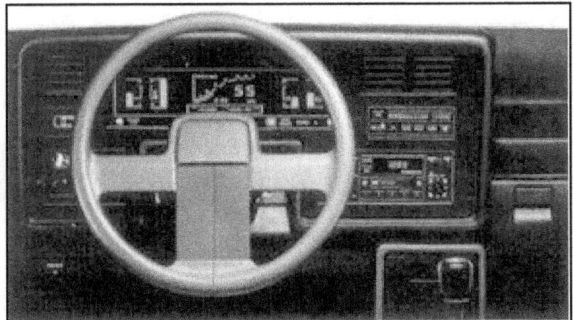
1986 Dodge Lancer ES electronic instruments

From the Brochure: "In the realm of front-drive technology, Dodge challenges any other car company in the world. And Dodge has the world's largest fleet of turbocharged cars. The strength of these two statements translates directly into the strength of the products we are building today. Our commitment to front-drive technology enables us to build cars that are lighter, more space-efficient and more fuel-efficient." — 1986 Dodge

1986 Dodge Daytona

1986 Dodge Conquest

1986 Dodge Lancer ES available leather interior

1986 Dodge Daytona Turbo Z

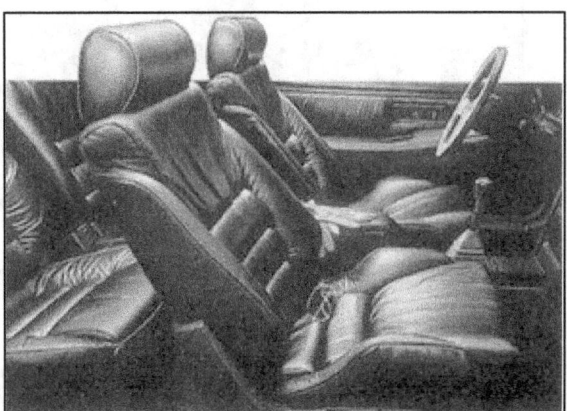
1986 Dodge Daytona Turbo Z leather interior

1986 Dodge Daytona Turbo Z

From the Brochure: "The credentials that define a performance sports car are multidimensional. In addition to outright speed, it must have open-road agility. Handling must be precise. Aerodynamics must work with the car. There must be outstanding stability under all conditions of braking and deceleration. The interior must be driver-oriented. In short, it must be a car in total balance."
— 1986 Dodge Daytona

Refreshed & Last Year Model: 1986 Dodge 600 convertible

1986 Dodge Aries K LE 4-door Sedan

> Aries K models include 2-doors and 4-doors in 3 trim series: base Aries K, elegant Aries K SE and luxurious Aries K LE. Wagons available in SE and LE trim levels only.

Refreshed & Last Year Model: 1986 Dodge 600 2-door Coupe

1986 Dodge Diplomat SE

1986 Dodge 600 SE 4-door interior

1986 Dodge Diplomat SE interior

1986 Dodge Colt E Sedan & Hatchback

1986 Dodge Charger 2.2 (back) & Charger

1986 Dodge Colt Vista 4WD Wagon

1986 Dodge Omni SE

1986 - FORD

A new 2.5 liter 4-cylinder is offered with a 3-speed auto or 5-speed manual. Most, are sold with a 3.0 liter multiple-port fuel-injected V6 & 4-speed auto overdrive.

New Model: 1986 Ford Taurus LX

1986 Ford Taurus GL interior

New Model: 1986 Ford Taurus LX Wagon

From the Brochure: "The 1986 Ford Taurus, *Motor Trend* Car of the Year, represents a remarkable combination of advanced design, interior roominess and all-around performance. It invites comparison to *any* car in the world today because its five years of planning were based on a 'best in class' philosophy."
- 1986 Ford Taurus

1986 Ford LTD Crown Victoria LX 4-door Sedan

1986 Ford LTD Crown Victoria LX interior

1986 Ford LTD Country Squire Wagon

Last Model Run: 1986 Ford LTD

Last Model Run: 1986 Ford LTD

1986 Ford Thunderbird

1986 Ford Thunderbird élan interior

1986 Ford LTD Crown Victoria instrument panel

1986 Ford LTD Crown Victoria 2-door Coupe

1986 Ford Mustang 2-door Sedan

1986 Ford Mustang GT interior

From the Brochure: "Sporty, spirited Ford Mustang model choices begin with the LX 2-door sedan, 2-door hatchback or convertible. Next is breathtaking performance: GT 2-door hatchback or convertible. Finally there's the sophistication of Mustang SVO."
- 1986 Ford Mustang

1986 Ford Escort LX 4-door Hatchback

New Escort engine: 1.9 liter 4-cylinder
Diesel engine dropped

1986 Ford Escort LX Wagon

1.9 liter 4-cylinder

Refreshed: 1986 Ford EXP Luxury Coupe

1986 Ford Escort LX interior

1986 Ford EXP Luxury Coupe interior

New Model: 1986 Ford Aerostar (Though truck based, unlike the Chrysler minivans, this was Ford's response to Chrysler's leading design.)

1986 Ford Tempo LX 2-door Coupe

1986 Ford Aerostar interior

Seating up to 7-passengers & cargo space up to 139.2 cu. ft.
2.3 liter EFI 4-cylinder standard with 2.8 liter V6 optional

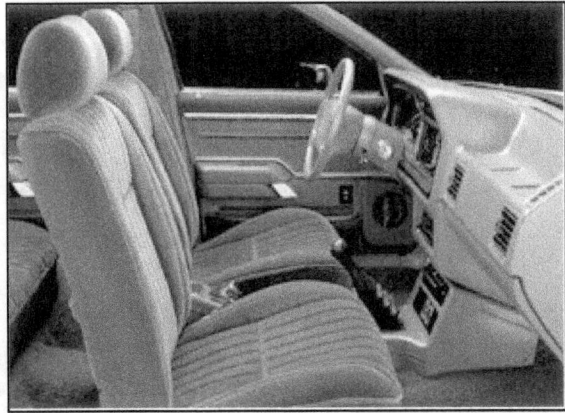
1986 Ford Tempo LX interior

Those '80s Cars

1986 - LINCOLN

1986 Lincoln Mark VII LSC

1986 Lincoln Mark VII LSC interior

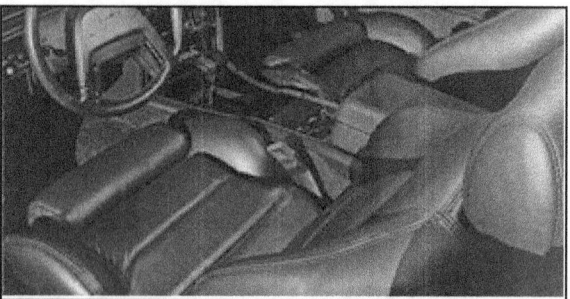

1986 Lincoln Mark VII LSC interior

1986 Lincoln Continental

1986 Lincoln Town Car

1986 - MERCURY

A new 2.5 liter 4-cylinder & 3.0 liter V6 engines

New Model: 1986 Mercury Sable LS Sedan

From the Brochure: "Sable is designed to change the way you think about contemporary automobiles. The new Mercury Sable is a sophisticated shape that blends contemporary style and efficient performance in the manner of great a European road car.

Sable was designed to fulfill the needs of today's discriminating buyer – spaciousness, comfort and superior driving characteristics." - 1986 Mercury Sable

New Model: 1986 Mercury LS Wagon

Last Model Run: 1986 Mercury Marquis

Last Model Run: 1986 Mercury Marquis Wagon

1986 Mercury Sable LS interior

1986 Mercury Marquis interior

From the Brochure: "Cougar XR-7 proves that a car can be strong on performance without being musclebound. The Cougar XR-7 is designed to use the wind to achieve practical, functional benefits."
- 1986 Mercury Cougar XR-7

1986 Mercury Cougar XR-7

1986 Mercury Cougar LS interior

1986 Mercury Topaz GS

1986 Mercury Topaz interior

Last Model Run: 1986 Mercury Capri

1986 Mercury Capri RS interior

Capri RS: 0 – 50 in under 6 seconds

Last Model Run: 1986 Mercury Capri RS 5.0

1986 Mercury Lynx XR3 interior

1986 Mercury Grand Marquis LS Sedan

1986 Mercury Grand Marquis Coupe & Colony Park Wagon

1986 Mercury Lynx GS Wagon

New Series: 1986 Mercury Lynx XR3

XR3 sports a new 1.9 liter EFI 4-cylinder engine, 15" aluminum wheels, fog lamps, front air dam, rear spoiler, special wheel spats and rocker panel moldings

1986 Mercury Grand Marquis LS interior

1986 - MERKUR

1986 Merkur XR4Ti (same as 1985)

Those '80s Cars

1986 - OLDSMOBILE

New Model: 1986 Oldsmobile Delta 88 Royale Brougham

In 1986, the Delta 88 is downsized and now has front-wheel drive with 3.0 & 3.8 liter V6 gas engine choices and a 4-speed automatic overdrive

1986 Oldsmobile Delta 88 Royale Brougham interior

New Model: 1986 Oldsmobile Delta 88 Royale Coupe

Oldsmobile drops diesel engine options after 1985

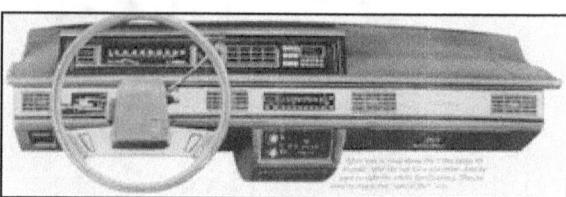

1986 Oldsmobile Delta 88 instrument panel

1986 Oldsmobile Custom Cruiser

1986 Oldsmobile Custom Cruiser interior

1986 Oldsmobile Ninety-Eight Regency Sedan & Coupe

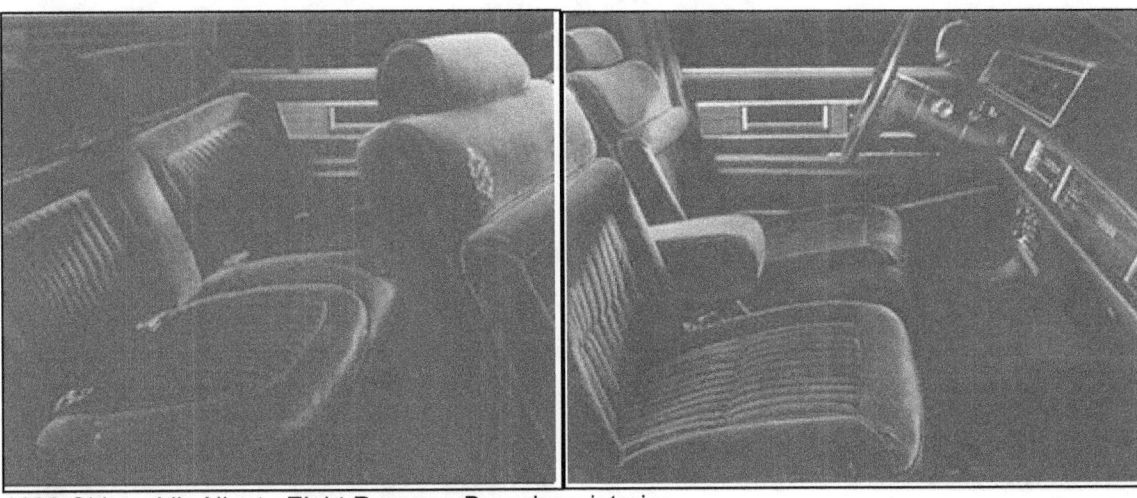
1986 Oldsmobile Ninety-Eight Regency Brougham interior

3.8 liter V6 w/4-speed auto & torque converter standard

New Model: 1986 Oldsmobile Toronado

1986 Oldsmobile Toronado available bucket seat with console interior

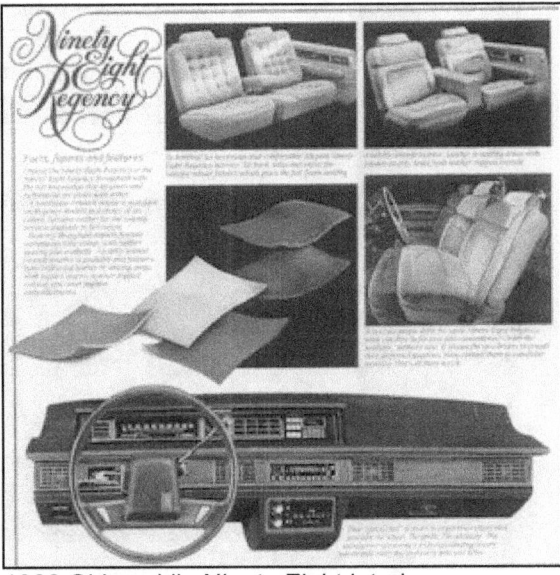
1986 Oldsmobile Ninety-Eight interiors

From the Brochure: "A generation ago, Oldsmobile introduced the first Toronado, and with it an entirely new category of driving experience, now referred to as the 'Personal Luxury Coupe.' A new Toronado emerges. Rethought. Reshaped. Reborn."
– 1986 Oldsmobile Toronado

1986 Oldsmobile Firenza Coupe

1986 Oldsmobile Cutlass Supreme Brougham Coupe & Sedan

1986 Oldsmobile Calais 4-door Sedan

Refreshed: 1986 Oldsmobile Cutlass Ciera S Coupe

Ciera adds 2.8 liter V6 engine option

1986 Oldsmobile Calais 2-door Coupe

1986 Oldsmobile Cutlass Ciera GT Sedan

1986 Oldsmobile Calais instrument panel

1986 Oldsmobile Cutlass Cruiser

1986 Oldsmobile Calais interior

1986 Oldsmobile Cutlass Ciera Brougham

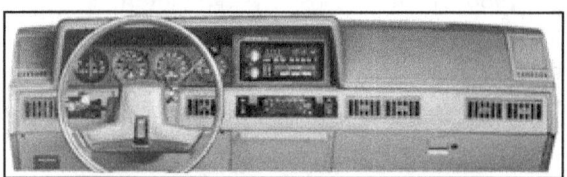
1986 Oldsmobile Ciera instrument panel

Those '80s Cars

1986 - PLYMOUTH

1986 Plymouth Reliant K LE 2-door Coupe

1986 Plymouth Reliant K LE 4-door Sedan

1986 Plymouth Reliant K SE Wagon

1986 Plymouth Reliant K instrument panel

1986 Plymouth Reliant K LE interior

1986 Plymouth Caravelle SE 4-door Sedan

New, optional 2.5 liter 4-cylinder with dual balance shafts

1986 Plymouth Caravelle SE 4-door Sedan

From the Brochure: "Style and value come together in today's most exciting family transportation, the 1986 Plymouth Caravelle SE. Caravelle SE is Plymouth's finest, combining six-passenger comfort with crisp handling and front-wheel drive."
– 1986 Plymouth Caravelle

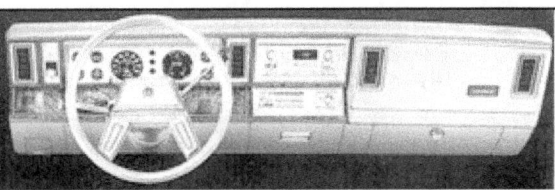
1986 Plymouth Caravelle SE instrument panel

1986 Plymouth Caravelle SE interior

Those '80s Cars

1986 Plymouth Horizon

1986 Plymouth Turismo 2.2

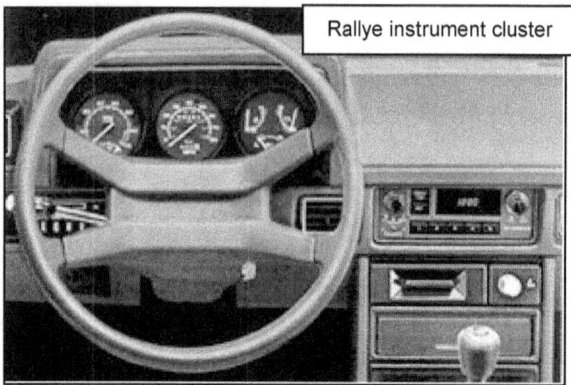
Rallye instrument cluster
1986 Plymouth Turismo 2.2 instrument panel

1986 Plymouth Turismo 2.2 interior

Standard 5.2 liter V8
1986 Plymouth Gran Fury Salon

1986 Plymouth Gran Fury Salon interior with optional velour and vinyl 60/40 front bench seat

1986 Plymouth Conquest/Colt Vista 4WD Wagon

1986 Plymouth Colt Sedan

1986 - PONTIAC

1986 Pontiac Firebird Trans Am

1986 Pontiac Firebird Trans Am instrument panel

1986 Pontiac Grand Am SE 4-door Sedan

1986 Pontiac Grand Am SE interior

1986 Pontiac Fiero SE

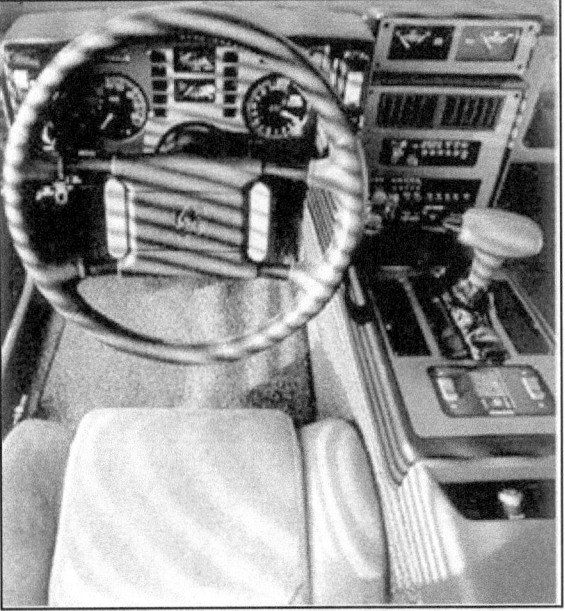
1986 Pontiac Fiero SE interior

1986 Pontiac Grand Am SE 2-door Coupe

1986 Pontiac Sunbird GT 2-door Hatchback

1986 Pontiac 1000 2-door & 4-door Hatchbacks

1986 Pontiac 1000 instrument panel

1986 Pontiac 1000 interior with optional cloth

1986 Pontiac Grand Prix LE

1986 Pontiac Sunbird Wagon

1986 Pontiac Sunbird GT interior

Sunbird GT: 1.8 liter turbocharged EFI 4-cylinder with choice of 5-speed & 4-speed manual or 3-speed automatic P215/60R14 Goodyear Eagle GT tires

1986 Pontiac Sunbird SE 2-door Coupe

Last Model Run: 1986 Pontiac Bonneville Brougham

1986 Pontiac Grand Prix LE instrument panel

1986 Pontiac 6000 STE

Pontiac drops remaining diesel options from 1985

1986 Pontiac Parisienne Brougham Wagon

1986 Pontiac Parisienne Brougham interior

1986 Pontiac Parisienne Brougham

1987

1987- Facts at Glance

News Headlines

- Oct 19 Stock Market crashes $508, dropping 22.6%
- Fox broadcasting debuts
- Televangelist Jim Bakker scandal breaks

Tops in Pop Culture

Music
- Walk Like an Egyptian, Bangles

Movies
- 3 Men and a Baby

TV Show
- The Cosby Show

Sports Champions

Basketball
- L.A. Lakers

Football
- N.Y. Giants

Baseball
- Minnesota Twins

Motor Trend – Car of the Year

Ford Thunderbird Turbo Coupe

1987 - AMC / EAGLE

1987 AMC / Eagle Wagon & Sedan

The performance and dependability of four-wheel drive. A sophisticated, soothing interior. The convenience of cargo space and superb trailering capabilities. Quite simply, Eagle's got it all.

Whether you choose Eagle wagon or sedan, you're making a very intelligent choice. Both come with an impressive list of standard features designed to give you maximum security and comfort. In addition, an extensive list of optional features lets you equip your Eagle to suit your needs.

Through the years, Eagle heritage has grown strong and proud. 1987 is no exception. Eagle truly is a breed apart.

1987 - BUICK

Regal Limited with Exterior Sport Package

Regal Turbo Package Engine with intercooler

Regal Grand National

Last Model Run: 1987 Buick Regal

1987 Buick LeSabre T Type 2-door Coupe

1987 Buick Century Limited 4-door Sedan

1987 Buick Riviera

1987 Buick Somerset Limited Coupe T Package

1987 Buick Skyhawk

1987 Buick Electra

Those '80s Cars   229

1987 - CADILLAC

1987 Cadillac Fleetwood d'Elegance Sedan

4.1 liter, high-output, V8 with electronic sequential-port fuel injection
New Model: 1987 Cadillac Allanté

1987 Cadillac Fleetwood d'Elegance interior

10-way power Recaro seats with power lumbar
1987 Cadillac Allanté interior

New Model: 1987 Cadillac Fleetwood Sixty Special

1987 Cadillac Cimarron

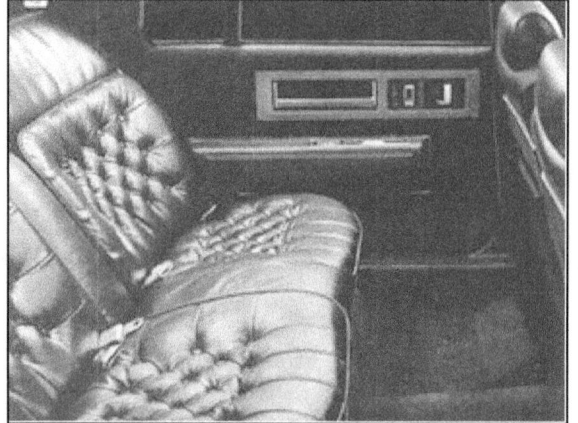
1987 Cadillac Fleetwood Sixty Special interior with foot rests

1987 Cadillac Cimarron interior

Those '80s Cars

1987 Cadillac Eldorado

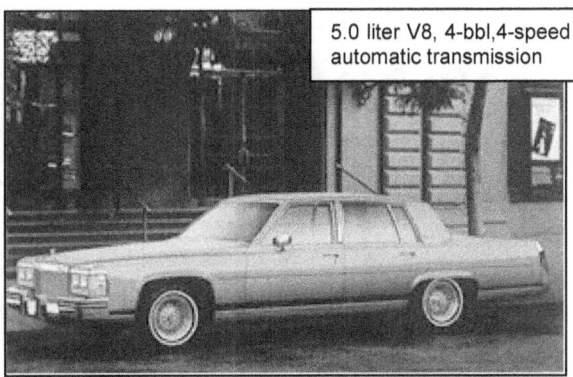
1987 Cadillac Brougham d'Elegance

> 5.0 liter V8, 4-bbl, 4-speed automatic transmission

1987 Cadillac Eldorado interior with optional leather

1987 Cadillac Brougham d'Elegance interior with optional leather

1987 Cadillac Seville interior with optional leather

1987 Cadillac Seville

From the Brochure: "Seville for 1987 is the elegant spirit of Cadillac. Upon closer inspection, you will see remarkable engineering advancements and electronic features. The reassuring traction and space-efficiency of a front-drive, transverse-mounted 4.1 liter V8 engine – a worldwide Cadillac exclusive." – 1987 Cadillac Seville

Those '80s Cars

1987 Cadillac Coupe deVille

1987 Cadillac Sedan deVille

1987 Cadillac Coupe deVille interior

1987 Cadillac Sedan deVille with optional leather

1987 Cadillac Touring Sedan

1987 Cadillac Touring Sedan interior

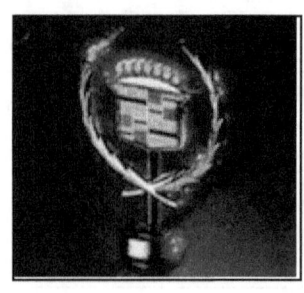

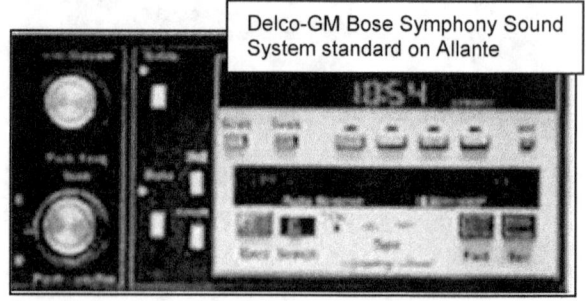
Delco-GM Bose Symphony Sound System standard on Allante

1987 - CHEVROLET

1987 Chevrolet Corvette

1987 Chevrolet Camaro Z28

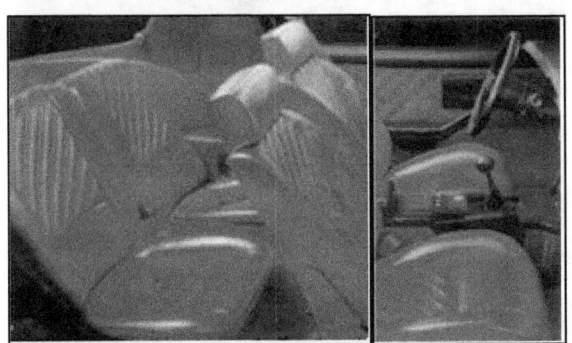
1987 Chevrolet Camaro optional leather interior

1987 Chevrolet Camaro Z28 instrument panel

1987 Chevrolet Corvette convertible

1987 Chevrolet Corvette Official Pace Car Indianapolis 500

1987 Chevrolet Camaro Z28

1987 Chevrolet Camaro

1987 Chevrolet Celebrity Eurosport 4-door Sedan

Those '80s Cars

New Series: 1987 Chevrolet Sprint Turbo, 1.0 L3

Last Model Run:
1987 Chevrolet El Camino

1987 Chevrolet Monte Carlo SS

1987 Chevrolet Spectrum

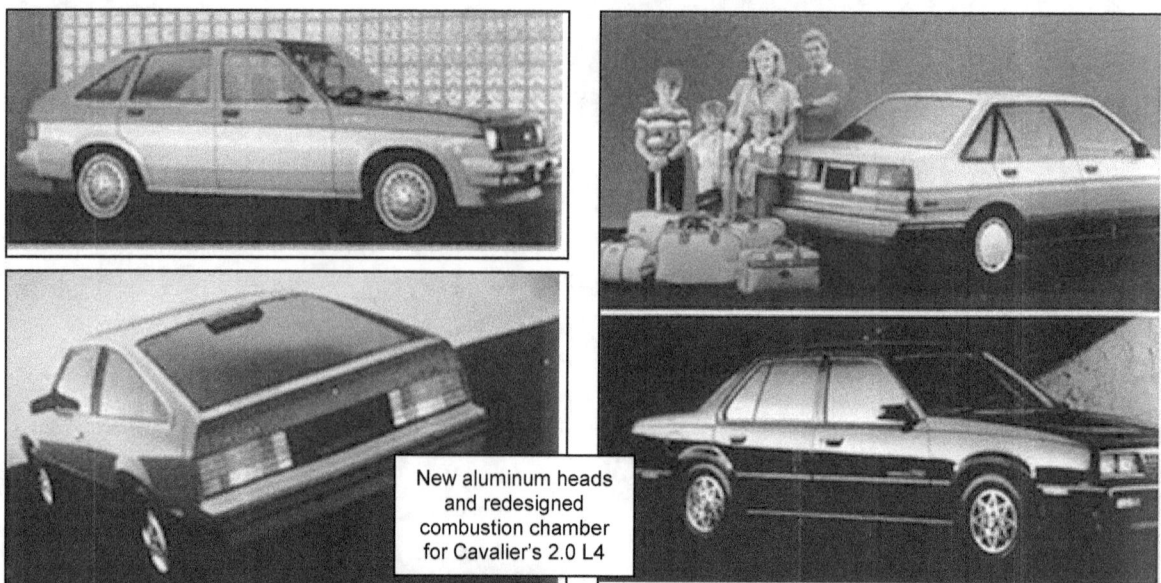

New aluminum heads and redesigned combustion chamber for Cavalier's 2.0 L4

Last Model Run: 1987 Chevrolet Chevette CS 4-door Hatchback
1987 Chevrolet Cavalier Hatchback

1987 Chevrolet Nova 4-door Sedan
1987 Chevrolet Cavalier RS 4-door Sedan

1987 Chevrolet Caprice Classic Sedan, Coupe & Wagon

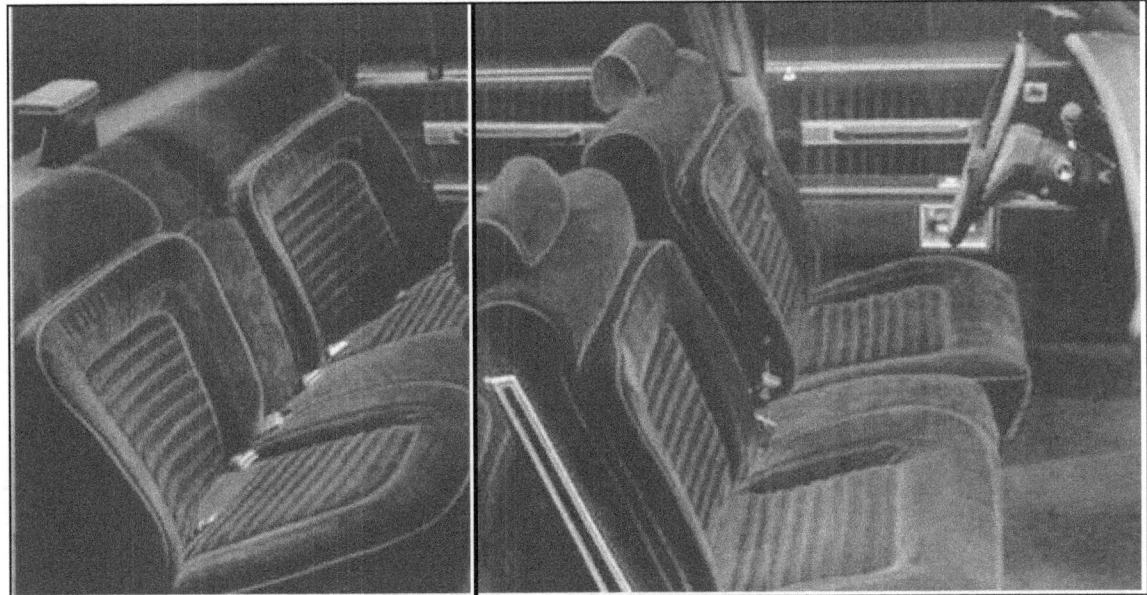
1987 Chevrolet Classic Brougham interior

1987 Chevrolet Classic

1987 - CHRYSLER

1987 Chrysler Fifth Avenue

1987 Chrysler Fifth Avenue optional leather interior

1987 Chrysler Fifth Avenue instrument panel

1987 Chrysler New Yorker

1987 Chrysler New Yorker leather interior

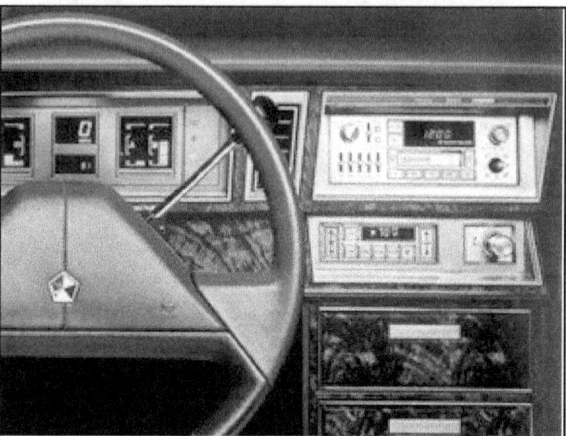

1987 Chrysler New Yorker instrument panel

From the Brochure: "A respect for tradition. That's what keeps classical New Yorker luxuriously comfortable. A resolve to improve. That's what makes contemporary New Yorker powerfully efficient. A union of the established and the innovative; a collaboration of the familiar and refined. That's how New Yorker became the ultimate high-technology luxury sedan."
- 1987 Chrysler New Yorker

1987 Chrysler LeBaron 4-door Sedan

1987 Chrysler LeBaron, Town & Country Wagon

1987 Chrysler LeBaron GTS

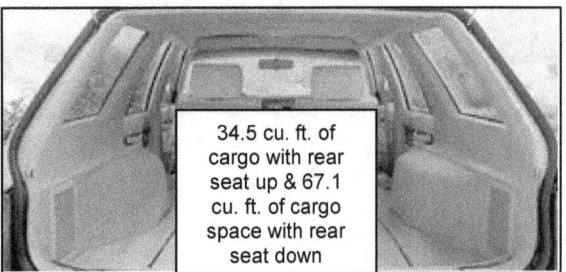

34.5 cu. ft. of cargo with rear seat up & 67.1 cu. ft. of cargo space with rear seat down

1987 Chrysler Town & Country Wagon

New Model: 1987 Chrysler Conquest (previously Plymouth & Dodge Conquest)

From the Brochure: "The 1987 Chrysler Town & Country Station Wagon continues to be a successful combination of traditional station wagon features, Chrysler's advanced front-wheel drive technology and Chrysler quality backed by the 5/50 Limited Warranty. Refinements for 1987 include a standard long-life stainless steel exhaust system, standard electronic instrument cluster and a new available electronic speed control for easier use during highway cruising."
- 1987 Chrysler Town & Country

1987 Chrysler Town & Country optional Mark Cross leather interior

Those '80s Cars

THE ALL-NEW CHRYSLER LE BARON.
BEAUTY... WITH A PASSION FOR DRIVING.

Shaped by wind, reason and a unique artistry, the design of the all-new LeBaron coupe is more than efficient aerodynamics...it is a triumph of elegance.

While the new LeBaron believes in cheating the wind, it has no intention of robbing the eye...it is an image of arresting beauty.

But beneath this beauty breathes a passion: LeBaron was created to drive. And drive it does! It attacks the road with a high torque, 2.5 fuel-injected engine. Its turbo option can blur the surface of any passing lane.

Handling is equally impressive. LeBaron's advanced front-wheel drive and positive-response suspension will calm the most demanding roads.

Even razor-sharp turns lose their menace.

Luxurious contoured leather seats comfort and support. Instrument readings are captured in a glance. Controls...positioned to minimize distraction.

And whether you buy or lease, LeBaron gives you Chrysler's new protection plan* that covers powertrain, engine and turbo for 7 years or 70,000 miles. And against outerbody rust-through for 7 years or 100,000 miles.

Its power will move you. Its beauty will stop you. The all-new Chrysler LeBaron. At your Chrysler-Plymouth dealer.

CHRYSLER. DRIVING TO BE THE BEST.

New Model: 1987 Chrysler LeBaron Coupe

From the Brochure: "LeBaron is a car for drivers who enjoy the roadway. It is a car to be appreciated by those who favor touches of luxury and convenience."

- 1987 Chrysler LeBaron Coupe

1987 - DODGE

1987 Dodge Diplomat SE

1987 Dodge 600 4-door Sedan

1987 Dodge Diplomat SE interior

1987 Dodge 600 SE 4-door interior

1987 Dodge Omni America

Lowest priced car of its class made in America

1987 Dodge Aries K LE 2-door Coupe

1987 Dodge Shelby Charger (back) & Charger

1987 Dodge Omni interior

Those '80s Cars

New Model: 1987 Dodge Shadow 2-door Coupe

45 standard features; more than any other car of its size

New Model: 1987 Dodge Shadow 4-door Sedan

1987 Dodge Shadow ES interior

1987 Dodge Caravan SE

1987 Dodge Caravan LE interior

1987 Dodge Lancer ES

Refreshed:
1987 Dodge Daytona Shelby Z

3 trims series: Daytona, Daytona Pacifica, Daytona Shelby Z

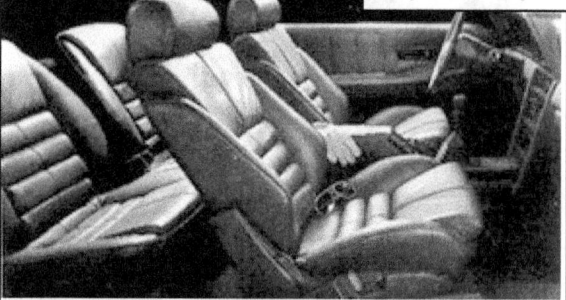
1987 Dodge Daytona Pacifica interior

1987 Dodge Colt Premier 4-door Sedan

1987 Dodge Colt E 3-Door Hatchback

1987 Dodge Colt Vista 4WD Wagon

1987 - FORD

Refreshed: 1987 Ford Mustang GT

New interior

1987 Ford Mustang LX interior with new dash

1987 Ford Mustang LX Coupe

1987 Ford Mustang Cobra GT Convertible

Cobra GT: 225 hp at 4,000 RPM
300 lb./ft. torque at 3,200 RPM

Refreshed: 1987 Ford Thunderbird LX

1987 Ford Thunderbird optional electronic instrument cluster

1987 Ford Thunderbird LX interior

New 2.3 turbo intercooled rated at 190 hp

Refreshed: 1987 Ford Thunderbird Turbo Coupe

Those '80s Cars

1987 Ford Taurus LX Sedan & Wagon

1987 Ford Taurus LX Sedan

1987 Ford Taurus LX interior

1987 Ford Escort GL 4-door Hatchback

1987 Ford Escort GL interior

1987 Ford LTD Crown Victoria LX Sedan

1987 Ford LTD Crown Victoria LX interior

1987 Ford Tempo All-Wheel Drive 4-door Sedan

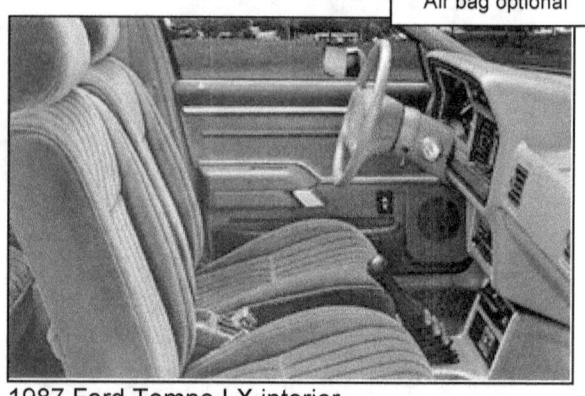
Air bag optional

1987 Ford Tempo LX interior

1987 Ford EXP Sport Coupe

1987 - LINCOLN

Last Model Run: 1987 Lincoln Continental Givenchy Edition

1987 Lincoln Mark VII LSC

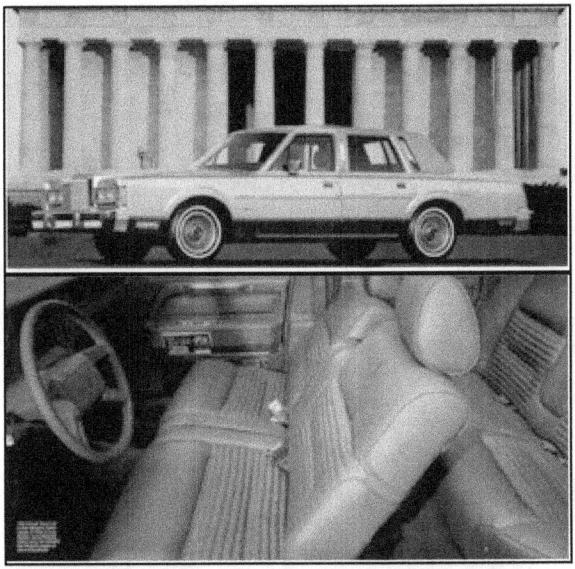

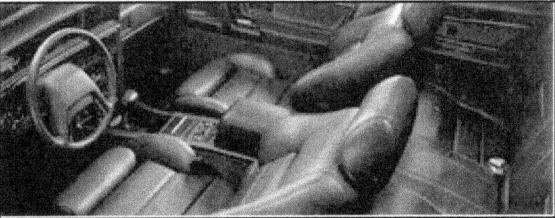
1987 Lincoln Mark VII interior

1987 Lincoln Town Car Cartier edition

1987 - MERCURY

1987 Mercury Sable GS Sedan

1987 Mercury Sable GS Wagon

Sable drops 2.5 liter engine, standard engine is 3.0 liter V6

1987 Mercury Grand Marquis Colony Park

1987 Mercury Grand Marquis LS Sedan

Last Model Run: 1987 Mercury Lynx Wagon

1987 Mercury Sable LS interior

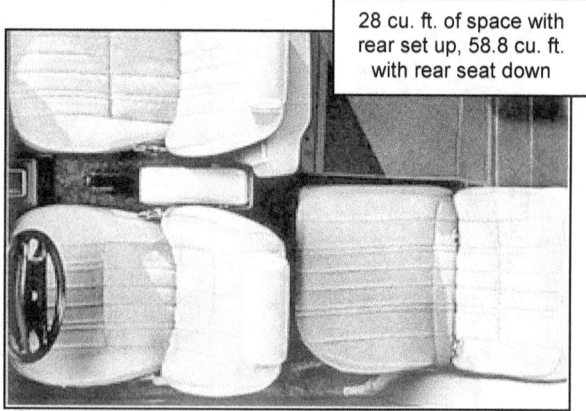
1987 Mercury Lynx GS wagon interior

28 cu. ft. of space with rear set up, 58.8 cu. ft. with rear seat down

Refreshed: 1987 Mercury Cougar

Refreshed: 1987 Mercury Cougar & XR-7 (right)

1987 Mercury Cougar LS interior

Air bag optional

1987 Mercury Topaz LS 4-door Sedan

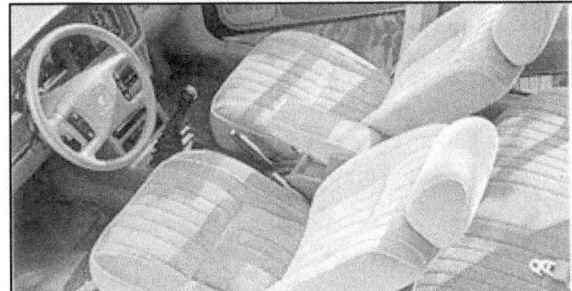
1987 Mercury Topaz LS interior

1987 Mercury Cougar XR-7 electronic instrumentation

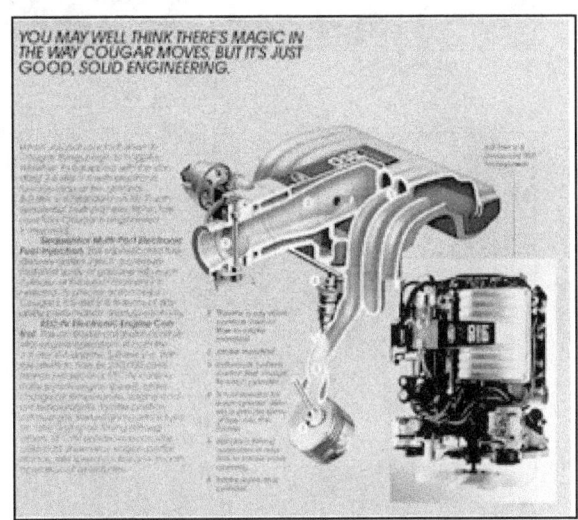

1987 Mercury Topaz All-Wheel Drive option

Those '80s Cars

1987 - MERKUR

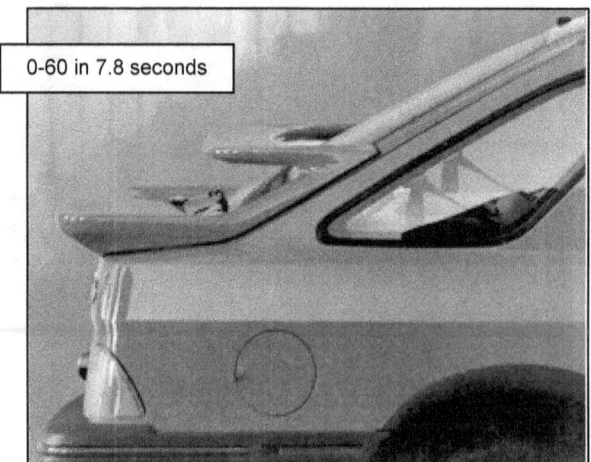

0-60 in 7.8 seconds

1987 Merkur XR4Ti

1987 Merkur XR4Ti

1987 Merkur XR4Ti interior

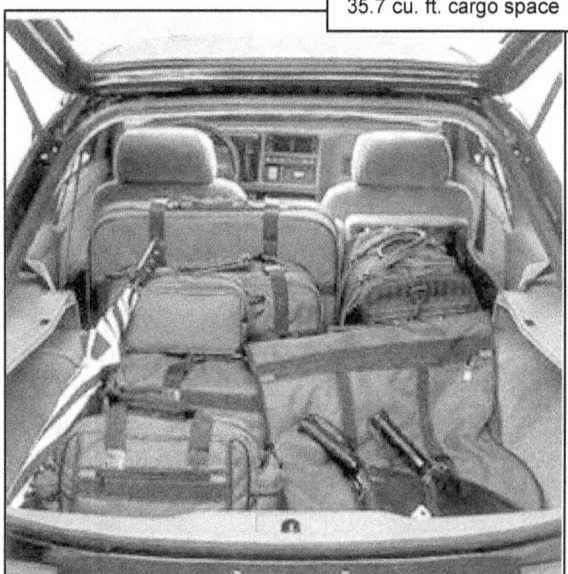

35.7 cu. ft. cargo space

1987 Merkur XR4Ti with rear seats folded provide 35.7 cu. ft. of space

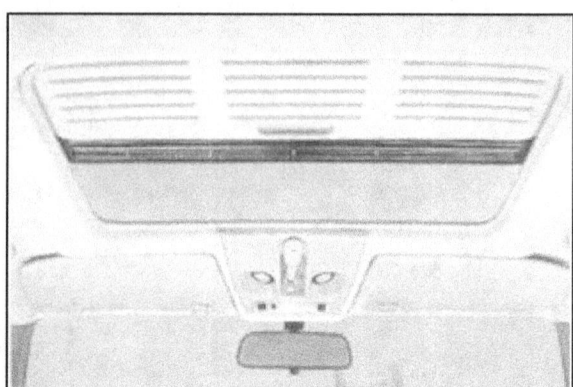

1987 Merkur XR4Ti optional moonroof

1987 Merkur XR4Ti instrument panel

From the Brochure: "Merkur XR4Ti. The performance coupe from Germany that is advancing the art of driving. It is from a country where the speed limit is often regulated only by the driver's skill and the automobile's design. Where the switchbacks of a narrow mountain road challenge both driver and machine. The XR4Ti sport coupe is the product of that attitude, an automobile for the kind of driver who would go a few miles out of the way to discover that 'perfect' road." – 1987 Merkur XR4Ti

1987 - OLDSMOBILE

1987 Oldsmobile Toronado Trofeo interior

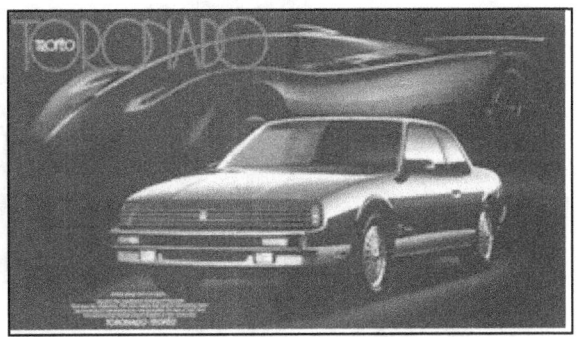
1987 Oldsmobile Trofeo

1987 Oldsmobile Toronado interior

1987 Oldsmobile Toronado

1987 Oldsmobile Toronado instrument panel

1987 Oldsmobile Ninety-Eight Regency interior

1987 Oldsmobile Ninety-Eight Regency Brougham Sedan

1987 Oldsmobile Ninety-Eight Regency Brougham Coupe

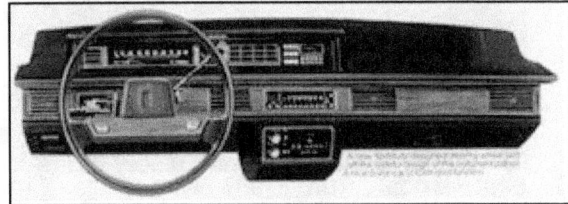
1987 Oldsmobile Ninety-Eight instrument panel

1987 Oldsmobile Delta 88 Royale Brougham

1987 Oldsmobile Delta 88 Royal Coupe

1987 Oldsmobile Custom Cruiser

1987 Oldsmobile Supreme Brougham Coupe

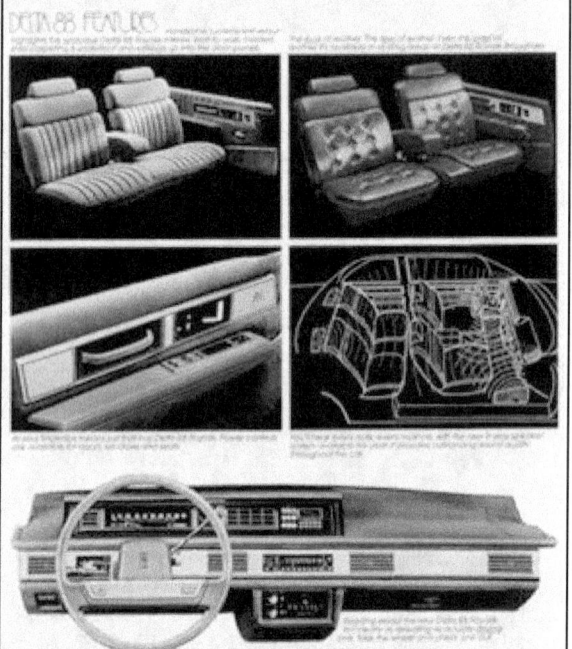
1987 Oldsmobile Delta 88 interiors & dash

Last Model Run: 1987 Oldsmobile Cutlass Supreme Brougham Sedan

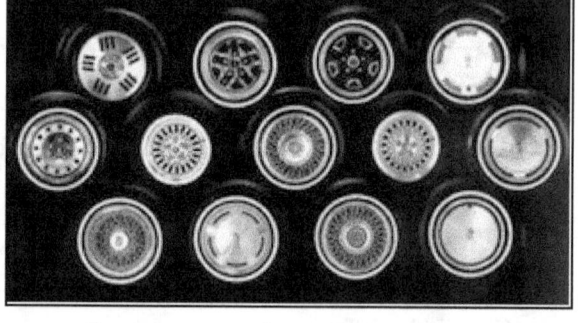

248

Those '80s Cars

1987 Oldsmobile Calais Supreme Sedan

1987 Oldsmobile Calais Supreme Coupe

1987 Oldsmobile Cutlass Ciera Brougham

1987 Oldsmobile Cutlass Ciera SL Coupe

1987 Oldsmobile Firenza LC Coupe

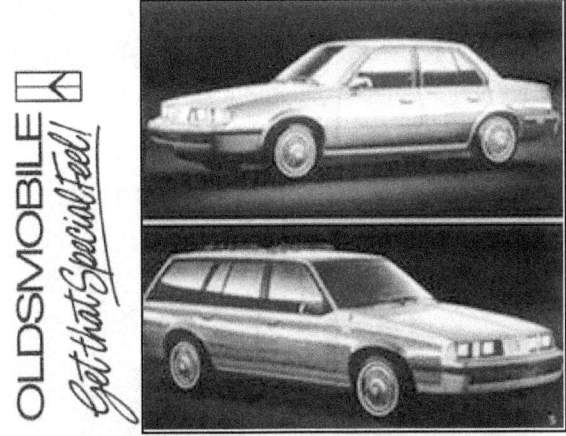
1987 Oldsmobile Firenza Sedan & Wagon

1987 Oldsmobile Cutlass Cruiser

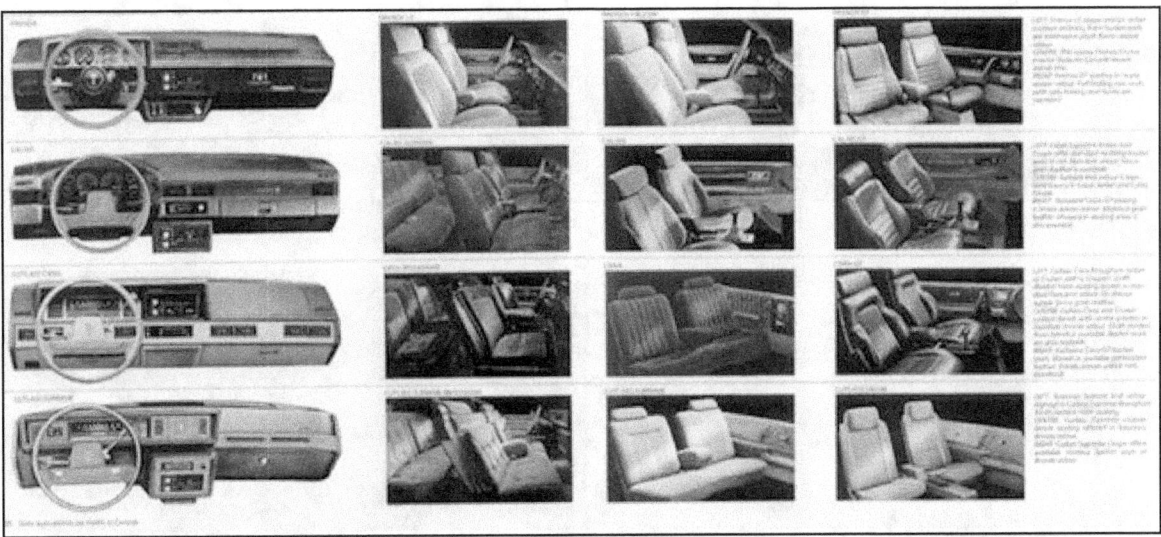
1987 Oldsmobile Firenza, Calais, Cutlass Ciera & Cutlass Supreme instrument panels & interiors

Those '80s Cars

1987 - PLYMOUTH

2.2 liter 4-cylinder standard
2.5 liter 4-cylinder optional

New Model: 1987 Plymouth Sundance 4-door (also available in coupe)

1987 Plymouth Caravelle SE 4-door

1987 Plymouth Reliant K LE 4-door Sedan

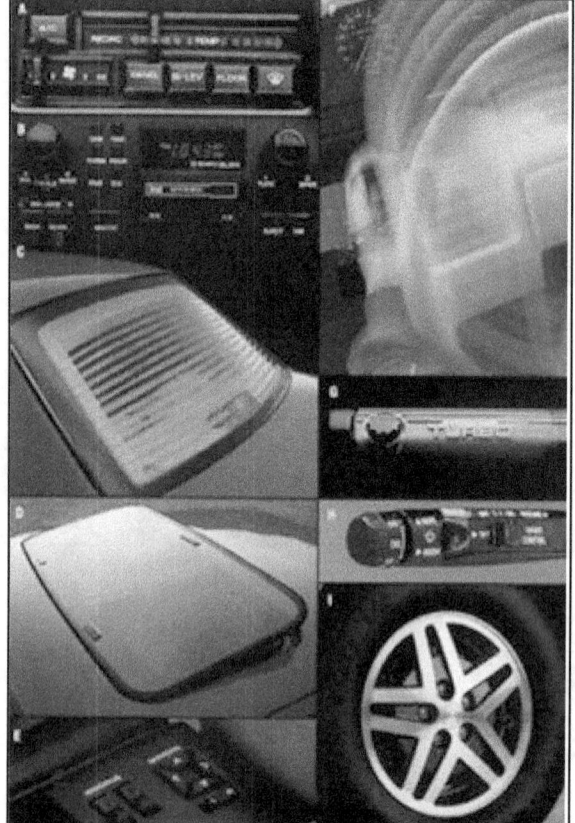

1987 Sundance Options

1987 Plymouth Reliant K LE interior

1987 Plymouth Gran Fury Salon

1987 Plymouth Gran Fury Salon

1987 Plymouth Colt Sedan

1987 Plymouth Colt Turbo instrument panel

1987 Plymouth Colt Vista 4WD Wagon

1987 Plymouth Conquest

1987 Plymouth Colt Hatchback

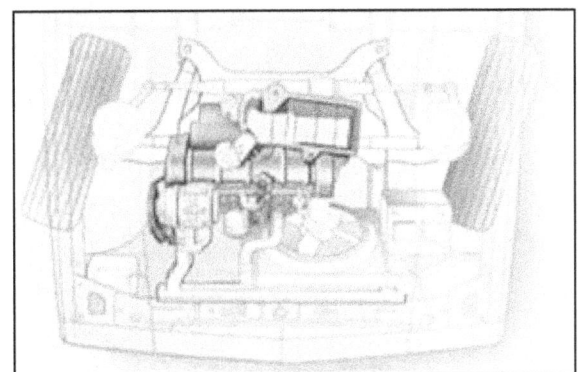

1987 Plymouth Turismo

1987 Plymouth Turismo

1987 Plymouth Horizon America

1987 - PONTIAC

1987 Pontiac Fiero GT

1987 Pontiac Fiero SE

1987 Pontiac Fiero instrument panel

From the Brochure: "Firebird Formula (shown below) returns with a 5-speed gearbox, Pontiac's famed WS6 performance package, and an available 5.7 liter V8.
- 1987 Pontiac Firebird Formula

1987 Pontiac Firebird Trans Am

1987 Pontiac Firebird Formula

1987 Pontiac Grand Am SE Sedan & Coupe

1987 Pontiac Grand Am SE interior

3.8 liter V6, 4-speed auto & front-wheel drive

New Model: Bonneville LE

1987 Pontiac Bonneville LE interior

1987 Pontiac Firebird interior

1987 Pontiac 6000 LE Sedan & SE Wagon

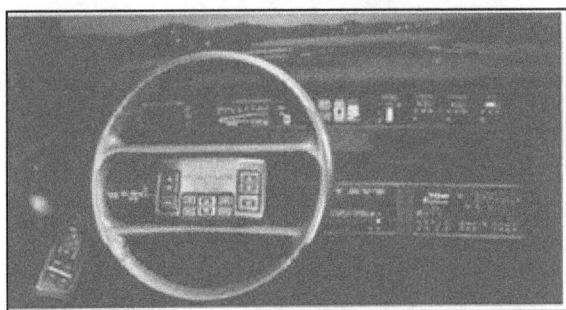
1987 Pontiac STE instrument panel

1987 Pontiac Safari Wagon

Those '80s Cars

Last Model Run: 1987 Pontiac Grand Prix

Last Model Run: 1987 Pontiac Grand Prix

From the Brochure: "Grand Prix LE for 1987 offers a new sport steering wheel, new 45/55 seats turbo finned aluminum wheels, power brakes and available hatch roof." – 1987 Pontiac Grand Prix

1987 Pontiac Sunbird LE Sedan

New Sunbird engine: 2.0 liter OHC MFI engine with a turbo option

1987 Pontiac 1000 4-door Hatchback

1987 Pontiac Sunbird Turbo GT convertible

1987 Pontiac 1000 instrument panel

1987 Pontiac Sunbird interior

1988

1988 Facts at Glance

News Headlines

- Iran/Iraq war ends
- Terrorist blow up Pan Am jet over Lockerbie
- Hubble space telescope placed in orbit
- Stealth bomber unveiled

Tops in Pop Culture

Music
- Faith, George Michael

Movies
- Rain Man

TV Show
- The Cosby Show

Sports Champions

Basketball
- L.A. Lakers

Football
- Washington Redskins

Baseball
- L.A. Dodgers

Motor Trend – Car of the Year

Pontiac Grand Prix

1988 - AMC / EAGLE

New Model: 1988 Eagle Premier ES – Now owned by Chrysler, Chrysler re-brands the franchise as Eagle and sells models from Renault, the previous owner of AMC/Eagle.

1988 Eagle Premier optional all-aluminum 3.0 liter V6 engine with multi-port fuel injection

2.5 liter 4-cylinder engine with 4-speed automatic overdrive transmission is standard equipment

Eagle Premier LX interior

Last Model Run: 1988 Eagle Wagon, formerly AMC Eagle

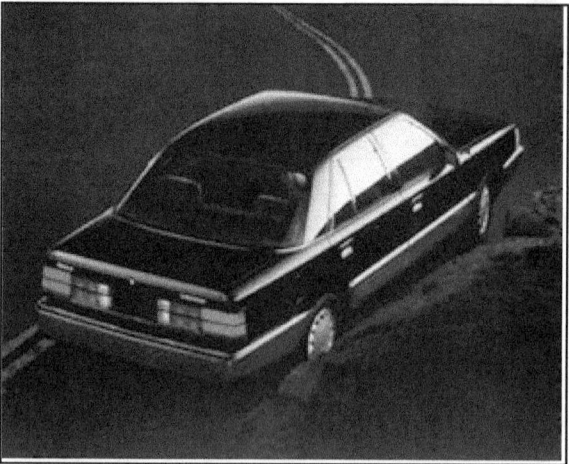

New Model: 1988 Eagle Premier ES

1988 - BUICK

3.8 V6, 4-speed auto, anti-lock brakes & Gran Touring suspension

New Model: 1988 Buick Reatta

New Model: 1988 Buick Reatta

1988 Buick Electra T Type

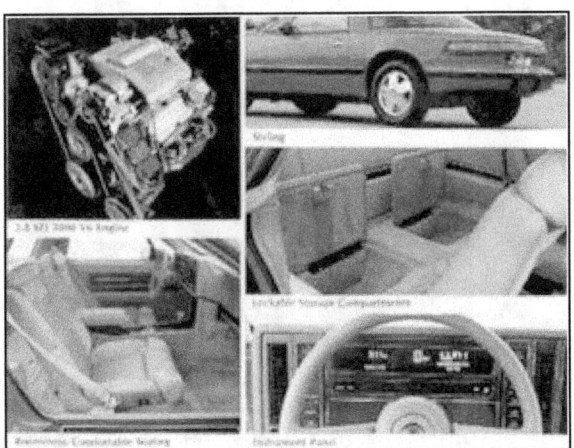

New Model: 1988 Buick Reatta

1988 Buick Electra Park Avenue interior

1988 Buick Riviera T Type (all Rivieras are Silver Anniversary editions)

1988 Buick Riviera interior

Those '80s Cars

.305 coefficient of drag

New Model: 1988 Buick Regal Gran Sport

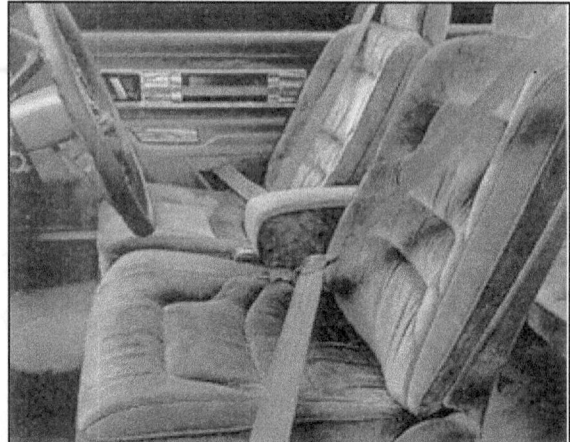

1988 Buick Regal Limited interior

1988 Buick Skylark Custom 4-door

1988 Buick Skylark Limited interior

New Model: 1988 Buick Regal Gran Sport

> **From the Brochure:** "The first example of the next generation of Buicks, is a totally new car for 1988. There's nothing else like it on the American road. The values held by the Regal owner are clearly reflected in the characteristics of the new Regal: quality, excellence of design and execution, and – above all – that special, spirited beauty that belongs only to automobiles that bear the Buick hallmark."
>   - 1988 Buick Regal

1988 Buick LeSabre T Type 2-door Coupe

1988 Buick LeSabre Limited 2-door Coupe

1988 Buick Electra Estate Wagon

1988 Buick Century Estate Wagon

1988 Buick LeSabre Limited interior

1988 Buick Skyhawk Wagon

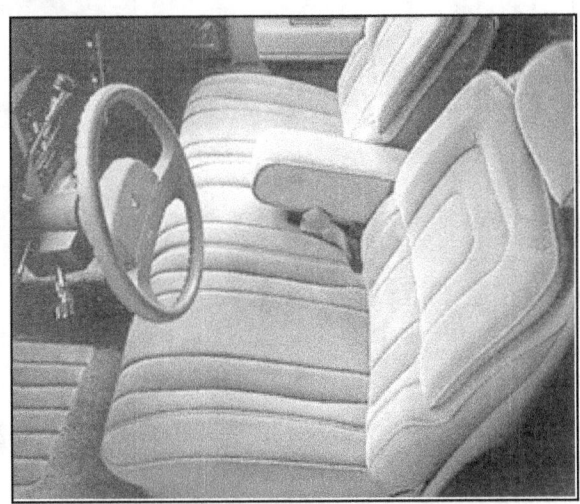
1988 Buick Century Limited interior

1988 Buick Skyhawk SE interior

Those '80s Cars

1988 - CADILLAC

1988 Cadillac Allanté

From the Brochure: "Using premium German steel and a unique Swiss aluminum alloy, Italian artisans handcraft its coachwork at the studios of Pininfarina, designer of Ferraris and Rolls-Royce Camargue. Then, specially modified 747s transport the sculpted bodies to one of the world's most advanced automotive facilities – a Cadillac facility here in the United States."

-1988 Cadillac Allanté

1988 Cadillac Allanté standard analog gauges

1988 Cadillac Allanté optional digital instruments

1988 Cadillac Touring Sedan

1988 Cadillac Eldorado Biarritz

1988 Cadillac Sedan deVille

1988 Cadillac Eldorado

1988 Cadillac Coupe deVille

New 4.5 liter V8 with digital fuel injection standard on deVille, Fleetwood, Eldorado & Seville

1988 Cadillac deVille leather interior

Retained accessory power

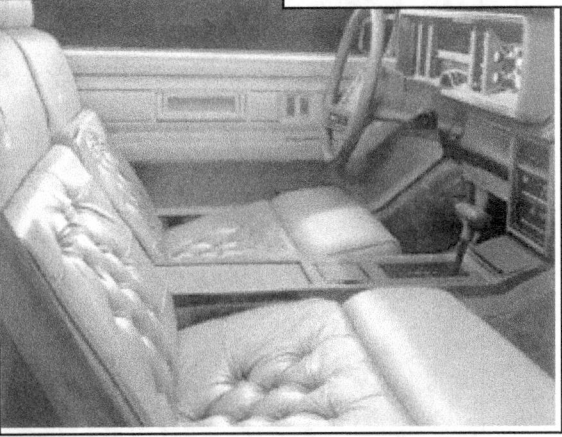
1988 Cadillac Eldorado Biarritz leather interior

1988 Cadillac Seville

1988 Cadillac Eldorado & Seville dash panel

1988 Cadillac Seville interior

Those '80s Cars

1988 Cadillac Fleetwood Sixty Special

From the Brochure: "The executive-class Cadillac says more about you than you can say yourself. The custom-crafted coachwork of the Fleetwood Sixty Special reflects your distinctive approach to conducting business." - Fleetwood Sixty Special

1988 Cadillac Fleetwood leather interior

1988 Cadillac Brougham

Last Model Run: 1988 Cadillac Cimarron

1988 Cadillac Brougham d'Elegance roofline

1988 Cadillac Cimarron leather interior with analog gauges

1988 Cadillac Brougham cloth interior

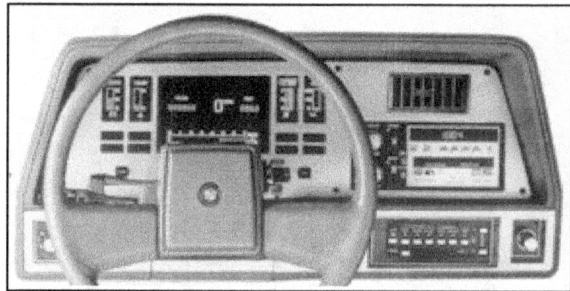
1988 Cadillac Cimarron optional digital dash cluster

262 Those '80s Cars

1988 - CHEVROLET

1988 Chevrolet Corvette convertible

1988 Chevrolet Corvette

1988 Chevrolet Camaro Z28

Standard 2.0 L4 EFI
New Model: 1988 Chevrolet Beretta

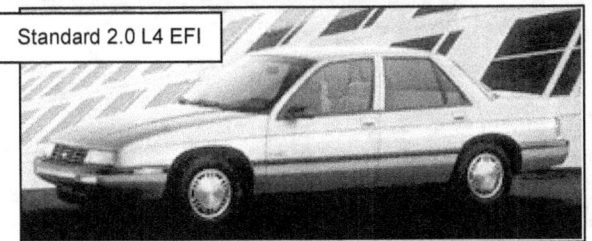
Standard 2.0 L4 EFI
New Model: 1988 Chevrolet Corsica

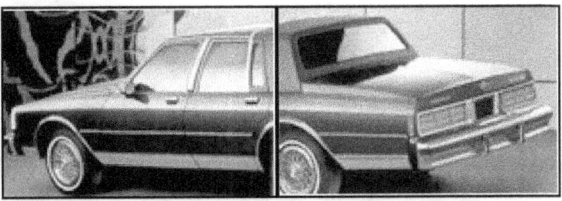
1988 Chevrolet Caprice Classic Brougham

1988 Chevrolet Caprice Classic Brougham interior with optional leather

1988 Chevrolet Caprice Classic line

1988 Chevrolet Celebrity Coupe, Sedan, Wagon

Those '80s Cars

1988 Chevrolet Celebrity Eurosport Wagon

Last Model Run: 1988 Chevrolet Monte Carlo SS & Coupe

Last Model Run: 1988 Chevrolet Monte Carlo

1988 Chevrolet Cavalier RS 4-door

New aero styling

1988 Chevrolet Cavalier Z24 2-door

1988 Chevrolet Nova CL Sedan

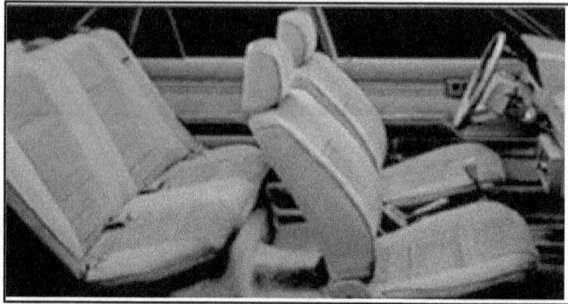
1988 Chevrolet Nova CL Custom cloth interior

1988 Chevrolet Sprint Turbo 2-door

1988 Chevrolet Sprint 4-door

1988 Chevrolet Spectrum 4-door Sedan

1988 Chevrolet Spectrum line

1988 - CHRYSLER

The New "New Yorkers" comes with a 3.0 V6

(from left)
New Models: 1988 Chrysler New Yorker Landau & New Yorker
Last Model Run: 1998 New Yorker Turbo (for 1988, this body style comes with the 2.2 turbo only)
1988 Chrysler Fifth Avenue

From the Brochure: "Luxury abounds. Prestigious, comfortably quiet, smoothly maneuverable luxury... in Chrysler's all-new New Yorker Landau. Distinctively styled in the traditional big-car manner. Accented with such elegant touches as a classically graceful grille and concealed headlights. Engineered for stability with front-wheel drive; for performance with V-6 power; for comfort and quiet with road-smoothing suspension. And for the most discriminating and demanding drivers, a most extensive list of standard features."

- 1988 Chrysler New Yorker Landau

1988 Chrysler New Yorker Landau interior

1988 Chrysler New Yorker Turbo leather interior

1988 Chrysler New Yorker standard interior

From the Brochure: "The New Yorker's suspension is tuned to provide a smooth, comfortable ride. In addition, a variable front-strut damping system helps reduce the noise and jarring effects of road hazards. Comfort prevails." – 1988 Chrysler New Yorker

1988 Chrysler Fifth Avenue leather interior

Those '80s Cars

1988 Chrysler LeBaron Convertible, LeBaron Coupe, and LeBaron GTS
Last Model Run: 1988 LeBaron Sedan and LeBaron Town & Country Wagon

1988 Chrysler LeBaron Premium Convertible

1988 Chrysler GTS Premium optional leather interior

> Its power will move you.
> Its beauty will stop you.

1988 Chrysler LeBaron Premium interior with optional leather seating

1988 Chrysler LeBaron 4-door sedan interior with available bucket seats

1988 Chrysler Conquest

1988 Chrysler LeBaron Town & Country optional Mark Cross leather interior

1988 - DODGE

2.5 liter 4-cylinder standard with available 3.0 liter multipoint fuel-injected V6

New Model: 1988 Dodge Dynasty LE Sedan

1988 Dodge Dynasty LE interior

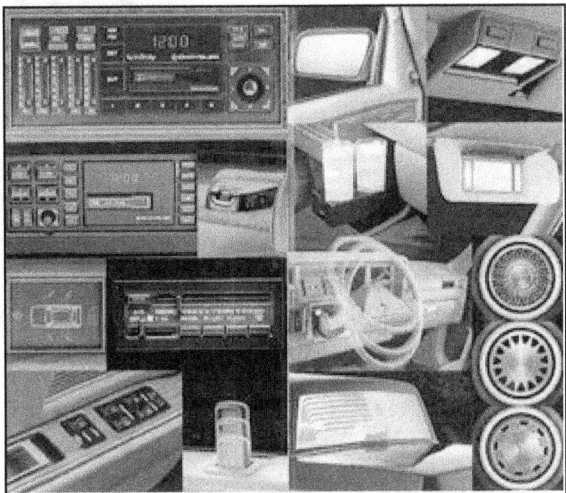

1988 Dodge Dynasty features & options

1988 Dodge Shadow ES 2-door

1988 Dodge Shadow ES 4-door

1988 Dodge Shadow ES interior

Those '80s Cars

1988 Dodge Daytona Shelby Z

1988 Dodge Lancer ES

New 7/70 Power Train & 7/100 Anti-Corrosion Warranties

1988 Dodge Aries America LE 4-door

1988 Dodge Aries America LE 2-door

1988 Dodge 600 & 600 SE (back)

1988 Dodge Diplomat SE

Fuel injection now standard

1988 Dodge Omni America

1988 Dodge Colt Premier Turbo Sedan

1988 Dodge Colt DL 2-door Hatchback

1988 Dodge Colt Vista 4WD Wagon

1988 - FORD

5.0 liter V8 & AOD

1988 Ford Thunderbird Sport

1988 Ford Thunderbird Turbo Coupe interior

1988 Ford Mustang GT

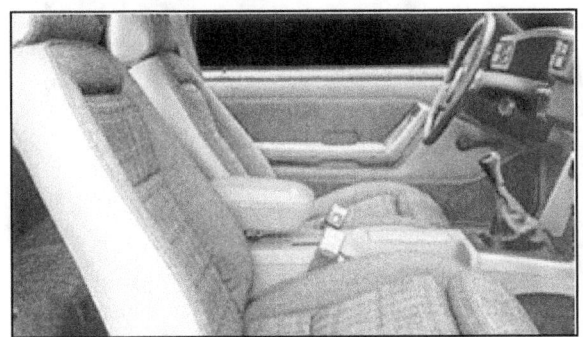

1988 Ford Mustang GT interior

New 3.8 liter V6 option

1988 Ford Taurus LX sedan

1988 Ford Taurus LX instrument panel

1988 Ford Taurus LX interior

Those '80s Cars 269

1988 Ford Escort GT 2-door Hatchback

1988 Ford EXP Luxury Coupe

1988 Ford Escort GT interior

1.3 liter 4-cylinder w/ 4- & 5-speed manuals & 3-speed auto

New Model: 1988 Ford Festiva

Refreshed: 1988 Ford Tempo GL

1988 Ford Tempo instrument panel

Refreshed: 1988 Ford LTD Crown Victoria 4-door Sedan

1988 LTD Crown Victoria is refreshed with updated front and rear end styling

Refreshed: 1988 Ford LTD Country Squire Wagon

1988 Ford LTD Crown Victoria LX interior

270   Those '80s Cars

1988 - LINCOLN

1988 Lincoln Continental Town Car

1988 Lincoln Town Car interior

1988 Lincoln Continental instrument panel

1988 Lincoln Continental cloth interior

1988 Lincoln Mark VII LSC

1988 Lincoln Mark VII LSC interior

1988 Lincoln Town Car

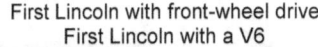
First Lincoln with front-wheel drive
First Lincoln with a V6

New Model: 1988 Lincoln Continental

New Model: 1988 Lincoln Continental

.35 drag

3.8 liter (232) V6
4-speed AOD

New Model: 1988 Lincoln Continental

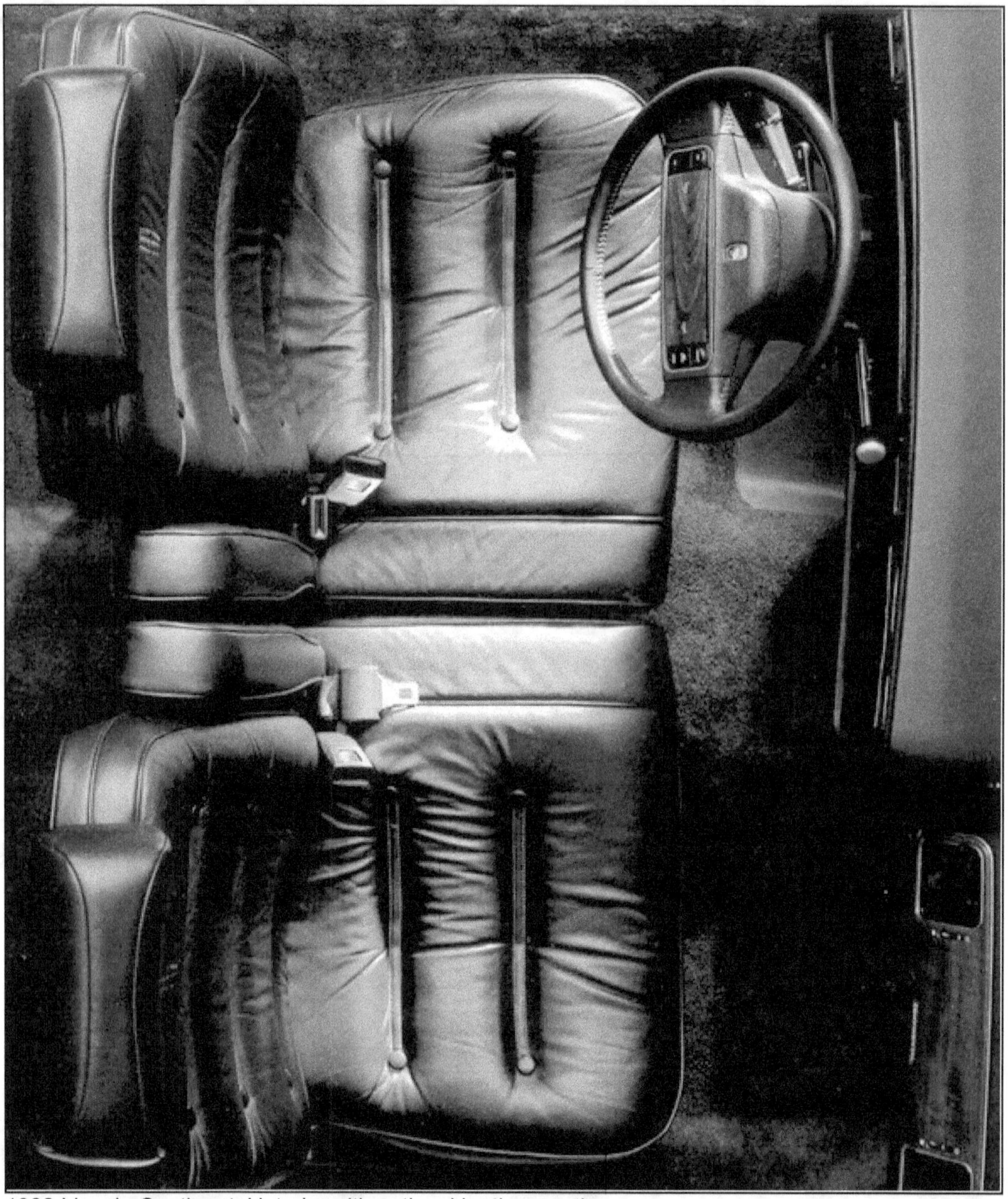

1988 Lincoln Continental interior with optional leather seating

1988 - MERCURY

5.0 liter V8 & AOD on XR-7 models

1988 Mercury Cougar XR-7

1988 Mercury Cougar XR-7 analog instruments

New Model: 1988 Mercury Tracer 2-door Hatchback

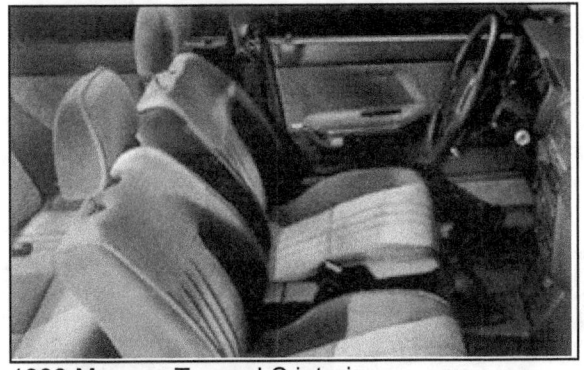

1988 Mercury Tracer LS interior

New Model: 1988 Mercury Tracer LS 4-door Hatchback

Tracers feature a 1.6 liter OHC multi-port electronic fuel injected 4-cylinder engine

New Model: 1988 Mercury Tracer LS Wagon

Those '80s Cars

Refreshed: 1988 Mercury Topaz XR5 2-door & LTS 4-door

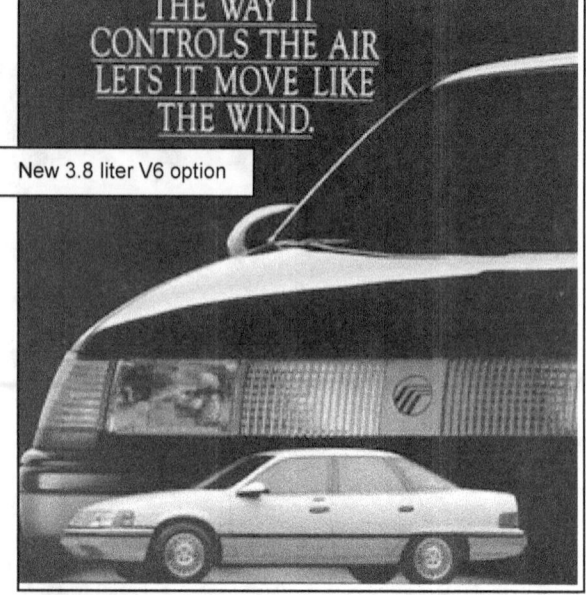

1988 Mercury Sable GS Sedan

1988 Mercury Topaz LS interior

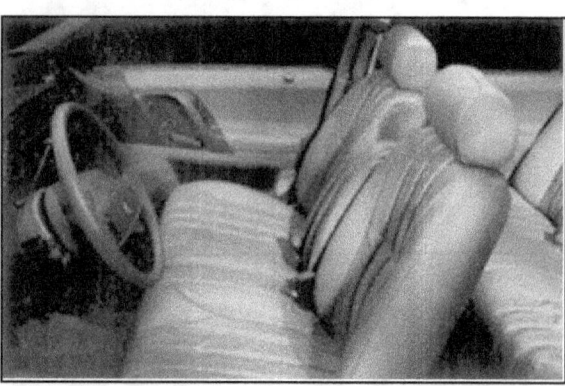

1988 Mercury Sable LS leather interior

1988 Mercury Grand Marquis Colony Park

1988 Mercury Grand Marquis LS

1988 Mercury Grand Marquis LS leather interior

1988 Mercury Grand Marquis LS cloth interior

1988 - MERKUR

1988 Merkur XR4Ti

2.9 liter V6, 140 hp

New Model: 1988 Merkur Scorpio 4-door Hatchback

1988 Merkur XR4Ti optional leather interior

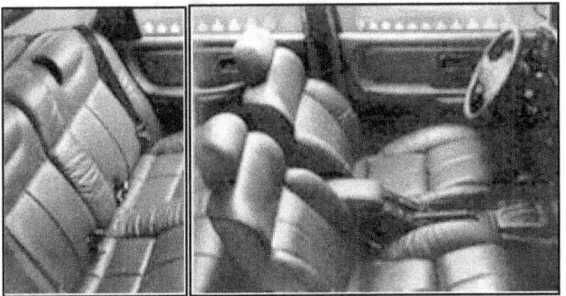
1988 Merkur Scorpio interior with optional leather

From the Brochure: "All the performance of a fine German sedan, but with a major difference. Exceptional interior comfort. Scorpio's interior appointments and obvious attention to personal comfort separate it from all other German sedans in an exceptional manner."
- 1988 Merkur Scorpio

5-speed manual & 4-speed automatic transmission availability

New Model: 1988 Merkur Scorpio 4-door Hatchback

1988 - OLDSMOBILE

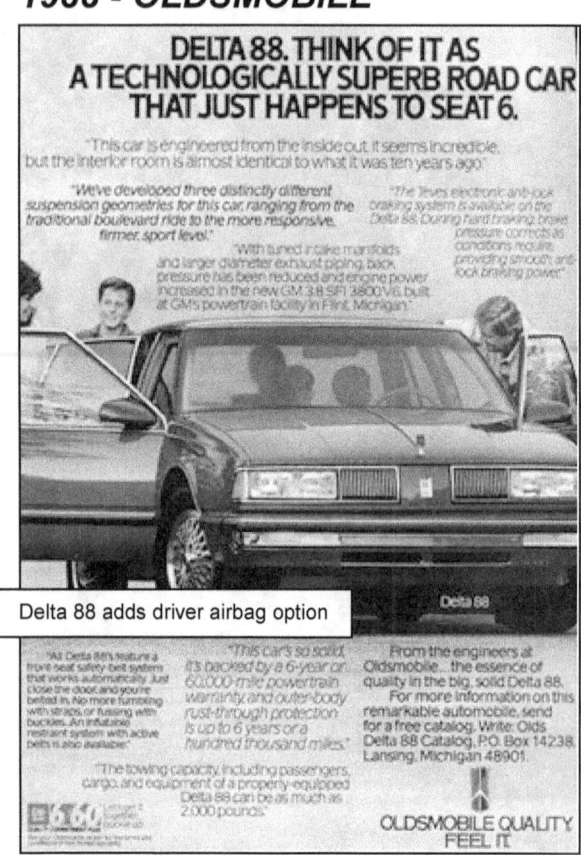

Delta 88 adds driver airbag option

1988 Oldsmobile Delta 88

Oldsmobile adds International Series on many models

Last Model Run: 1988 Oldsmobile Cutlass Supreme Classic (5.0 liter V8 & 4-speed AOD)

1988 Oldsmobile Cutlass Supreme Brougham

New 3.8 liter SFI V6

1988 Oldsmobile Ninety-Eight Touring Sedan

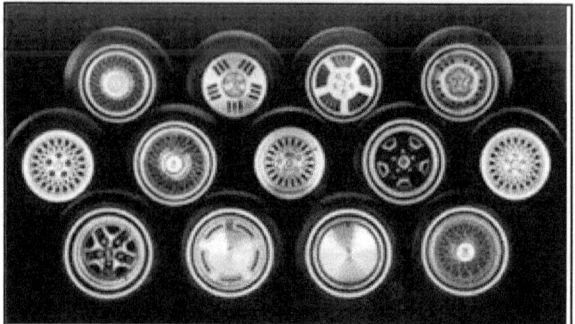

1988 Oldsmobile Wheels & Wheel Covers

1988 Oldsmobile Toronado

1988 Oldsmobile Cutlass Supreme dash panel

1988 Oldsmobile Cutlass Calais Sedan

1988 Oldsmobile Cutlass Calais Coupe

New "Quad 4" 2.3 liter DOC 16-valve 4-cylinder engine

1988 Oldsmobile Cutlass Calais SL interior with optional leather

1988 Oldsmobile Cutlass Ciera SL Coupe

1988 Oldsmobile Cutlass Ciera Sedan

1988 Oldsmobile Firenza Coupe

New front-end

1988 Oldsmobile Firenza Sedan

1988 Oldsmobile Firenza Cruiser

1988 Oldsmobile Firenza interior

1988 Oldsmobile Cutlass Cruiser

1988 Oldsmobile Cutlass Ciera International Series interior with optional leather

1988 - PLYMOUTH

Last Model Run: 1988 Plymouth Caravelle SE

1988 Plymouth Reliant America LE 4-Door

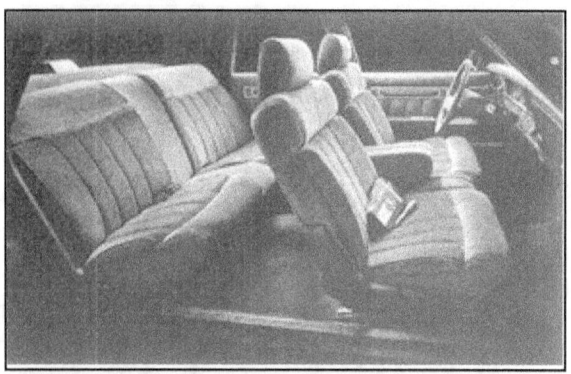

1988 Plymouth Caravelle SE interior

1988 Plymouth Reliant America LE 2-Door

1988 Plymouth Sundance RS

1988 Plymouth Reliant interior

1988 Plymouth Sundance

1988 Plymouth Sundance Turbo RS

1988 Plymouth Horizon America interior

Fuel injection now standard

1988 Plymouth Horizon America

1988 Plymouth Colt Premier Turbo 4-Door

1988 Plymouth Colt E 3-Door Colt DL 4-Door Colt Turbo 3-Door

1988 Plymouth Colt DL 3-Door

Those '80s Cars 279

1988 - PONTIAC

1988 Pontiac Bonneville SE

1988 Pontiac Bonneville SSE interior

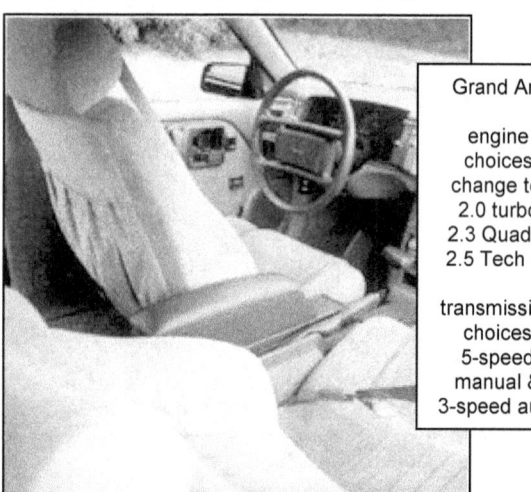
1988 Pontiac Grand Am SE interior

Grand Am

engine choices change to:
2.0 turbo
2.3 Quad 4
2.5 Tech IV

transmission choices
5-speed manual &
3-speed auto

1988 Pontiac Parisienne Brougham Wagon

New Model: 1988 Pontiac Grand Prix

1988 Pontiac Grand Am SE Coupe

1988 Pontiac Grand Am Sedan

New Model: 1988 Pontiac LeMans SE Sedan

1988 Pontiac LeMans interior

LeMans power: 1.6 liter 4-cylinder w/ 4- & 5-speed manual and 3-speed auto

1988 Pontiac 6000 S/E Sedan

1988 Pontiac 6000 STE

1988 Pontiac Firebird Formula

1988 Pontiac Sunbird GT Coupe

New Model: 1988 Pontiac LeMans 2-door Hatchback

1988 Pontiac 6000 STE interior

1988 Pontiac Fiero Formula

1988 Pontiac Sunbird GT Turbo Convertible

Those '80s Cars

1989

1989 - Facts at Glance

News Headlines

- USSR pulls out of Afghanistan
- George Bush Sr inaugurated as President
- Exxon Valdez spills 240,000 barrels of oil
- Leona Helmsley convicted on tax fraud
- Ford buys Jaguar
- Berlin Wall comes down

Tops in Pop Culture

Music
- Look Away, Chicago

Movies
- Batman

TV Show
- Roseanne

Sports Champions

Basketball
- Detroit Pistons

Football
- San Francisco 49ers

Baseball
- Oakland A's

Motor Trend – Car of the Year

Ford Thunderbird SC

1989 - AMC / EAGLE

1989 Eagle Premier ES Limited

1989 Eagle Summit optional 1.6 liter 16-valve DOHC

2.2 liter 4-cylinder electronically fuel-injected, independent rear suspension, front-wheel drive

New Model: 1989 Eagle Summit LX Sedan

1989 Eagle Medallion LX Sedan (previously sold as Renault Medallion in '87 & '88)

Optional 3rd row forward-facing seat

1989 Eagle Medallion DL Wagon

1989 Eagle Summit LX interior

1989 Eagle Medallion DL interior

Those '80s Cars

1989 - BUICK

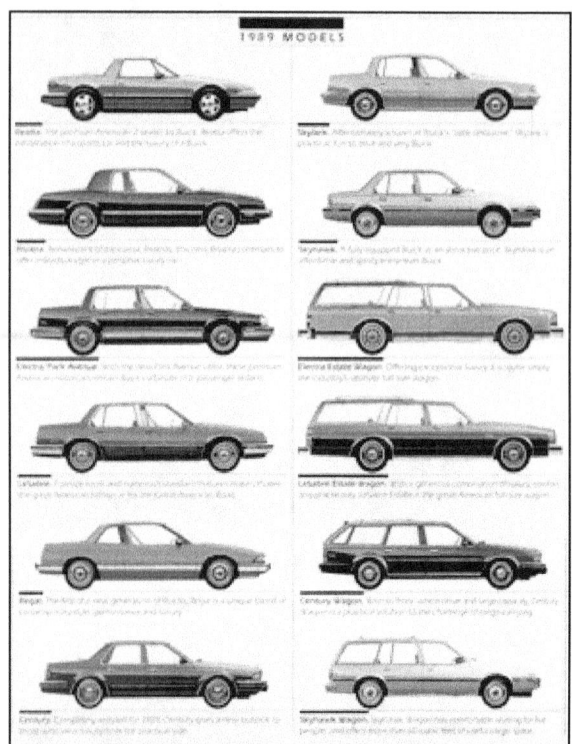

Refreshed: 1989 Buick Riviera — 11 inches longer

Refreshed: 1989 Buick Riviera

1989 Buick Riviera instrument panel

1989 Buick Riviera interior with available leather

Refreshed: 1989 Buick Riviera

1989 Buick Century Limited Sedan

1989 Buick Century instrument panel

1989 Buick Century Limited interior

Those '80s Cars

1989 Buick Reatta

1989 Buick Reatta interior

1989 Buick Reatta instrument panel

1989 Buick Park Avenue Ultra

New Series
Ultra: special 15" wheels, unique grille & tail lamps, 2-tone paint, padded roof and 20-way power designer, Giorgio Giugiaro seats

1989 Buick Park Avenue Ultra interior

1989 Buick Regal Gran Sport 2-door Coupe

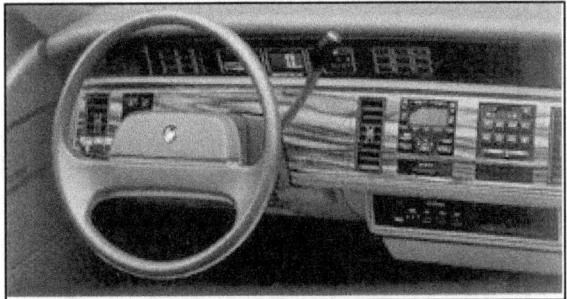
1989 Buick Regal instrument panel

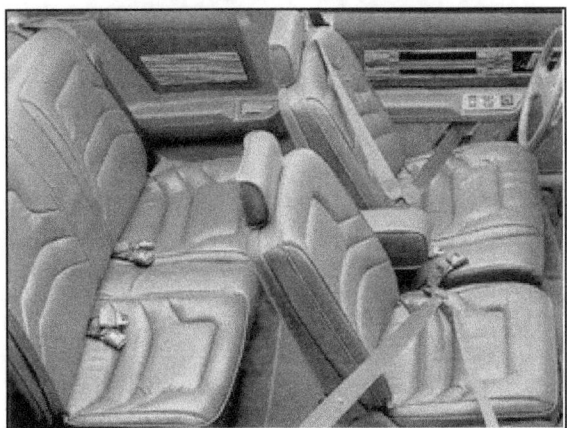
1989 Buick Regal Limited available leather interior

1989 Buick LeSabre T Type Coupe

1989 Buick LeSabre instrument panel

Those '80s Cars

1989 Buick Park Avenue instrument panel

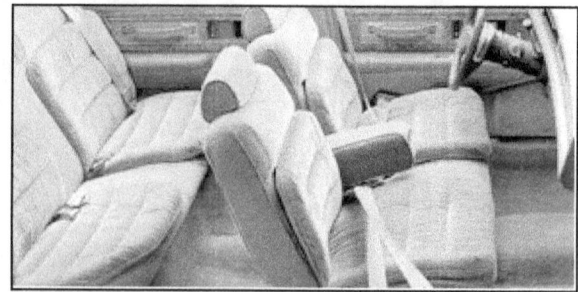
1989 Buick LeSabre Limited interior

1989 Buick Skylark with Gran Touring Package

1989 Buick Park Avenue interior

1989 Buick Skylark instrument panel

Last Model Run: 1989 Buick Skyhawk Coupe

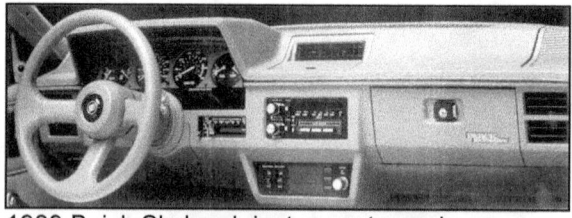
1989 Buick Skyhawk instrument panel

Buick calls the Skylark the "little limousine"

1989 Buick Skylark interior

Reclining bucket seats standard

1989 Buick Skyhawk interior

1989 - CADILLAC

1989 Cadillac Eldorado

1989 Cadillac Allanté

1989 Cadillac Seville

Refreshed: 1989 Cadillac Fleetwood Coupe

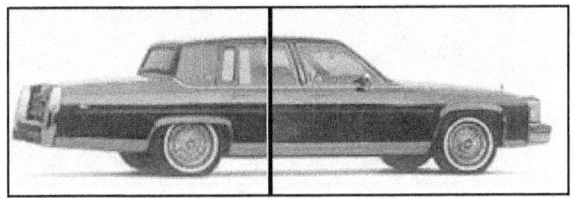
1989 Cadillac Brougham

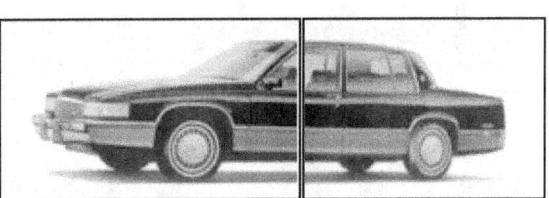
Refreshed: 1989 Cadillac Sedan deVille

Refreshed: 1989 Cadillac Fleetwood

Those '80s Cars

1989 - CHEVROLET

New RS series introduced

1989 Chevrolet Camaro IROC-Z Convertible

1989 Chevrolet Camaro IROC-Z Custom interior

1989 Chevrolet Corvette Convertible

1989 Chevrolet Cavalier RS sedan

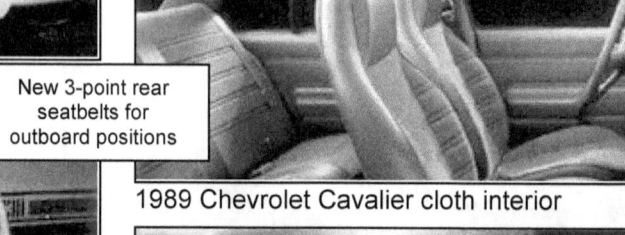
1989 Chevrolet Cavalier Coupe

New 3-point rear seatbelts for outboard positions

1989 Chevrolet Cavalier RS instrument panel

1989 Chevrolet Cavalier cloth interior

1989 Chevrolet Celebrity Eurosport Sedan

1989 Chevrolet Caprice Classic sedan

1989 Chevrolet Caprice Classic interior

1989 Chevrolet Beretta GTU Coupe

1989 Chevrolet Beretta interior

1989 Chevrolet Geo Sprint

1989 Chevrolet Geo Spectrum Sedan

1989 Chevrolet Spectrum interior

1989 Chevrolet Celebrity interior

New LTZ series introduced

1989 Chevrolet Corsica Sedan

New Model: 1989 Chevrolet Geo Tracker

New Model: 1989 Chevrolet Geo Metro

Those '80s Cars

1989 - CHRYSLER

New Model: 1989 Chrysler's TC by Maserati

From the Brochure: "Style is beauty… and performance. The best of two traditions. A blend of Italian craftsmanship and American engineering. The result is the TC… Chrysler's Turbo Convertible built by Maserati. TC is a luxury sport coupe whose stunning style is hand-hewn by Maserati coachworkers who meticulously form, fit and finish automobiles… as if each were one of a kind. The style of its appearance is enhanced on the road by Chrysler engineering… whose refinements include a gas-charged touring suspension system."   – 1989 Chrysler's TC by Maserati

1989 Chrysler LeBaron GTS Turbo

1989 Chrysler LeBaron GTS optional leather interior

1989 Chrysler LeBaron Convertible

1989 Chrysler LeBaron Coupe

1989 Chrysler New Yorker Landau

1989 New Yorker introduces Chrysler's new 4-speed, fully adaptive electronic control Ultradrive transaxle

1989 Chrysler New Yorker Landau optional leather interior

Last Model Run: 1989 Chrysler Fifth Avenue

1989 Chrysler New Yorker

1989 Chrysler New Yorker interior

Last Model Run: 1989 Chrysler Fifth Avenue

1989 Chrysler Fifth Avenue optional leather interior

Those '80s Cars

1989 - DODGE

1989 Dodge Dynasty LE

From the Brochure: "Dynasty and Dynasty LE. An artful blend of time-honored heritage and state-of-the-art technology. Bringing together such traditional family sedan qualities as impressive ride."
 - 1989 Dodge Dynasty

1989 Dodge Caravan LE & Caravan SE

1989 Dodge Caravan LE optional leather interior

New Model: 1989 Dodge Spirit ES

New Model: 1989 Dodge Spirit ES

From the Brochure: "Available with an array of performance engines, such as the 2.5-liter turbo. With multipoint fuel-injection. Four cylinders. Single overhead cam. And a turbocharger that responds quickly to provide low- and mid-range performance, such as 150 horsepower at 4,800 RPM."
 - 1989 Dodge Spirit

Power Trip

1989 Dodge Lancer Shelby

Exclusive Appeal

Last Model Run: 1989 Dodge Diplomat SE

Generous Value

Last Model Run: 1989 Dodge Aries America

Great Value

1989 Dodge Omni America

1989 Dodge Colt DL 4WD Wagon

Wild

1989 Dodge Daytona

1989 Dodge Shadow Coupe

1989 Dodge Shadow interior

Affordable quality from Japan. Dodge Colt.

1989 Dodge Colt E

1989 Dodge Colt Vista 4WD Wagon

Those '80s Cars

1989 - FORD

New Model: 1989 Ford Thunderbird Super Coupe

4-wheel anti-lock brakes, Automatic Ride Control suspension, super-charged intercooled 3.8 liter V6 & 5-speed manual

1989 Ford Thunderbird LX interior

1989 Ford Mustang GT Hatchback

1989 Ford Mustang LX Coupe

New Series: 1989 Ford Taurus SHO

3.0 liter V6, 4 valves per cylinder, DOHC, 220hp with 5-speed manual transmission only

1989 Ford Taurus LX instrument panel

2.2 liter 4-cylinder, with turbo option

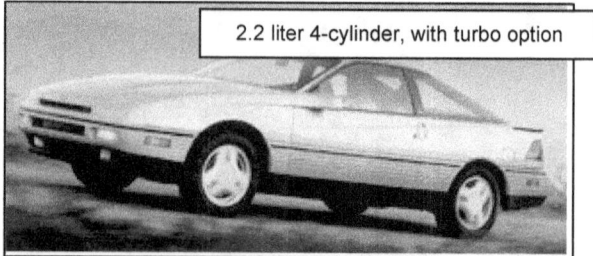
New Model: 1989 Ford Probe GT

1989 Ford Probe instrument panel

5-speed manual & 4-speed automatic

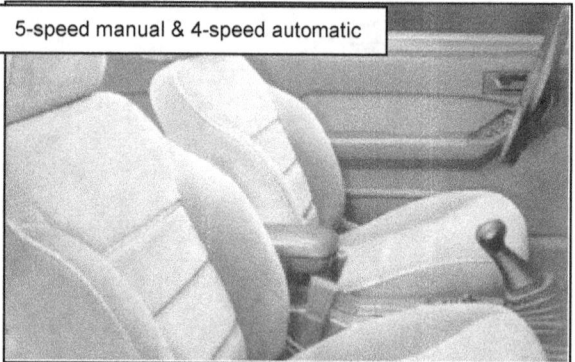
1989 Ford Probe interior

294   Those '80s Cars

1989 Ford Tempo AWD

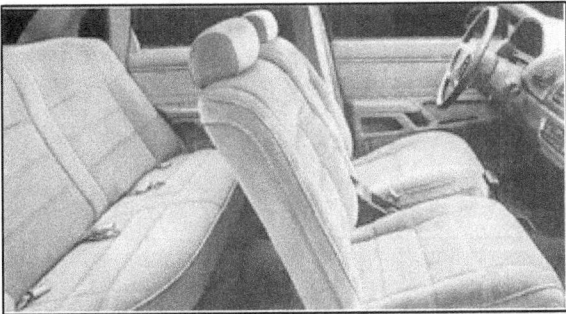
1989 Ford Tempo LX interior

1989 Ford Tempo GLS instrument panel

1989 Ford LTD Crown Victoria

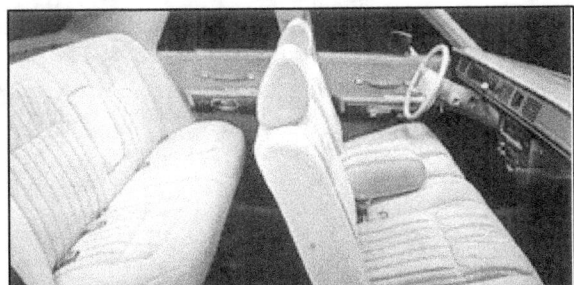
1989 Ford LTD Crown Victoria LX interior

1989 Ford Festiva

1989 Ford Escort LX Wagon

3 Escort series: Pony, LX & GT

1989 Ford Escort GT

1989 Ford Escort instrument panel

From the Brochure: "Escort features front-wheel drive, electronic fuel-injected performance, 4-wheel independent suspension and an interior environment designed to be both comfortable and practical."
- 1989 Ford Escort

Those '80s Cars

1989 - LINCOLN

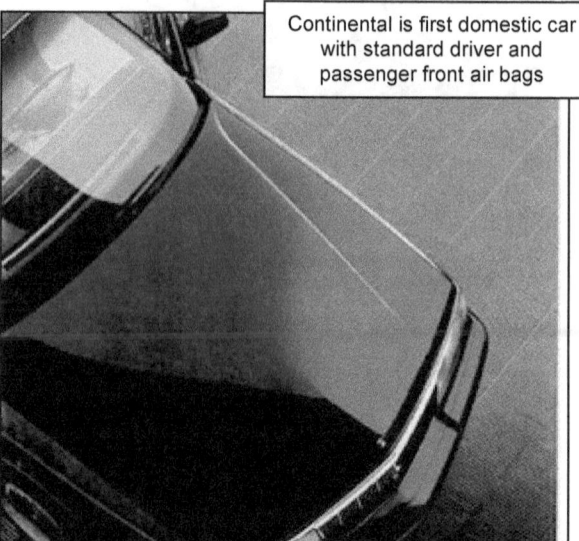

Continental is first domestic car with standard driver and passenger front air bags

1989 Lincoln Continental

1989 Lincoln Mark VII LSC

Last Model Run: 1989 Lincoln Town Car

1989 Lincoln Mark VII LSC instrument panel

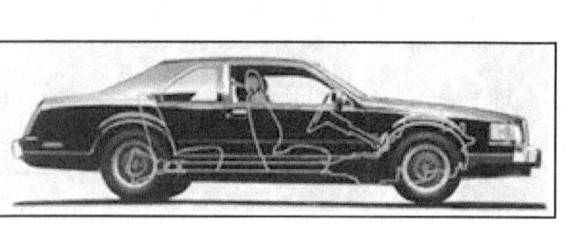

1989 Lincoln Town Car Cartier interior

1989 - MERCURY

1989 Mercury Sedan Line

1989 Mercury Tracer 4-door Hatchback

1989 Mercury Sable LS

1989 Mercury Sable LS

1989 Mercury Sable LS optional leather interior

1989 Mercury Tracer interior

68 standard features

Those '80s Cars

297

New Model: 1989 Mercury Cougar XR7

After many years being badged as "XR-7", in 1989, the dash is dropped and it is now badged "XR7"

1989 Mercury Cougar XR7 instrument panel

Standard Cougar models come with a 3.8 liter V6 producing 140 horsepower at 3,800 RPM

1989 Mercury Cougar LS interior

1989 Mercury Topaz

1989 Mercury Topaz LS Sedan

1989 Mercury Topaz LTS interior

From the Brochure: "Cougar XR7. Comfort just got a shot of adrenaline. The objective was to combine comfort and control with uncommon quickness. The result is the new Cougar XR7. Its adrenaline takes the form of a 210-horsepower supercharged V-6 with intercooler. It delivers load of performance that will draw more than just a passing glance from enthusiasts."

- 1989 Mercury Cougar XR7

1989 Mercury Wagons: Tracer, Grand Marquis Colony Park and Sable LS

1989 Mercury Grand Marquis

1989 Mercury Grand Marquis LS interior

From the Brochure: "Mercury Grand Marquis. Comfort and control on a grand scale. Grand Marquis is one automobile that doesn't ask its driver or passengers to compromise. Its interior possess more room than 99 percent of today's automobiles. There's body-on-frame construction and the control that comes with a V-8 engine, power brakes, nitrogen gas-pressurized shocks and a four-speed automatic transmission.

Grand Marquis sedans and Colony Park wagons are available with a number of additional comfort and convenience features. In addition to the standard electronic AM/FM stereo radio with four speakers there are three other radio options. You may wish to consider the high-level electronic AM stereo/FM stereo cassette audio system with a power amplifier and six speakers.

Both sedans and wagons can be ordered with the Trailer Tow III option."
- 1989 Mercury Grand Marquis

1989 - MERKUR

Last Model Run: 1989 Merkur XR4Ti

Last Model Run: 1989 Merkur Scorpio Sedan & XR4Ti Coupe

From the Brochure: "The bold, rakish design of the XR4Ti promises a driving experience that is clearly a cut above the norm. And on the road, the XR4Ti fulfills that promise with a striking combination of performance and comfort."
- 1989 MerkurXR4Ti

1989 Merkur XR4Ti standard cloth interior

1989 Merkur XR4Ti optional leather interior

1989 - OLDSMOBILE

2.8 liter V6 with 5-speed manual & 4-speed auto

New Model: 1989 Oldsmobile Cutlass Supreme International Series Coupe

1989 Oldsmobile Cutlass Supreme International Series interior with optional leather

From the Brochure: "1989 Cutlass Supreme is not your father's Oldsmobile. It's the new generation of Olds."

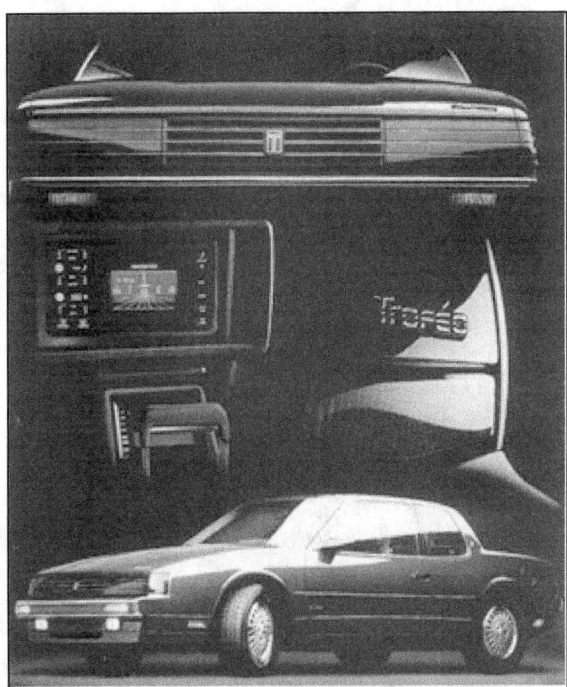

1989 Oldsmobile Toronado Trofeo

1989 Oldsmobile Cutlass Supreme International Series instrument panel

1989 Oldsmobile Toronado Trofeo interior

Those '80s Cars

1989 Oldsmobile Cutlass Calais International Series interior

New 3.3 liter multiport EFI V6

1989 Oldsmobile Calais Sedan

1989 Oldsmobile Cutlass Ciera International Series Coupe

1989 Oldsmobile Calais International Series Coupe

Maximum 74.4 cu. ft.

1989 Oldsmobile Cutlass Cruiser

1989 Oldsmobile Touring Sedan

> **From the Brochure:** "Inside, Touring Sedan takes ergonomics to new heights The Lear Siegler bucket seats are deep and thick. They feature individual controls for 11 power adjustments, including seat back recliners, side bolsters, lumbar and thigh, plus articulating headrest."
> — 1989 Oldsmobile Touring Sedan

1989 Oldsmobile Eighty-Eight Royale Brougham Sedan and interior

1989 Oldsmobile Custom Cruiser

1989 Oldsmobile Touring Sedan

1989 Oldsmobile Touring Sedan interior

1989 Oldsmobile Eighty-Eight Royale Brougham Coupe

1989 Oldsmobile Custom Cruiser

Those '80s Cars

1989 - PLYMOUTH

Available 3.0 liter V6 with Ultradrive fully adaptive 4-speed automatic

New Model: 1989 Plymouth Acclaim LX

1989 Plymouth Acclaim LX interior

From the Brochure: "Abundant room and comfort in a midsize car, front-wheel drive, and more than 50 standard features help make the Acclaim the optimum family vehicle." – 1989 Plymouth Acclaim

1989 Plymouth Sundance RS Sedan

New 2.5 liter Turbo I MPI engine option

1989 Plymouth Sundance RS Coupe

1989 Plymouth Sundance RS interior

304

Those '80s Cars

1989 Plymouth Horizon America & **Last Model Run:** 1989 Plymouth Reliant America (back)

1989 Plymouth Reliant America interior

1.6 liter 16-valve DOHC turbo MPI 4-cylinder engine

1989 Plymouth Colt GT Turbo

1989 Plymouth Colt DL 4WD Wagon

1989 Plymouth Omni America interior

1989 Plymouth Colt Vista 4WD Wagon

Those '80s Cars

1989 - PONTIAC

1989 Pontiac Bonneville

165 hp
1989 Pontiac Bonneville SSE

1989 Pontiac Bonneville instrument panel

1989 Pontiac Bonneville SSE interior

1989 Pontiac Firebird GTA interior

225 hp
1989 Pontiac Firebird GTA

2.8 liter V6, 5-speed manual or 4-speed auto & front-wheel drive

1989 Pontiac Grand Prix LE

1989 Pontiac Prix LE interior

1989 Pontiac Grand Am LE Coupe

1989 Pontiac 6000 LE Sedan

1989 Pontiac Grand Am LE Sedan

1989 Pontiac 6000 Wagon

1989 Pontiac Grand Am LE interior

Those '80s Cars

1989 Pontiac Sunbird LE Coupe

1989 Pontiac Sunbird LE Sedan

1989 Pontiac Sunbird instrument panel

1989 Pontiac LeMans GSE interior

Last Model Run: 1989 Pontiac Safari Wagon

1989 Pontiac Safari Wagon interior

1989 Pontiac LeMans GSE 2-door Hatchback

1989 Pontiac LeMans SE Sedan

Index

Table of Contents 2
Foreword 3
The 80's Measured 4
1980 5
   1980 - Facts at Glance 5
   1980 - AMC / EAGLE 6
   1980 - BUICK 8
   1980 - CADILLAC 11
   1980 - CHEVROLET 13
   1980 - CHRYSLER 16
   1980 - DODGE 19
   1980 - FORD 21
   1980 - LINCOLN 24
   1980 - MERCURY 26
   1980 - OLDSMOBILE 29
   1980 - PLYMOUTH 32
   1980 - PONTIAC 34
1981 38
   1981 - Facts at Glance 38
   1981 - AMC / EAGLE 39
   1981 - BUICK 41
   1981 - CADILLAC 44
   1981 - CHEVROLET 46
   1981 - CHRYSLER / IMPERIAL 50
   1981 - DODGE 53
   1981 - FORD 57
   1981 - LINCOLN 60
   1981 - MERCURY 63
   1981 - OLDSMOBILE 65
   1981 - PLYMOUTH 69
   1981 - PONTIAC 71
1982 .... Error! Bookmark not defined.
   1982 - Facts at Glance 74
   1982 - AMC / EAGLE 75
   1982 - BUICK 77
   1982 - CADILLAC 80
   1982 - CHEVROLET 81
   1982 - CHRYSLER / IMPERIAL 85
   1982 - DODGE 87
   1982 - FORD 89
   1982 - LINCOLN 92
   1982 - MERCURY 94
   1982 - OLDSMOBILE 97
   1982 - PLYMOUTH 100
   1982 - PONTIAC 102

1983 .... *Error! Bookmark not defined.*
- 1983 - Facts at Glance 106
- 1983 - AMC / EAGLE 107
- 1983 - BUICK 109
- 1983 - CADILLAC 112
- 1983 - CHEVROLET 116
- 1983 - CHRYSLER / IMPERIAL 118
- 1983 - DODGE 121
- 1983 - FORD 124
- 1983 - LINCOLN 126
- 1983 - MERCURY 127
- 1983 - OLDSMOBILE 129
- 1983 - PLYMOUTH 132
- 1983 - PONTIAC 134

1984 .... *Error! Bookmark not defined.*
- 1984 - Facts at Glance 138
- 1984 - AMC / EAGLE 139
- 1984 - BUICK 140
- 1984 - CADILLAC 142
- 1984 - CHEVROLET 145
- 1984 - CHRYSLER 148
- 1984 - DODGE 150
- 1984 - FORD 153
- 1984 - LINCOLN 156
- 1984 - MERCURY 158
- 1984 - OLDSMOBILE 160
- 1984 - PLYMOUTH 163
- 1984 - PONTIAC 164

1985 167
- 1985 - Facts at Glance 167
- 1985 - AMC / EAGLE 168
- 1985 - BUICK 169
- 1985 - CADILLAC 172
- 1985 - CHEVROLET 175
- 1985 - CHRYSLER 178
- 1985 - DODGE 180
- 1985 - FORD 183
- 1985 - LINCOLN 185
- 1985 - MERCURY 186
- 1985 - MERKUR 188
- 1985 - OLDSMOBILE 189
- 1985 - PLYMOUTH 191
- 1985 - PONTIAC 193

1986 195
- 1986 - Facts at Glance 195
- 1986 - AMC / EAGLE 196
- 1986 - BUICK 197
- 1986 - CADILLAC 201
- 1986 - CHEVROLET 204
- 1986 - CHRYSLER 207
- 1986 - DODGE 209
- 1986 - FORD 211
- 1986 - LINCOLN 214
- 1986 - MERCURY 215
- 1986 - MERKUR 217
- 1986 - OLDSMOBILE 218
- 1986 - PLYMOUTH 221
- 1986 - PONTIAC 223

1987 .... *Error! Bookmark not defined.*
- **1987- Facts at Glance** 226
- **1987 - AMC / EAGLE** 227
- **1987 - BUICK** 228
- **1987 - CADILLAC** 230
- **1987 - CHEVROLET** 233
- **1987 - CHRYSLER** 236
- **1987 - DODGE** 239
- **1987 - FORD** 241
- **1987 - LINCOLN** 243
- **1987 - MERCURY** 244
- **1987 - MERKUR** 246
- **1987 - OLDSMOBILE** 247
- **1987 - PLYMOUTH** 250
- **1987 - PONTIAC** 252

1988 255
- **1988 Facts at Glance** 255
- **1988 - AMC / EAGLE** 256
- **1988 - BUICK** 257
- **1988 - CADILLAC** 260
- **1988 - CHEVROLET** 263
- **1988 - CHRYSLER** 265
- **1988 - DODGE** 267
- **1988 - FORD** 269
- **1988 - LINCOLN** 271
- **1988 - MERCURY** 273
- **1988 - MERKUR** 275
- **1988 - OLDSMOBILE** 276
- **1988 - PLYMOUTH** 278
- **1988 - PONTIAC** 280

1989 282
- **1989 - Facts at Glance** 282
- **1989 - AMC / EAGLE** 283
- **1989 - BUICK** 284
- **1989 - CADILLAC** 287
- **1989 - CHEVROLET** 288
- **1989 - CHRYSLER** 290
- **1989 - DODGE** 292
- **1989 - FORD** 294
- **1989 - LINCOLN** 296
- **1989 - MERCURY** 297
- **1989 - MERKUR** 300
- **1989 - OLDSMOBILE** 301
- **1989 - PLYMOUTH** 304
- **1989 - PONTIAC** 306

www.ingramcontent.com/pod-product-compliance
Lightning Source LLC
Chambersburg PA
CBHW081210230426
43666CB00015B/2694